Self Improvement for Women

Hypnosis and meditation to take over your life: Boost your confidence to achieve high self-esteem, overcome anxiety and shyness and become the woman you always wanted to be.

COPYRIGHT

This document is geared towards providing exact and reliable information with regard to the topic and issue covered. The publication is sold with the idea that the publisher is not required to render accounting, officially permitted or otherwise qualified services. If advice is necessary, legal or professional, a practiced individual in the profession should be ordered. - From a Declaration of Principles which was accepted and approved equally by a Committee of the American Bar Association and a Committee of Publishers and Associations.

In no way is it legal to reproduce, duplicate, or transmit any part of this document in either electronic means or in printed format. Recording of this publication is strictly prohibited, and any storage of this document is not allowed unless with written permission from the publisher. All rights reserved. The information provided herein is stated to be truthful and consistent, in that any liability, in terms of inattention or otherwise, by any usage or abuse of any policies, processes, or directions contained within is the solitary and utter responsibility of the recipient reader.

Under no circumstances will any legal responsibility or blame be held against the publisher for any reparation, damages, or monetary loss due to the information herein, either directly or indirectly. Respective authors own all copyrights not held by the publisher.

The information herein is offered for informational purposes solely and is universal as so. The presentation of the information is without contract or any type of guarantee assurance.

CONTENTS

INTRODUCTION

Just as the term implies, self-esteem simply means the confidence exhibited by oneself. Confidence may also be compared to fueling out internal capacity to meet and surpass expectations. For example, folks with self-confidence tend to face specific hurdles with unwavering thoughts that the scenario is a win-win for them. Even in case they fail life challenges particularly, they often have the will to and inbuilt, infused encouragement to try again with the assurance of making a difference.

When your life is affected by anxiety, it is time for a change. You may feel that you are resigned to this difficult life forever, but that is not so. There are actually numerous coping techniques and even cures for what you feel. This book is one of the best first steps that you can take for yourself. This book will show you how to take control of your thoughts when they run wild and put an end to the crippling fears that rule your existence.

For the past ten years of my life, I have dealt with anxiety. I received the formal diagnosis of General Anxiety Disorder when I was eighteen, but I suspect that I suffered from this disorder starting at a much earlier age. I know how is it is to be ruled by fear and to have difficulty enjoying life like other people. I also know how it is to "ruin" relationships because of mental illness. While it has taken me a long while to get control over this disorder, I have learned to not let it rule me. In addition, I have learned to stop blaming myself. This is a mental disorder that I suffer, not something that is my choice.

While anxiety is not your fault or your choice, it is also not your slave master. You have the ability to gain control over it and prevent it from manifesting and ruining your life. You can stop anxiety in its tracks and live life the way that you choose. You just have to learn how, and this book will show you. Overcoming anxiety is an intensely mental and personal process that you should dedicate some time to accomplishing. The rewards will be rich.

I will show you some of the things that I have learned over the years about anxiety so that you can understand your disorder better. I will also show you the many tricks and tips I have learned over the years. From meditation to mindfulness as a skill to loving yourself, I will teach you how to think better in order to avoid the patterns of thinking that lead to anxiety. Keep in mind that these things take work. You cannot just overcome something crippling like anxiety overnight. However, you really can minimize the effects of anxiety on your life very easily and quickly. Almost immediately, you will start to notice results if you employ the methods in this book. Still, some of these things take time. Be patient with yourself and with these techniques. Don't give up just because you do not see immediate results.

In this book, we will cover what hypnosis is, how to use it, and how to practice it in daily life following yourself to enact effective changes on yourself and your psyche for better living. We will straightforwardly go about this, first by defining hypnosis in practical terms anyone can understand and apply to daily life. Then, we will go over what power hypnosis can have on daily living, the benefits and effects you can see from its practice, the simple steps to perform hypnosis, and ways to practice and hone the skill. There will also be practical exercises to partake daily to master the skill, ways specifically to address problems in the subconscious mind that can be altered through the practice of hypnosis, including trauma, ways that hypnosis can be applied directly to affect your confidence and self-esteem, and, ultimately, ways that hypnosis can be mastered altogether

6

to achieve the much-desired health, greater wealth, and all-around abundance in your daily living. We will take these grand concepts and break them down so they will be understood and thoroughly digested by the entire self, melded into the psyche permanently, and become a part of your daily life. That way, you can practice these concepts every day when you wake up, when you're out and about, and when you come back home before you sleep.

CHAPTER 1: Hypnosis andSelf-Hypnosis

How hard can it be to define a concept so it can be readily understood by any single person who hears the word? To many people, hypnosis is a very esoteric concept with little practical use in daily living. It is magic, something practiced by higher beings, maybe something that doesn't even exist, or something that only exists in fantasy. Little do most people know that hypnosis is actually a part of our daily lives, whether we realize it. Self-talk is the things we tell ourselves internally and externally. The things we say like "I am ugly," "I am stupid," "You could've done this or that better," "They will never love you,"—these are hypnotic phrases that program our mind in ways we take for granted. The practice of hypnosis is merely becoming aware of the power we have over our own minds and honing it, grabbing hold of it like a wild beast, taming it, taking control of it, and using it to do what we want it to do. Once this concept is grasped, hypnosis becomes many real, solid, tangible things that we can hold onto, keep in our toolbox, and pull out when we need it. All concepts of hypnosis have stemmed from this.

But hypnosis is also more than this. This is just branching off point. To get more specific, hypnosis involves honing the will, of the focus and attention, and, therefore, intention of the subject. The subject is the one who is being hypnotized. Generally, the subject and the practitioner are two separate people. The practitioner can be a magician. I'm sure you've seen one at the state fair or the amusement park asking for volunteers, but in more practical terms, the practitioner can be a licensed clinical therapist. This is because hypnotism can have a very powerful effect on the betterment of the subject. Therapists often use hypnotism to break down barriers in the psyche and address problems head-on in ways that can't be done through a simple conversation, ways that are traditionally blocked by the conscious, protecting the sub-conscious. But, alas, the practitioner and the subject can most importantly be the same person. You can perform hypnosis on yourself and for your own betterment. It involves a very strong understanding of the patterns of the conscious and subconscious mind and a very solid awareness of where your mind goes and what it is focusing on at any given time.

Traditionally, hypnosis involves the summoning of a relaxed, almost trance-like state—a state where the conscious mind is less guarded over what comes and goes from its sub-conscious brother. This can be achieved in a large, almost infinite number of ways, several of which we will go over later in this book. Once a state of relaxation is achieved, simple core concepts are introduced, or extracted from, the sub-conscious mind, depending on the intended effect the hypnosis is to have. Say, you want a person to quit smoking. Once the state of relaxation of the conscious mind is achieved, a story can be told to the subject that would involve a narrative of them waking up, desiring a cigarette, going outside to smoke the cigarette, and the cigarette making them very ill to the point of extreme nausea. This will become a legitimate memory in the subject's subconscious that will be triggered in their conscious state when they desire a cigarette. They will feel a wave of great and powerful nausea overtake them, and they will gradually feel less and less of a strong desire to smoke a cigarette. This is a very simple breakdown of very prevalent hypnotic practice. Besides false memories that can be implanted for positive goals, such as this, real memories that have been repressed by the conscious mind can be extracted; a big reason clinical practitioners practice hypnosis. Hypnosis gets to the core of past trauma. This will come into play later as we realize the power hypnosis can have on changing ingrained patterns of behavior that we have learned and developed over time that negatively affect us in one way or another in our daily living, which will come to be the largest point this book will make.

Besides the concept of implanting or detracting false and real memories, a very simple practice of hypnosis involves the implantation of simple positive core concepts that positively benefit the core beings—things as simple as saying, "I am loved," or "I am not stupid," or "I can do this." To continue the smoking example, instead of implanting a false memory with inherent sensations and feelings associated with it that will continue to trigger, said sensations and feelings in the waking life of the subject, the practitioner could simply, while the subject is in the relaxed state, say "I do not crave cigarettes, "Cigarettes make me ill," or "I have no addictions. I am a free being." Post-hypnotic suggestions are the clinical term for these phrases when induced to the subject after achieving what is called the hypnotic state, or trance state, the desired state of relaxation is the one that strives for in hypnosis. This is another very powerful concept in hypnosis. When practiced on the self, these positive phrases can be repeated over and over. These affirmations will be known to us as "mantras." This is a word to remember here.

So, where did hypnosis originate? How legitimate is it? How long has it been practiced, and where? This is almost like tracing back the origins of religion or life itself. Simply put, for as long as man and his consciousness have existed, so have ideas and practices associated with manipulating that consciousness and breaking down its barriers into higher states of being. To understand this fully, we must first realize the inherent parallels between hypnosis and the simple act of meditation. Meditation is most simply any state of reflection and awareness of the conscious acting mind. For as long as man has existed, man has been alone in his mind, having full ability to look into his mind and see what is there, what he is thinking, how he is acting, how he is feeling, so long as he would choose to exercise this awareness. Concepts of awareness of the psyche have grown over history to where we as a people living today have unlimited bounds of knowledge to apply to the awareness of our living selves. One very early dated example of hypnosis comes from the religious practice of Hindus experiencing illnesses. They go into the temples of their gods and meditating for long periods of time on the very experience of being in the presence of the symbols of their deities. In this instance, the meditation and extended period of relaxation inherently summoned the relaxed state while the "suggestion" brought forth in the hypnotic state was the presence of this symbol of their divine deities, giving the humans a supernatural power beyond their waking lives—this being the very purpose of their religion. Positivity and psychic energy would become known to cure the sick.

Fast-forward over the years, and many more people became aware of this undefined and natural manipulation of consciousness. Before it even had a name, it was a school of thought passed down through generations. The continued religious use of prayer, mantra, incantations repeated over and over to "exorcise" demons, or, in other words, conquer negativity. A man named Franz Mesmer, the father of the word

11

"mesmerism," practiced his entire life on the ability of a person to implant positive energy by touch onto others and surrounding objects. He said there was a magical, magnetic force in the consciousness of man, which he coined as "animal magnetism" that could physically embed positivity into the subject. While largely regarded with skepticism, this proved very influential and can still be applied, in part or whole, to concepts of hypnotism to this day, hence the staying power of his name.

While hypnotism, as what has been established, has been around in practice for near millennia, it would seem, the origin of the term itself is surprisingly much more recent. "Hypnotism," as a term, is attributed to a doctor from Scotland named James Braid. He himself made many great strides in the field, as should come as no surprise. Braid founded himself in near-direct opposition to the "mesmerism" of Franz Mesmer. The positive effects that Mesmer believed to be stemmed from the application of a magical force, Braid attributed to a separate, but altogether a different, powerful force, not that of any spirit or magnetism, but the human mind. Braid postulated that the human mind, if focused on a particular space or idea for a long period of time, would relax to a degree where seemingly "magical" changes could occur, or be made to occur, in the subject. Specifically, a large part of Braid's body of work was focused on the eyes, believing when the eyes were forced to focus on a specific point in space for a large period of time, this very action caused the relaxation of the mind and the induction of a hypnotic state. Think of the stereotypical notion of a practitioner swinging a pendulum in front of the face of the subject and asking them to follow the trajectory of the pendulum with their eyes for an extended period of time while luring thesubject verbally into a trance-like state. This notion, while reminiscent of caricature, still holds up in modern hypnotism. However, later in his life, Braid's ideas began to expand to incorporate a variety of concepts, all stemming from ancient modes of knowledge, about all kinds of mediums to enact this relaxed, suggestible state, a state which, shortly after his death, and stemming from his coining of the term "hypnotism," would come to be called "hypnosis." The origin of these words comes from the words "upnos," a Greek word meaning "sleep" and "osis" meaning a state or condition, referring crudely to the relaxed, meditative state of the subject as a "sleep-like state or condition." Braid's attention was put all around the globe to all variety of concepts, yogic, religious, esoteric, ancient practices and modern practices alike, and at the end of his life, he began to see how this "hypnotism" was no new invention but merely a word to describe a phenomenon as old as man himself.

So, coming full circle, in order to truly understand ourselves and our capabilities, who we are when we are functioning at our highest levels, it seems necessary that we understand this absolutely inherent and holistic concept that we have come to call hypnotism. We must understand where it came from so we know how intertwined it is with our very being—our very consciousness. We must understand where it has been, so we know what it is capable of. We must understand where it is now and how to use it so that we can apply it unto ourselves and in our daily life so as to better ourselves and make our everyday selves the ultimate manifestations of our true, desired being. We will call this application of hypnosis "self-hypnotism," and we will begin its practice.

So, having truly defined hypnosis and hypnotism as both vague and specific concepts, let's begin to define, more specifically, "self-hypnotism" where you are both the practitioner and the subject. It is merely a process of moving variables; you become the inductee of the relaxed state and the one who suggests the positive ideas for change on yourself. You are both the guide into the relaxed state and the one experiencing the relaxed state. While this might seem like it ups the ante and makes the process much more complicated just by increasing your number of roles and responsibilities, it is actually much simpler than you could ever imagine.

Relaxation is key here, and the pathways to it are many and numbered. What relaxes you? It can be listening to music, reading a book, or watching television. When you do any of these things, your conscious mind is being "hypnotized" by your own actions. The song, the book, the film—these are the pendulums we are swinging in front of our own eyes. And what is being suggested to us by them? The things our mind consumes every day are post- hypnotic suggestions we are feeding to our sub-conscious mind. We must become aware of them. If the song you are listening to says, "I want to die. I am sick of this world," you will come to want to die and be sick of this world. If the film or television program you are watching is negativistic, you will become negativistic. If the book you are reading promotes hate-speech, you will come to be a hateful person. It is the very nature of learning—what we focus on is what grows in our psyche. We must thoroughly understand the power of focus and intention, will, and willpower. We must meditate on where our focus is going in our daily living and make the decisions to focus on more positive areas of infinite being. This goes beyond outside influences such as media and other people we interact with all the way up to the most important influential factor on our wellbeing, our thoughts and feelings, our beliefs, that being ourselves.

We are our own best friends. There is no one you spend time with more than yourself. There is no place you spend more time in than your own body, your own mind, your soul, and your consciousness; it is your temple. How many times have you heard this? And how true is it now? Is your temple clean? The Hindus would go to the temples of their gods and meditate on the power they would give them; do you feel such power emanating from your own temple? We must go into our temples with a mop and a bucket and clean them up. We must go into our temples with mounds of clay and fashion new deities in the image of our ultimate desires, our happiness, what we genuinely wish to be. We must go into our temples with prayer and positivity, reciting mantras of power, and wishes of peace. We must eliminate from our temples forever the ne' er-do-wells and "demons" that have set up camp in our being, negativity from outside sources, things that are keeping us down, are telling us who we are, and who we can be. We must eliminate all preconceived notions of the self, of dreaded tangibility, of fate. We must embrace the infinite potential of our own consciousness, the ways it can transform reality. We are the layers of the stone. We are the ones who choose our destiny. When we were created, we were created with the power to change anything, over time, and we were given the tools to do so. The most potent weapon was consciousness. Hypnotism, the art of affecting the consciousness, will be where and how we sharpen our knives.

15

Self-hypnotism will be you, in reality, finding a safe place, sitting down, breathing in and out in peace, and heading inside— heading inside your brain, or your heart, or your soul, heading inside of your consciousness. See who you are, who you view yourself as, what you think, what you do, then tell yourself who you are going to be. Tell yourself what you are going to assume

from here on out. How you are going to feel about yourself going forward. "I am health. I am wellness. I am my own master. No one controls me. I control my destiny. I am the decider of my actions. I am not indebted to anyone or anything. I am free. I am great. I will be the best that I can be."

Find your mantras. What do you desire? Do you want peace? Your mantra can be, "I will be at peace." Relax, take several deep breaths, envision yourself floating on a cloud, in the hands of a powerful deity, like the Hindus, or at the core of the brightest star in the universe, having it emanates from you, and say, over and over, louder and louder, firmer and firmer, "I am peace." You are what you desire. Hone your desires. Understand where your focus and intentions are. Your mind is a wild animal. Lasso it, tame it, give it a name, and ride it into the sunset.

Self-hypnotism is something that is practiced by every single person every single day. It is unconscious. Our subconscious minds have a void that needs to be filled by intention; it is a continually running program consuming information. Find your inner peace. Find your temple. Find your mantra. Examine yourself from an outside perspective and find out who you really want to be, what you would like to see looking in the mirror and what you would believe to be your absolute, ultimate peak. Is that who you are now? If it is not, then why is it not? We will create a bridge over the ocean of the infinite, a bridge from where you are now to where you are going. That bridge will be the conscious practice of the manipulation of the sub- conscious, the control over the aspects of our thinking mind over which we feel we have no control. We will create a way to understand and develop more positive modes of thinking. We will erase the pathways in our mind that lead us to stumble blindly into the negative spaces we know so well and carve out new pathways that lead us into brand new positive paradises that

we can only imagine. And we will do it, quite simply, by the very act of imagining them itself. The power of our thoughts cannot be overstated. You are what you think you are. You are not what anyone else thinks you are. You are not what you are. You are whatever you want to be. Dream.

Practical application

It is a common misconception to relate self-hypnosis or hypnosis in this matter to sleep. Being in a hypnotic state makes you even more aware of what you are doing than normal. This allows better concentration while doing an act allowing you to block any form of distraction that may come externally. This is why people say they enter a trance while being hypnotized. You do not forget about yourself, and you are just stopping the other parts of you that prevent a better performance while doing a certain action.

You must understand that hypnosis will not work with those who are not willing to be hypnotized. The reason behind this can be related to the fact that hypnosis taps into the subconscious of a person. Unwillingness to go through things will trigger your subconscious self to resist any effects in your body. This is true not only in hypnosis but in other areas as well, such as trying to work on a job you do not like to have. Thus, if you are going to use self-hypnosis as a way to help you out improve your life, you must be willing to do so and not force yourself to go through this process jut because of the lack of another option.

Benefits

It will also increase the level of intuition a person can use in day to day life; we are allowing them to react better. Further, some mental illnesses can also be mitigated and even cured through self-hypnosis.

In terms of physical health, self-hypnosis allows the lowering of a person's heart rate. This lower workload given to the heart helps prevent high blood pressure and lower the possibility of cardiac arrest. The relaxed state induced by self-hypnosis also helps in expelling toxins the human body can produce while in a stressful situation. This can then even lead to the prevention of cancer since the cells of the body will be given proper nutrition by allowing the internal organs to function the best they can. It can also help out a person trying to manage personal weight since the routine in self- hypnosis can be focused on weight loss.

Self-hypnosis can help in many areas of your life – depending on your creativity in deciding how you use this tool. I have used self- hypnosis to overcome procrastination, think more positively, and change habits of all sorts. I have used self-hypnosis to focus on eating the "right" foods, meaning I now (most of the time) reach for a fruit or a vegetable when I feel like a snack, instead of the biscuits or chocolates that I used to do so often. Self-hypnosis helped me kick the habit of smoking – no other intervention was needed, only the intention of what I wanted to change and the action to follow through with the self-hypnosis.

Help in People's Lives

But the benefits are not limited to long term effects. Self-hypnosis can also help a person improve daily living by allowing better performance in daily tasks. Reading this book, for example, can give you some information you need to know about self-hypnosis. But if you read this same book after you are in a self-induced hypnotic state, you will be able to see that each chapter was designed for you to be able to slowly realize on your own why it is best to practice self-hypnosis in your life. This is somewhat like a spoiler, but it can only be proven real if you try it out willingly yourself.

Another daily life benefit taps into the claim of gaining better concentration. A basketball player enters what is called "the zone" if a certain situation during the game triggers the self-hypnotic state practiced by that player, this is often related to an improved game for that particular player. The trigger, of course, varies from person to person like being on the verge of being defeated or having a certain number of fouls. But this trigger will then allow the player to be more conscious of the game, and thus better concentration is given. This improved concentration then becomes the means to be able to do the basics better and allow for better plays as well. This heightened consciousness blocks all other aspects of the game and makes the player focus more on his performance.

Of course, this improved concentration and performance can also be applied in other fields. A business transaction, for example, can be done more smoothly if distractions are set aside. Studying can also give more output and better retention if a student can concentrate more on the task. In a sense, self-hypnosis can benefit you no matter what field you are in, and no matter what, you want to improve.

Although it can be argued that these can be done without self-hypnosis, the goal is technically not just doing it; it is doing it easier for you to conserve your energy for other tasks later on.

Reasons To Start Now

If you believe that you need to rewire your way of thinking to improve your life, then that would be reason enough to start practicing self-hypnosis. Remember that you must be willing yourself and not be forced to do so otherwise, it will not work. You need to want to change, and you must allow self-hypnosis to change you. This willingness becomes your first step into experiencing the trance that could lead to a better performance in the aspect you wish to improve on. It will also serve as your motivation to push yourself to make the method work. If the willingness is missing, then even if you believe it works, you will not be able to take advantage of its full potential. A slight distraction will pull you out from hypnosis and thus putting a halt in the entire process. Practice self-hypnosis.

This information can only serve as a background that will prepare you to practice self-hypnosis. But again, the background can only open the door for you. You must have the will to step through the door to experience self- hypnosis & the benefit it brings first hand. The only way to truly prove it to yourself is by trying it out to see how it affects your daily routine. Once you notice the changes, you'll begin to have stronger insight into what might be possible. Many people see results from the first few times of practice, which only gets better over time.

Self-Improvement Through Self-hypnosis

This happens due to the fact that while you are in a hypnotic state, you are more susceptible to suggestions by the person who put you in this state. In the case of self-hypnosis, the person who made you enter the trance of hypnotism is yourself. Thus, the only person who can give you suggestions that can change your attitude in this method is you and you alone.

Again, you must forget the misconception that hypnosis is like sleeping because if it is, then it would be impossible to give autosuggestions to yourself. Try to think about it like being in a vivid daydream where you can control every aspect of the situation you are in. This gives you the ability to change anything that may bother and hinder you from achieving the best possible result. If you are able to pull it off properly, then the possibility of improving yourself after the constant practice of the method will just be a few steps away.

Career

People say that motivation is the key to improve in your career. But no matter how you love your career, you must admit that there are aspects of your work that you really do not like doing. Even if it is a fact that you are good at the other tasks, there is that one duty that you dread. And every time you encounter this specific chore, you seem to be slowed down and thus lessening

21

your productivity at work. This is where self-hypnosis comes into play.

The first thing you need to do is find that task you do not like. In some cases there might be multiple of them depending on your personality and how you feel about your job. Now, try to look at why you do not like that task and do simple research on how to make the job a lot simpler. You can then start conditioning yourself to use the simple method every time you do the job.

After you are able to condition your state of mind to do the task, each time you encounter, it will become the trigger for your trance and thus giving you the ability to perform it better. You will not be able to tell the difference since you will not mind it at all. Your coworkers and superiors though, will definitely notice the change in your work style and in your productivity.

Family

It is easy to improve in a career. But to improve your relationship with your family can be a little trickier. Yet, self-hypnosis can still reprogram you to interact with your family members better by modifying how you react to the way they act. You will have the ability to adjust your way of thinking depending on the situation. This then allows you to respond in the most positive way possible no matter how dreadful the scenario may be.

If you are in a fight with your husband/wife for example, the normal reaction is to flare up and face fire with fire. The problem with this approach is it usually engulfs the entire relationship which might eventually lead up to separation. Being in a hypnotic state in this instance then can help you think clearly and change the impulse of saying words without thinking the through. Anger will still be there of course, that is the healthy way. But anger now under self-hypnosis can be channeled and stop being a raging inferno, you can turn it into a steady bonfire that can help you and your partner find common ground for whatever issue you are facing. The same applies in dealing with sibling or children. If you are able to condition your mind to think more rationally or to get into the perspective of others, then you can have better family/friends relationships.

Health And Physical Activities

Losing weight can be the most common reason why people will use self- hypnosis in terms of health and physical activities. But this is just one part of it. Self-hypnosis can give you a lot more to improve this aspect of your life. It works the same way while working out.

Most people tend to give up their exercise program due to the exhaustion they think they can no longer take. But through self-hypnosis, you will be able to tell yourself that the exhaustion is lessened and thus allowing you to finish the entire routine. Keep in mind though that your mind must never be conditioned to forget exhaustion, it must only not mind it until the end of the exercise. Forgetting it completely might lead you to not stopping to work out until your energy is depleted. It becomes counterproductive in this case.

Having a healthy diet can also be influenced by self-hypnosis. Conditioning your mind to avoid unhealthy food can be done. Thus, hypnosis will be triggered each you are tempted to eat a meal you are conditioned to consider as unhealthy. Your eating habit then can change to benefit you to improve your overall health.

23

Mental, Emotional And Spiritual Needs

Since self-hypnosis deals directly in how you think, it is then no secret that it can greatly improve your mental, emotional and spiritual needs. A clear mind can give your brain the ability to have more rational thoughts. Rationality then leads to better decision making and easy absorption and retention of information you might need to improve your mental capacity. You must set your expectations though; this does not work like magic that can turn you into a genius. The process takes time depending on how far you are want to go, how much you want to achieve. Thus, the effects will only be limited by how much you are able to condition your mind.

In terms of emotional needs, self-hypnosis cannot make you feel differently in certain situations. But it can condition you to take in each scenario a little lighter and make you deal with them better. Others think that getting rid of emotion can be the best course of action if you are truly able to rewire your brain. But they seem to forget that even though rational thinking is often influenced negatively by emotion, it is still necessary for you to decide on things basing on the common ethics and aesthetics of the real world. Self- hypnosis then can channel your emotion to work in a more positive way in terms of decision making and dealing with emotional hurdles and problems.

Spiritual need on the other hand is far easier to influence when it comes to doing self-hypnosis. As a matter of fact, most people with spiritual beliefs are able to do self-hypnosis each time they practice what they believe in. A deep prayer for instance is a way to self hypnotize yourself to enter the trance to feel closer to a Divine existence. Chanting and meditation done by other religions also leads and have the same goal. Even the songs during a mass or praise and worship triggers self-hypnosis depending if the person allows them to do so.

Still, the improvements can only be achieved if you condition yourself that you are ready to accept them. The willingness to put an effort must also be there. An effortless hypnosis will only create the illusion that you are improving and thus will not give you the satisfaction of achieving your goal in reality.

CHAPTER 2: DEFINITION OF SELF-ESTEEM

The American Heritage Dictionary of the English Language defines self- esteem as "Pride in oneself." While some may consider this an adequate definition, self-esteem is a complex and important part of our makeup. Our self-esteem measures how we view ourselves about the world in which we live and others who live in our world. Our self- esteem is the grade we give ourselves as individuals.

Most of us fill our mental report cards with some A's, some B's some C's, and lower grades in a few particular areas. The person with low self-esteem, on the other hand, starts at the bottom with the red F's, may give himself a few C's, fewer B's, and even fewer—if any—A's.

Self-esteem gives us our opinions about whether or not we are capable of accomplishing much or little in our world. It gives us an unsolicited, often erroneous, evaluation of our intelligence, talents, abilities, and potential.

Self-esteem is a paradox. It is the strength within us that tells us we can take on challenges and risks with a firm belief in our ability to win. It gives us confidence that we can challenge and overcome superior forces, but it is also the cause of butterflies in our stomachs, the tremble in our knees, and the tightness in our throats when we are asked to speak the local Cub Scout pack. It can be as tough as a diamond or as fragile as crystal. The conditions are necessary for a person to have healthy, high self-esteem have been described in many ways. Dr. Harris Clemes, Ph.D., and Dr. Reynold Bean, Ed.M., in their books on developing self-esteem, describe only four conditions. The degree to which these conditions are reflects the level of a person's self- esteem. For a person to have high self-esteem, all of the following conditions must be met.

Connectedness Or Sense of Belonging:

A person needs a feeling of belonging to a family, to a group, or to some unit—even if it is called a gang—to connect with the people who are important in her life. In the workplace, this means having a feeling of belonging or being a part of the group of co-workers with whom she works. Employees treated by their supervisor as expendable, work-producing units rather than human beings who are making valuable contributions to the organization will have little feeling of being a part of the workgroup. They will have little feeling of value to the organization, will have a low level of self-esteem as measured by their work contribution, and, as a result, will have little or no feeling of dedication to the organization. The employee who has no feeling of belonging to the organization may become the withdrawn, low production loner in the group.

The supervisor's role in giving the employee a sense of belonging to the group should be obvious. The supervisor should, from the time the employee comes into the group, let the employee know that the work he is doing is important in meeting the goals of the organization and how his work fits into the overall operation. The employee who enters a job and is simply told, "sit here and do this," and is ignored by the other workers and the supervisor— except to be handed additional work—will find little satisfaction in her work and will have a low sense of self-worth because of her apparent lack of acceptance in and importance to the workgroup.

A SENSE OF POWER OR CONTROL

A sense of power or control comes from a person's feeling that he possesses the skills, the resources, the capability, and the opportunity to influence his life circumstances, make choices, and be responsible for his actions. When an employee believes he is being denied the right to make decisions affecting his work even though he feels he can correctly make those decisions, and that his destiny is totally under the control of others, the employee may resort to other methods of gaining control such as becoming rebellious or argumentative.

When a person has a sense of control over his work and life situation, he will be willing to put forth greater effort, won't be as easily stopped when confronted with problems, and will be willing to work longer and harder to meet a goal. Also, people with a sense of control over their lives have fewer illnesses and recover more quickly from those they do have. They react to fewer events in a stress-producing manner, so they have fewer stress-related illnesses.

When the worker is given a feeling of some degree of control over his job and his destiny, such as making decisions on some matters concerning his work or being delegated authority to carry out certain responsibilities or approve certain actions without consulting his supervisor, he will have a greater sense of control over the work and his future. When he has some vision of potential career growth within the organization based on his performance, he develops a sense of having some responsibility for and control over the future of his career. The supervisor, the organization that gives to their employees these feelings of control or power, will have a better satisfied, better working, and more dedicated workgroup.

A SENSE OF UNIQUENESS:

Every human being wants and needs to be treated as a unique individual: one who possesses his own set of physical characteristics, talents, skills, knowledge, thoughts, and opinions. He needs to recognize his own uniqueness, but, even

28

more, he needs the recognition of his parents, his peers, his co-workers, his supervisor, and even strangers that he is an individual unlike any other person on earth.

If a supervisor fails to recognize employees' uniqueness under his direction, he will deny each of them the opportunity to develop this sense or condition necessary for them to have high self-esteem. He will also deny the organization the benefit of the unique capabilities that each employee could contribute to the organization.

The supervisor, who boasts, "I treat all my employees alike," is either fooling himself or is a very difficult person to work for.

A supervisor works with a group of individuals who are administratively assigned to her organizational entity, but that supervisor does not supervise or motivate the group. Instead, he supervises and attempts to motivate the individuals who make up that group. To do so, he must recognize the differences in these people in order to identify their individual needs and to identify their best, most productive qualities in order to use them to the fullest for the good of both the organization and the person.

Military basic training attempts to cast all members of a group into a single fighting unit. Everyone is treated the same. They all receive the same training, fire the same rifles, perform the same dirty work, and pass the same inspections. Ultimately, it is the rigidity of the training that brings out the uniqueness of the individual soldier. Because of the individual's need for recognition as a unique person, those with the strongest need to display this uniqueness will emerge as the strongest, the best shot, or the informal leader of the organization. Those are the soldiers with the high self-esteem necessary to show themselves as having unique skills, talents, strengths.

Each shows his uniqueness, even that of being the best scrounger in the outfit. The wise commander recognizes these traits as they emerge and takes advantage of this knowledge in order to build the best possible unit.

This is true for the supervisor of any organization. To develop the best unit or group possible, he must utilize the knowledge, skills, and talent available to him. It is incumbent on the supervisor to help each employee to display his uniqueness, to recognize those traits, and to use them the same as he would utilize other resources available to him. Every supervisor should realize that only by bringing out the best in his people will he ever be able to demonstrate the best in himself by utilizing all resources available to him.

A SENSE OF MODELS:

To acquire good self-regard or self-esteem, a person must be able to distinguish between right and wrong and between appropriate and inappropriate behavior.

As children, we have role models who influence us in forming our behavior standards. We look to the ways our parents, other adults, and our peers act or react in situations and derive our standards from what we see and hear. The key to developing a good set of standards is to have role models who act and react consistently in a manner that is acceptable to society. Later, as we mature and have various experiences, we build on the standards we have developed as children by observing the responses of others to our actions. The role model who is inconsistent in the manner in which he acts or reacts sends confusing messages that fail to provide a solid base upon which we can develop our own standards of conduct.

In the work situation, an employee must be able to look first and foremost to her supervisor as a role model who provides appropriate and correct behavior on the job. The supervisor who demands punctuality but frequently arrives late for work, one who misses deadlines, or one who demands that employees keep

30

their noses to the grindstone for eight full hours a day –or even more– while he chats, reads, disappears for long periods of time, or otherwise wastes company time cannot serve as an acceptable role model for his employees. The supervisor who works by the old adage, "Don't do as I do, do as I say ," may find that his subordinates do as he says do while he is present, but quickly resort to doing as he does when he leaves the work area for even a short time. They may feel, albeit unconsciously, that goofing off, leaving the work area, or chatting is actually acceptable behavior because that is the behavior that has been modeled by their supervisor.

The supervisor who displays enthusiasm, and interest in the work, a sense of value to the organization and its goals, and observes the rules of the business, will serve as a positive role model who can expect the same behavior from his employees as he gives the organization. Model the behavior you desire.

Under certain circumstances, each of us has had or will have feelings of inadequacy or self-doubt. These feelings likely reflect situations that took place earlier in our life when we didn't perform up to our expectations or to the expectations of others who were important in our lives. In most instances we brace ourselves and go ahead and try, not because we have overcome these feelings, but in spite of the fact that we have them. If we do well we will most likely be elated and that particular situation will no longer present so great a challenge. If we do not perform as well as we think we should have, most of us have the ability and the strength to set aside the disappointment in ourselves and accept the fact that we may not be as skilled, talented, and trained in that particular area as some others might be. We can do that without harboring a continuing feeling of inadequacy and without labeling ourselves as failures. But what about the person with low self-esteem?

A person suffering from low self-esteem may feel inadequate or incapable of meeting the demands placed upon her, particularly the demands of a job that presents any degree of challenge. That person may reach for nothing but the least demanding, lowest paying job or she may resort to the life of the chronically unemployed or under employed. He may see no future for himself in a society that honors, rewards, and virtually idolizes the high achiever.

The person with low self-esteem may view any situation that presents even the slightest challenge as having the potential of showing the world his inadequacy and inability, and the potential to add one more failure to a life filled with failure. Low self-esteem results in fear. It is fear of life's demands that robs him of the power to say, "yes" to life's challenges.

Unfortunately, when a person grows up with these degrading opinions of himself, it is extremely difficult to overcome these poor self-evaluations. Often, it cannot be done without the help of others who know and care about that person.

In the business world there will always be employees who never live up to their true potential because they never have a true picture of what they can accomplish. They never believe themselves capable of meeting the challenges imposed by more complex work or higher levels of responsibility. Employees who live in this self-imposed world of restricted performance delude themselves, delude their families, delude the organization in which they work, and delude society by not giving them the products of their minds and talents that would be possible if they could shed their fear of failure and live up to their true potential.

HOW OUR SELF-ESTEEM IS DEVELOPED

Why do so many people grow up with such poor regard for themselves in aworld filled with opportunities? Our feelings of self-regard/self-esteem are rooted in the nurturing, the attitudes, the responses, and the acceptance of us by our parents, our teachers, other adults, and our peers during our early years.

PARENTAL INPUT

We are all familiar with stories of parents who physically abuse their children with beating, burning, scalding, etc. but we hear little of those who emotionally abuse their children with actions and words. These are the parents who ignore the children or treat them with indifference, or destroy their possibility of developing positive self-esteem by convincing the child that, "...you'll never amount to anything," " ...you can never do anything right," "...you're too stupid to ever learn to do that." Fortunately, these parents are relatively few, but such abuse frequently results in a debilitating low self-esteem in a person who could have accomplished a great deal if he had not been constantly told that he couldn't.

Most parents would never consciously do anything to hurt their children. They might, however, injure them unconsciously by comparing their child's accomplishments, talents, or appearance with siblings or peers who make higher grades, throw a baseball better, or are chosen Miss Something-or- other. Even a casual remark such as, "I wish you were as popular as Mary," can be a devastating put down for a child who interprets the remark as, "You are not pretty or as popular as Mary," or "I wish Mary were my daughter." Making positive remarks and responses, giving praise, actively listening, being a good role model, and using

33

positive, consistent discipline are important factors in helping a child develop high self-esteem.

TEACHER INPUT

Teachers play an important role in the formation of child's self-esteem. They can help build a child's positive self-esteem by encouraging and helping, or

they can make an unsure student even unsure of herself. They sometimes make remarks about a student's work or compare the student with one who makes higher grades. The target child may take the remark to mean that she is stupid, or a failure, or that she is incapable of doing the work.

An "F" on a test means only that the student did not meet the teacher's standard for a passing grade on those particular questions on that particular subject on that particular day. But the student who frequently receives F's may brand herself a failure not just on those test scores, but in all phases of her life. She may picture herself as a failure to the extent that she develops a failure complex and will not be willing to risk doing anything because she believes she is destined to fail. Actually, she may be perfectly capable of performing very well if she would put as much energy into risking as in convincing herself that she will fail if she tries.

PEER/SIBLING INPUT

Our reaction to the treatment we receive from our peers as we grow up has a direct relationship to the level of our self-esteem. Children are very frank in what they say and can be brutal in their treatment of their peers. If a child hears from his siblings or schoolmates that he is stupid, or a nerd, or that he is funny looking, it can be difficult for that child to ignore the epithets, so they may become a part of his personal belief system. Being the last chosen for a game becomes a loud and clear statement that he is not as good as the others in the game. In that case, the child does not have a sense of belonging to the group, of having any power or control, or models, and is not in a position at that time to demonstrate his uniqueness. His feelings may extend to other parts of his life.

YOUR ROLE AS A SUPERVISOR.

An insensitive supervisor can easily add to a person's self-imposed concept of his inadequacy. If an employee is poorly or improperly trained he may be

prone to errors from the beginning of his employment. When those errors are immediately and perhaps rudely, pointed out, the employee with low self- esteem may find his negative feeling about himself further verified. The result can be that he will become extremely cautious in his work. This may result in a supervisor's evaluation that he is not only prone to errors but is too slow in his work. The stress from his anxiety in the work place can result in even more errors and more cautious performance.

As his belief of inadequacy is further verified by the words and actions of the supervisor, the next result may be habitual absence or tardiness as a way of avoiding more negatives. He may become the "job hopper" who moves from one job to another until he finds one that makes few demands and offers little potential.

In some cases, a person with low self-esteem may find an area in which he can perform well. He may then over-compensate by becoming an over- achiever in that particular part of his life in order to make up for the self- ordained deficiencies in other aspects of his life.

Most of us do not suffer from such low self-esteem as those described above, but some who appear to have healthy self-esteem may have a problem but hide it well. They may find it difficult to meet people, to take on new tasks, to go through a job interview, or to do other things necessary to get ahead and fully participate in the activities of their world. They have to push themselves through a lifetime of anxiety to reach only a fraction of their potential.

The supervisor's role in developing self-esteem in their employees is one of many characters. She must become the supervisor who maintains responsibility for the work of the group while serving as the role model, mentor, trainer, coach, and cheerleader, for the group and the individuals who make up that group. She recognizes good work, accomplishment, and potential with even more enthusiasm than she recognizes errors or lapses in

judgment. She praises in public, disciplines in private.

THE SUPERVISOR'S SELF-ESTEEM

Feelings of inadequacy are not limited to the lower level personnel in an organization. Most often, the tyrannical, autocratic, abrasive, perfectionist supervisor or manager is attempting to hide a deep-rooted poor self-concept that makes him doubt his deserving of his position. By being autocratic and demanding, he shields himself from questions, challenges, or input from his employees whom he fears will uncover his inability or lack of knowledge. Because of his intimidating behavior, workers may carry out orders or instructions that they know are wrong, or do their work in a prescribed way even though there are better, more efficient ways to do it in order to avoid further intimidation or even retaliation. They certainly would not feel free to bring the supervisor's errors to his attention.

In this situation, employees have been known to resort to what is called "malicious compliance." The supervisor gives an order that will, if carried out as he directs, cause repercussions and possibly get the supervisor in trouble with his own boss. The knowing employees smile at each other and carefully, openly, carry out their supervisor's instructions to the letter.

The other extreme of supervisory behavior influenced by low self-esteem is the boss who is never able to make a decision. Frequently she becomes the private office recluse who has little personal contact with his employees, sometimes abdicating her supervisory authority and responsibility to a stronger subordinate who becomes the informal but actual leader of the group.

The perfectionist may be covering up his feelings of inferiority by attempting to appear perfect in his work and demanding perfection from his employees.

His own perfectionism may come in the form of something relatively minor in the work of the group, such as punctuation in correspondence. But he may attempt to demand perfection from the workers in all parts of their jobs. What he doesn't realize is that having to be right all the time has an opposite effect of making the workers fear being wrong all the time, thus negating their willingness to risk or to find new and better ways to do the work. The more a supervisor demands perfection, the more imperfection he will find.

CHAPTER 3: DEVELOP SELF-ESTEEM

Let us try to understand how self-esteem develops. Why is this important? A thorough understanding of these factors is important to let them not negatively affect our self-esteem. Let us look at these factors in detail now.

Home

Home is where our learning begins as a child and continues till the day we die. This is the first place where we learn to understand what relationships mean. Hence it can be rightly said that home is where our self-esteem begins to nurture. How our family treats us and perceives us plays an important role in the way, we perceive us. When you were a kid, we try to imitate the members of our family because we are not mature enough to do things our own way. Suppose, you have an elder sibling who has self-esteem issues, you will pick that from him, as you grow up. This is because our family members are in a better position to influence us, especially when we are kids.

When a child grows up in a family that is content and reeks of positive energy, he will turn out to be an individual with high levels of self-esteem. The child starts valuing himself as he grows up; when he notices that his family members also value themselves a lot. When you grow up in a family that is supportive and has respect for one another, you will exhibit these values as well. In this environment, the child is encouraged to do what he believes his strengths are. For instance, if the child wishes to pursue a vocation, he is encouraged to do so. This encouragement makes the child believe in his strengths and talents. He will learn to respect himself for his values and traits this way.

Now let us look at the other side of the coin. When you grow up in a family that is not supportive of you, you will not value yourself much. When a child is surrounded by family members that think it is fine to always think that they do not deserve to be treated well, the child also develops that mindset as he grows. Another problem with dysfunctional families is that they are abusive in nature. When a child grows up in an abusive family, he develops an inferiority complex. Over time, he thinks that he deserves to be bullied around and treated in an ill fashion. He learns to accept this abusive behavior. By the time he grows up, he is not bothered by physical abuse anymore. He begins to believe that abuse is part and parcel of one's life. He grows up to be a bully. He ends up abusing others and thinks that they deserve to be treated that way.

On the other hand, when a child grows up in a family that constantly discourages him, he will not have any confidence left. He will not have any faith in his strengths or talents. When his family members keep discouraging him, over a period of time, the child believes that he is worth nothing. He begins to believe that he is not capable of achieving anything. He grows up to be an individual who does not have any confidence in his strengths whatsoever. He is prepared to fail at all times. This lost attitude will definitely not help the individual to succeed. Lack of success will not help the person to improve his confidence at all.

School

After home, a child spends most of the time in school. School plays an important role in nurturing the child's confidence. School is the first place where the child learns to make new friends. Choosing the right kind of friends is again very important. It plays a key role in influencing the confidence of the child.

For instance, if the child becomes friends with the right kind of people, he will grow up in an environment where he inspires his friends and is, in turn, inspired by his friends. As we all know, friends play an important role in motivating us and making us believe that success is not far away. Most of the time, our friends are our sources of strength and support. When a child has good and supporting friends, he will be motivated to build on his talents and taste success. He will grow up to be an individual who believes that his goals are achievable and is focused on achieving his targets. He values himself and also values the people around him. He is motivated to take up new challenges.

On the other hand, if a child falls into bad company, his self-esteem will be affected drastically. For instance, if he becomes friends with the school bully, he will eventually believe that it is normal to abuse others. Or worse, if he becomes the bully's sidekick, he will start believing that it is acceptable to be abused. The child will eventually grow up to be an individual who lets everybody around him take advantage of him and abuse him. He will not be able to stand up to abuse. He will never learn to value himself.

Similarly, if the teachers in the school do not encourage the child enough, the child will not be confident enough to showcase his talents. On the other hand, if the child has even one encouraging teacher, he will not be afraid to exhibit his talents. He will not be afraid to believe in his convictions. Teachers play an important role in nurturing the child's talents and encouraging them to believe in themselves. When this is absent, the child grows up to be an individual with very low self-esteem.

This is why school plays an important role in the development of self-esteem in the individual.

Society

The society that we live in is a constant teacher to all of us. We learn something or the other; every day from the various people we interact with within our society. It may be from our neighbor or from the milkman or even the guy at the billing department in the nearby grocery store. We are influenced by the various people in our society. We make most decisions, keeping what the society will think of it, in mind. This is because we are brought up to think that way.

When we grow up in a conservative society, which is not very accepting, we grow up with a narrow mindset as well. If the society does not approve of failures, we condemn ourselves for these failures. We do not take these failures in the right way. We blame ourselves too much for even one small failure, and that dampens our morale for good. When we grow up in a society where it is normal to demean someone for the smallest of mistakes, we think it is normal to criticize ourselves too much for the smallest of setbacks.

On the other hand, when we grow up in an accepting and forgiving society, we learn to respect others in society as well. We learn to forgive others for their mistakes and respect them for what they are and not let one bad experience change it all. We learn to be easy on ourselves for committing a silly mistake as well. We learn to forgive ourselves for any possible mistake and learn to move on. We understand that it is normal to make mistakes, and it is part and parcel of life.

Our personality is also dependent on the kind of society we grow up in. Hence it is highly essential that we pick only the right things from the people around us.

Media

In today's world, the media plays an important role in your life, especially if you are a teenager or a young adult. When you grow up, you look for inspiration on media. You idolize these music stars and other celebrities and try to ape them. I will not be exaggerating when I say that the media has a negative impact on our morale. This is because of the stuff projected by media.

For instance, teenage girls draw references from the celebrities shown on the media. They begin having body issues. They are carried away by the size zero fad and other things and end up spoiling their health. Research shows that most teenage girls suffer from anorexia because of their desire to stay fit and slim. They think that their beauty is defined by their height and weight. They think it is fine to starve themselves to appear slim. They start giving more importance to the external appearance and rely on it way too much. They begin judging people for the way they look and not for the way they behave. This judgmental attitude is not just restricted to others. They often employ it on themselves too. They are too harsh on themselves for being fat or dark or short. They blame themselves for not being pretty like the models they see on television. This need to perpetually look pretty has made them get addicted to cosmetics. They end up dabbing too much of these chemical-laden cosmetics without realizing the harm it poses for the health of their skin and hair. Similarly, they go to the extent of having plastic surgeries done to look pretty. Everything is fine, so long as the surgery is successful. I do not want to comment about the surgeries that have failed and resulted in these young girls losing whatever little confidence they had.

These girls do not appreciate their traits or talents. They don't make it a point to explore their talents. They have absolutely no sound value systems in place. They blindly follow what their favorite celebrity endorses. They stop analyzing and do not utilize their decision-making skills. They leave the decision making to their favorite celebrities. They judge other girls who focus on other serious life choices such as academics, careers, etc. and make life harder for them. So when it comes to being a teenager in today's world, you either follow the mob, or you get frowned at for being an exception.

The story gets sadder when it comes to boys and young men. They again tend to draw inspiration from their favorite sportsman or movie star. They do not think twice before following their footsteps, without thinking about the applicability of it in their lifestyle. They get into bad habits such as narcotics and other drugs, alcoholism, etc. at a very young age to imitate their favorite celebrities. They set standards for themselves, keeping these celebrities as parameters. When they fail to meet these parameters, they get depressed and dejected.

This is the influence of media on us. It is up to us to let it affect our self- esteem and tell us who we are. We can choose to ignore the negative aspects of media and just watch it purely for entertainment. Hence it is up to us to get affected by media.

Feedback

Feedback plays an important role in our growth as an individual. Whether we like it or not, there will be people who will be giving us feedback on our work. We do not realize the impact of this feedbacks on our morale. When the people around us constantly give us negative feedback, we end up believing that our work is entirely flawed. When people around us constantly criticize us, we end up doubting ourselves. We end up getting frustrated when we are constantly criticized. We end up not having any self-respect. We do not value ourselves. We end up being a victim of low self-esteem. We have already seen the repercussions of having low levels of self-esteem.

Another important aspect of feedback is how we take this feedback. Sometimes, our friends and family will be giving us negative feedback only with the intention to correct our mistakes. If we end up losing our confidence because of this, then it is entirely our fault. On the other hand, if we don't really appreciate the positive feedback, it will not have an impact on our morale. Hence, the huge responsibility of taking this feedbacks in the right way lies in us.

Consequences And Events

The events that occur in our life also have an impact on our self-esteem. This is so relevant, especially in the case of a child. When the child is often made to go through negative experiences, it has a negative impact on him. Their morale and self-esteem often stem from their experiences.

Now let us take the examples of children who had to grow up in an abusive home. The negative experiences, the children go through affects their self- esteem. When they are abused constantly, they believe that it is fine not to value themselves. They end up believing that they deserve to be treated in an abusive fashion. This, in turn, results in the child growing up to be an individual with very low self-esteem.

When we are an adult, the experiences, life offers us plays an important role in the development of our self-esteem. It is not always possible to have only good experiences. Instead of looking at our bad experiences with contempt, we should look at them as opportunities to learn. This way, our morale, and confidence will not be affected even if we encounter bad experiences down the line.

Apart from the intensity of the experience itself, the way we tackle it also matters a lot. When tackling a bad experience bravely, our confidence is tremendously improved. We start

44

believing in our problem-solving skills. This will, in turn, have a positive impact on our self-esteem.

Challenges And Opportunities

Challenges and opportunities go hand in hand. Our life is never devoid of them but seldom do we realize their presence before it is too late. Life is not interesting without these challenges or opportunities. It is plain and dull when we don't have anything interesting happening.

Apart from adding an interesting quotient to our lives, challenges and opportunities play an important role in influencing our confidence. Not clear? Well, how individual encounters the challenges that come his way and how he makes the best use of the opportunities that present themselves, define the person's confidence.

When a person is met with a challenge, he has two options – to deal with it or sulk. When an individual learns to deal with the challenge and figure out a solution for it, he will be impressed by his analytical skills. This will, in turn, develop his confidence and, in turn, self-esteem. On the other hand, when the person sits and sulks around, at the brink of a challenge, they will not be able to move on. They will feel powerless and feel discouraged from doing anything productive. Their confidence gets easily affected and makes them believe that they are not fit for anything.

The same approach goes for opportunities. Let us assume a lucrative opportunity presents itself. When you accept this opportunity and benefit from it, you will be motivated to not let go of such opportunities in the future. This will, in turn, increase your confidence. You will be able to take up newer opportunities in the future with zest and enthusiasm. On the other hand, when you let go of a good opportunity, you will forever regret it. You will not be able to forgive yourself easily for letting go of such a lucrative offer. This will have a negative impact on your morale. This will, in turn, decrease your confidence and results in you having low self-esteem.

Success

We all run behind success. All our actions are driven by our thirst to succeed. Why does success play such a crucial role in our lives? This is because we have been brought up saying that success is the one thing that defines us. It does not matter how talented we are. It does not matter how emotionally strong we are. If we don't taste success at least once, we will not be able to gain the respect of others. People don't respect us when we don't succeed.

This perception of success has a huge impact on our confidence. When we begin to use success as a parameter for defining our efforts, we will be dejected when we don't succeed in the conventional way. We lose faith in our efforts and talents when we do not succeed. This, in turn will affect our morale and confidence. When our confidence is shattered, the next to follow suit, will be our self-esteem.

Failures are the stepping-stones to success. But most of us don't see it that way. We look at temporary failures as permanent setbacks and get dejected. We do not look past these failures and end up getting affected by them for a long period of time. We look at failures as negative elements in our life, when in reality; these failures can actually help us learn a lot. Failures intimidate us. This fear of failure also has a negative impact on our confidence.

On the other hand, when we learn to look at failures as learning experiences, we will be able to realize that even failures have a positive impact on us. When we stop running towards success

46

blindly, we will be able to appreciate the other facets of life. This will teach us to remain confident, whether we succeed or fail. We learn to remain level headed irrespective of the results. This will make us respect our efforts. When we respect and believe in our efforts, success is no longer an issue. Your efforts will yield you the desired results.

When you realize that your efforts are not affected by the results, your confidence will improve tremendously. You will grow up into a strong individual who firmly believes in his efforts no matter what. You will be labeled as a success or failure, only when you believe in those labels. When these are nothing but labels to you, you will truly be able to realize your confidence.

Popularity

Fame is a fickle thing. We come to know the meaning of the word 'popular', the minute we step into school. We understand the implications of being popular from noticing the preferential treatment the individual is getting. When a child sees that a popular student is being treated differently from the others, he begins to believe that popularity is everything. He believes that popularity improves one's confidence. When he grows up into an individual, he carries that notion with him still, though not in the same intensity.

When a person is treated like a celebrity for some reason, his confidence automatically improves and so does his self-esteem. On the other hand, if the people around him seldom like a person, he will not end up liking himself. This will, in turn, affect his confidence and self-esteem as well.

Everybody wants to be loved and celebrated by others for this very same reason. They believe in themselves more, when others praise them. They feel good about themselves, when others

47

compliment them. Appreciations and compliments can make a lot of difference to one's self-esteem.

Competence

When an individual believes that he is talented, his confidence improves tremendously. All of us are talented. But some of us are more talented than an average individual. This is because they go the extra mile in identifying their hidden talents, by means of introspection. Our talents can help us gain popularity in no time, if our efforts are consistent.

On the other hand, if we don't build on our talents, we will not be able to achieve our full potential. Sometimes, we do not take the extra effort to identify our talents. This results in us believing that we do not have any talents at all. This will dampen our confidence. This will in turn lower your self-esteem.

Signs of low Self-Esteem

To help ourselves from falling into the trap of having low self-esteem, it is essential to know what the symptoms or the warning signs are. Then we can address whatever the cause is and work on bettering that aspect of ourselves and turning it into a positive.

We exude our state of emotional wellbeing to the outside world. Thus, how we feel and what we think about can be seen by those who cross our path. We attract what we put out into the world – this is known as the "law of attraction."

So, when our self-esteem is low, we will attract more of the same in our lives.

But when we have a healthy level of self-esteem, we will attract more positivity, joy, happiness, and a sense of wellbeing and abundance. We will find that life will have more appeal to us than when our self-esteem is low.

When we are happy and have a healthy level of self-esteem, we have the desire to do things and a desire to achieve and better our lives. You then have a sense of zest for life, which may urge you to live a very sociable life.

We do experience days where we feel a little "down," but this is where it is important to know what the signs and symptoms are of low self-esteem, so you can take action, if action is needed.

Some of the most common signs of low self-esteem that one should look out for are the following:

- Lack of confidence

- Fearful behavior

- Inability to be assertive

- Pretentiousness

- Anti-social behavior

- Indecisiveness

- Rebelliousness

- Lack of generosity or empathy

- Materialism Lack of Confidence

When we have low self-esteem, this results in a lack of self-confidence. People who have low self-confidence have little or no faith in themselves and/or their abilities. They normally seek the approval of others. Although they may not need their approval, these individuals have a dire need to feel appreciated.

Generally, people who have low self-confidence do not have a very high opinion of themselves and may feel that they somehow "fall short" compared to others. Some also tend to appear shy or introverted.

Another sign of low self-confidence is boastfulness. Some people boast about their existent and/or non-existent achievements. They have a need to feel superior to others, but in reality, they know that they are not over-achievers, and they are, in fact, not achieving anything better than anyone else.

Confidence and self-esteem affect how we think, how we feel about ourselves, and about others and how successful we deem ourselves to be. Fearful Behavior

Generally, these individuals are fearful of everything in life. They will try to hide from anybody, be invisible, blend into a crowd, and insignificant.

Such individuals generally have a fear of change and a fear of trying new things in life. They do not particularly enjoy facing new situations in their lives. They prefer not to draw any attention to themselves.

Some people also fear attending functions where they are faced with the possibility of meeting new people and their uncertainty of how they will fit in.

This could also include a fear of traveling alone and a fear of taking risks in life. For some, this even includes the fear of leaving their home. (Which serves as a "safety blanket" for them.

They generally prefer things to stay as they are. These individuals are also prone to pleasing and/or obeying everyone except themselves.

Inability to be Assertive

These individuals generally find it very difficult to say "no" to anybody or even stand up for their rights. They are unable to assert themselves.

People who lack assertiveness find it difficult to express their opinions, feelings, and beliefs towards others openly and honestly.

Individuals who lack assertiveness generally cannot put their ideas and thoughts forward. They are also often not straight forward and tend to sell themselves short. They may also come across to others as being submissive.

These individuals are generally non-confrontational, as they feel unable to defend themselves and stand up for what they believe. They may land up in situations where they are under too much pressure but cannot say so.

On a negative note, they can often be aggressive. But, this aggression is indicative of "false inner strength." These individuals are not aggressive, as aggressive behavior is more indicative of self-enhancing behavior.

Being assertive means having the ability to "speak your mind" (in a gentle manner) and to say "no" when you feel the need to... Pretentiousness

These individuals pretend to be someone or something which they are not, purely to keep up appearances. They spend money that they cannot afford and tend to buy things they do not need.

They will generally try to impress everyone in any possible way they can. These individuals have a dire need to be admired and respected by others. They also need to fit in and be accepted.

At a social gathering, these individuals could be labeled as the "light of the party." They generally enjoy the attention and tend to overspend when entertaining friends and family.

They tend to overcompensate with material possessions and the manner in which they come across to others. It is not about making other people feel bad about themselves. It is more about their need to feel good about themselves.

Anti-Social Behavior

These individuals are often also attention seekers as they are generally ignored by people and will resort to doing things that will gain the attention of others.

Sometimes these individuals will also commit acts that attract negative attention. But, they perceive negative attention as still being attention. To them, some form of attention is better than no attention at all.

Anti-social behavior is generally considered as either disobedient or angry (aggressive) behavior, or it may also be considered as rebellious or uncooperative behavior.

People who show signs of anti-social behavior generally tend to be withdrawn. They can resort to either aggressive or uncooperative behavior.

But this depends on the individual and various other factors.

Most of the time, people tend to show anti-social behavior when they are in their teens. However, in such a case where this is not just a "teenage phase," these teenagers can grow up having personality disorders later in their lives.

A good example of anti-social behavior would be the "very popular naughty child."

Indecisiveness

These individuals find it difficult to make a decision. There are various factors which may hinder their ability to make a firm decision.

They have a fear of being criticized, judged, and even a lack of courage prohibit these individuals from making decisions. Thus, absolving them from any form of responsibility.

They can be indecisive about anything, from doing something very small, choosing something from a menu, or taking a new job. On a bigger scale, they could be indecisive about making serious life-changing decisions.

Fear is one of the big driving forces behind indecisiveness and can prevent these individuals from finding happiness, from finding the right life partner and from changing their lives.

This hinders self-growth, self-confidence, and to an extent, ones level of independence and individuality. Thus, this can also affect various areas of one's life.

Not making a decision, is like choosing to do nothing at all... Rebellious Behavior

These individuals will rebel either in a positive or a negative way. This is another form of seeking attention and/or getting their point across.

Once again, also to these individuals any form of attention, is still attention. Whether this is in a negative or a positive form.

One good example of such behavior is when someone has been told or urged not to do something and yet the person will turn around and do exactly that, out of a sense of "spite" to others.

There are individuals who will act rebelliously, just for rebelling, despite the fact that they may know that they are wrong in some way.

This can rather be seen as a cry for attention or help, rather than an act performed out of sheer spite to another. Sometimes these individuals do not even realize what signals their behavior is sending out to others.

Lack of Generosity and Empathy

These individuals lack a sense of generosity and empathy. They perceive themselves as being underserving. They are not really "givers".

They cannot give, because for them they cannot receive, as they feel unworthy of receiving. They find it difficult to compliment others or even receive compliments themselves.

Generally, when these people receive a compliment, they will not thank the person for it, but rather comment on how old something is or respond with a question, such as "are you sure?"

This is not out of disrespect or ungratefulness, but rather their own sense of unworthiness. They do not feel that they are deserving of any compliments. This is nearly a foreign concept to some.

It is even difficult for them to help others and support charities and/or donate money towards a worthy cause. They tend to hold on to what they have and do not get rid of just anything.

Materialism

These individuals attach a lot of value to material possessions and wealth. They generally judge others not by their qualities, but by their material possessions.

One will find that there exists a lot of competition in the lives of people who are materialistic. There is always one person competing with another and there is a dire need to own the best of everything.

They would generally try to be "one up" on the next person and these individuals are not necessarily shy about showcasing their material possessions.

They generally tend to look down on those who are less fortunate and to them the only people who really count are people of the same monetary and/or social standing as themselves.

They tend to perceive rich people as more valuable (and important) than poor people; irrespective of the qualities they may possess.

CHAPTER 4: PROTECT YOURSELF FROM ENERGY VAMPIRES

Energy vampires are people who can drain a great deal of energy from you. They tend to have problem after problem, and they constantly come to you, asking for more than a reasonable amount of support. As an Empath, you feel into their position, empathize with them, and find yourself personally responsible for providing them with the energy required to do what is needed from you. This quickly turns into a treadmill, where you are constantly running to meet the person's energy needs, but you are never able to fulfill their needs. This is because they are an energy vampire.

To protect yourself from energy vampires, you need to teach yourself how to say "no." Learning to say no and stand behind it is important. This is how you can support yourself in feeling confident and protected in saying no. When you say no to an energy vampire, make sure that you consciously say no with your energy as well. Some people will envision their protective shield blocking out the request, preventing the energy from coming into their space altogether. Keeping out the energy of the energy vampire is important. If you let it in, it can begin to create empathic sensations within you that might cause you to change your mind. This is less of a worry when you become stronger in protecting yourself, but early on you are susceptible to changing your mind as a result of this energy.

Recognizing energy vampires and learning how to say no to them will also require you to protect yourself from shouldering any further responsibility. Affirming to yourself that it is not your duty to fulfill other people's needs beyond what you feel is reasonable is important. If you are not doing it out of love for yourself and the other person, you are not doing it for the right person. If you are doing something that extends your energy more than you can reasonably give, you are giving too much. Ensure that you educate yourself on saying no and that you consciously clear your energy field from the request. This will protect you against the energy, the request, and the energy vampire. You also want to minimize the amount of time you spend around the energy vampire as much as possible and practice setting stronger boundaries with them regarding what you are willing to listen to and engage with to create a stronger sense of protection against the energy vampire. This way, you do not feel like you are constantly in protection mode and you give yourself space to breathe and enjoy life.

Save Yourself from Time Vampires Too

In addition to energy vampires, there are also time vampires. Frequently, an energy vampire may also be a time vampire. However, not all time vampires are energy vampires. Time vampires are people who take up far too much of your time. You may find yourself constantly doing things for them, spending excessive time with them, or investing a lot of time worrying about them. As a result, they end up taking up far too much of your precious time.

The best way to deal with a time vampire is to limit the time that you are willing to share with them. Decide what your boundary needs to be, set it, and stand behind it. Begin reinforcing it by only giving them the allotted amount of time and then saying no when the boundary is reached. This also counts when you are thinking about them. If you find yourself worrying about the person, say no to yourself and set a boundary with yourself.

Reducing the amount of time you are willing to spend on a person, especially one that is toxic toward you (whether consciously or unconsciously), can protect you.

Even though it is nice to help people and you want to help others feel good in their lives, it is not your responsibility. Have an honest conversation with yourself about why you feel personally responsible for others and then begin to enforce boundaries with yourself as well. Creating these personal boundaries will make it easier for you to prevent yourself from feeling personally responsible for everyone else's needs and feelings. Then, it will become easier for you to say no and protect your time. When you do say no, make sure that you fulfill that time instead with a genuine act of self-love. The more you take good care of yourself, the easier it is to understand why you deserve your time, energy, and attention even more than anyone else. Even if that does not feel natural or "right" to you in the beginning. Soon, you will understand that it is a necessary protection and self-care practice. Not only does it help you feel great, but it will also amplify your ability to help others.

Preserve and Protect Your Energy

You must learn to preserve and protect your energy as an Empath. Knowing how to "tune out" of the world from time to time to give yourself the space to recharge is important. One great way to do this is by getting a high-quality set of noise-cancelling headphones and putting them on when you go out in public or in a noisy environment. While you may not be able to do this every time, using them in certain circumstances can support you in staying focused on the music's energy rather than the environment around you. Consider using music that is uplifting and upbeat so that it amplifies your energy, rather than you going out and coming home feeling depleted.

Another way to protect your energy is to begin practicing energetic boundaries. This means that you make yourself unavailable to tune into the energies of those around you unless you permit yourself to do so. Set the boundary with yourself that you are not going to tune into any energy.

Learning to switch your gift "on" and "off" can take practice, and the best way to do it is to start. Soon, you will learn to be firm and consistent, and your boundaries will be effortless to uphold. This means that you begin gaining power and control over your Empath gift to no longer feel like you are being ruled by it. Instead, you can rule the gift and use it as you need to support you in your life and soul purpose, as well as lead a quality life.

Shielding is a powerful practice that Empaths use to protect themselves from external energies. This is a form of creating an energetic boundary that can stay in place and keep you feeling protected without you always having to be consciously working toward it. In the beginning, your energetic shield may need continuous conscious reinforcement. Once you become more skilled with it, however, it becomes a lot easier.

The best shield to consider using when you are going out in public, or anywhere that your gift may be overly activated, is called a bubble shield. This shield is created by you envisioning a white light glowing in your solar plexus. This light then grows, purifies your body and energy field, and fills it with white light. Let this light grow until it forms a bubble that extends four feet away from your body in either direction, including down into the Earth. This shield is one that, once built, will stay in place as long as you desire. If you feel that your shield is down or you have taken it down by accident, you can always recreate it using the same strategy. Some people even choose to create a new one every morning to support them in staying protected throughout the day. Any time that you feel your energy is being threatened visualize your shield to reinforce it and keep unwanted energies out.

Energy Vampires and Empaths

Anna is an empath. She has a beautiful soul that lights up her surroundings. She does not only feel other people's emotions, she also absorbs them. When someone is happy, she is also happy. When someone is sad, she is also sad.

Her officemate, Glenda, is a beautiful woman. She has a good life – a three-bedroom house, two cars, two kids, and a good husband. However, she does not seem to appreciate everything she has. She complains about everything in her life.

Anna feels weak when she is near Glenda. It is as if she is sucking her energy. She feels drained after talking to her.

Glenda is an energy vampire. She is beyond toxic. However, what is an energy vampire? Why do they drain all your energy? How can you spot them?

You see, every interaction with another human being is an energy exchange. Some people (like the empaths) give us good energy, while others (like the energy vampires) sap it.

Let us say that you just were fired from work and you are really angry and sad. Therefore, you decided to talk to your mom about it. Your mom is warm,

welcoming, and loving demeanor calms you down. It gives you hope. It makes you realize that life is not very bad.

Your mother is what we call an "energy-giver". She has this rejuvenating effect. She makes you feel safe and secure.

Now, let us say that you lost your job and you decided to talk to your father. He is not as warm as your mom is. He is a harsh critic. After you told him your problem, he started saying things like "you'll never find another job because you're stupid" and "well, that's expected because you're good for nothing". Your dad, in this scenario, is what we call an energy vampire.

Energy vampires are emotionally immature people who feel like the world revolves around them. They have an underdeveloped psyche, so they feed off other people's emotional and psychic energy.

They are sometimes overly dramatic. They engage in erratic behavior. Some energy vampires are just plain pessimistic. Some of them are harsh critics. However, some of these toxic people are extremely dangerous – sociopaths, narcissists, and even psychopaths.

Here are the common characteristics of toxic people:

You feel sick and tired after talking to them.

Energy vampires are difficult to talk to. They complain and they criticize everything you say. They make you feel stupid.

61

After you talk to a toxic person, your shoulders feel heavy. It is as if you carried two sacks of rice or two hollow blocks.

They kill your hopes and dreams.

Eleanor wanted to be a ballet dancer when she was young. However, she was from a poor family and her parents cannot afford ballet lessons. Her mother said that dancing is a hobby and not a profession. Therefore, she chose to be a teacher instead.

Even if she is good at her job, Eleanor grew bitter because she did not achieve her childhood dreams.

Instead of lifting her students, she craps on their dreams. She tells her students that they are too ugly to become celebrities or too stupid to become entrepreneurs. She would come up with over a million reasons why her students cannot do whatever they want to do.

You would be surprised to know that there are many teachers who think and act like Eleanor. However, toxic naysayers are not only found in the academe. You can find them everywhere. They can be your sister, friends, co-worker, romantic partner, and even your parents.

They say things like:

"Are you sure you have enough experience?" "I don't know if that would work."

"It's already done before." "It's unproven."

"I'm not sure if someone would pay for it." "That sounds dangerous."

"It's going to be difficult."

Most naysayers have not achieved their own goals and dreams. They do not have an inspired existence. They are cloaked in self-loathing, jealousy, and fear, so they project these fears onto other people.

They make you feel bad about your life.

Toxic people will make you feel bad about your life. They make you feel like you are not good enough. They use their passive aggressive nature to make you feel like you are stuck and can never escape your job or your problems.

They only pay attention to you when they need something from you.

We all have that one friend who only calls us when they need a favor. Toxic people only give you attention when it serves them. They will use you and take everything you have until there is nothing left.

They hold grudges.

Joel was married to Diana for 7 years. They have a picture-perfect marriage. They have two kids and they look like they love each other. They seem like they have it all.

One day, Diana talked to Joel. She told him that she is no longer happy with their marriage and that she has been having an affair with her boss in the last two months.

Joel was beyond devastated. He started to stir up drama on social media and made sure that his friends know about Diana's affair.

However, 2 years later, Joel is still as bitter as he was when Diana broke his heart. He has become toxic. He is angry all the time and defames the mother of his children whenever he can. He just cannot let everything go.

Toxic people hold grudges. They bring up your past mistakes to create drama. They just cannot move on. They exude the negative energy that makes you feel weak and dizzy.

They do not take responsibility for their actions.

Nothing is ever their fault. They blame their problems on other people. They do not take responsibility for their actions and their lives.

They are inconsistent.

It almost feels like they have multiple personality disorder. They change their attitude, behavior, and personality to manipulate other people and get what they want.

They are colder than ice.

They are not supportive. They withhold love to manipulate you and get you to do whatever they want.

They lack empathy.

Empathy is a strong indication of a healthy personality. Energy vampires often have no empathy. They have a hard time understanding what other people are going through. They have a huge ego.

Toxic people often have an inflated self-image. They feel like they are smarter and better than the people around them are. They feel like they know everything.

They are abusive.

Some toxic people are just plain "evil". They can be both physically and emotionally abusive. They would humiliate and bully you. They would force you to give up your power so they can do whatever they want.

Different Types of Energy Vampires

Energy vampires are generally drawn to empaths because of their warmth and compassion. They often feast on empaths' energy.

If you are an empath or a highly sensitive person, you should try to stay away from the following energy vampires.

Drama Queen

Ara is a successful film producer. She is intelligent and has mad writing skills. She has a sharp wit and a captivating beauty. However, she constantly craves for attention and engages in attention-seeking behavior. She has a strong sense of entitlement.

She constantly stirs up dramatic situations. She will manipulate other people. She loves to create gossip just to start a conflict. She loves to pit her friends against each other just for her own entertainment. In addition, she is obsessed about looking and being perfect. She gets hysterical over the smallest things. Drama queens have zero accountability for their life and behavior. They start gossip just to create drama and conflict. They like pitting people against each other. They often recruit minions to help them tear down their targets.

These people are not only toxic. They are also shallow. They feel like the world is going to end just because they are having a bad day. They like being the center of attention.

Jealous Jane

Marie has a great life. She is an American living in the beautiful island of Capri. Everything in his r life seems perfect.

However, when she opens her Instagram account, she sees her friends going frolicking in exotic islands like Bali and Maldives. She sees her friends' wedding photos and she felt like she is missing out a lot in life.

She is chronically unhappy and complains about every little thing. She does not appreciate everything she has.

Jealous people carry the heavy, negative energy that is extremely dangerous to empaths. These people have low self-esteem. They are emotionally unstable. They berate others to cover up their feelings of inadequacy.

Temperamental Tom

Albert is a good man most of the time. He is kind and generous. However, he has a short temper. He gets angry over small things and he has a hard time controlling his anger.

When he is mad, he would throw anything he can get his hands on. He uses everyone around him as an emotional toilet. He dumps emotional crap whenever he can.

Temperamental Toms are draining and scary. Regular exposure to these toxic people can lead to extreme emotional trauma.

Manipulating Mark

Manipulating Marks are tricky and deceptive people who will pose as your friend. They will take time to know the things that can make you happy. They will use this information to manipulate you to do what they want you to do.

These toxic people often play the victim. They would exaggerate their personal issues, so you would sympathize with them. They tell half-truths to get what they want.

They will often pressure you or engage in passive aggressive behavior just to get you to see things their way.

Arrogant Arman

Arrogant people see everything as a competition. They believe that they are superior to others and sometimes, too cocky.

These people exaggerate their abilities to make you feel bad about yourself. They constantly brag about their accomplishments. They are often rude and mean.

Being around arrogant people can be extremely draining, especially for empaths.

Blaming Bens

Blaming Bens love to play the victim. They like to blame all their misfortunes to other people. They do not take responsibility for their actions or their life in general.

Selfish Sam

Selfish Sam's are people who prioritize their self-interest. These people have a little bit of a narcissistic streak. They will do everything just to get what they want.

The Critic

We can all use a constructive criticism every now and then. However, the Critic does not give other feedback to build them up. They just want to rip other people apart so they can feel good about themselves.

Let us take Gina as an example. She used to be a beauty queen, but her good looks have already faded. This made her feel bitter and angry.

Her bitterness pushed her to criticize everyone around her. She would tell her daughter that she is fat even if she is only 125 pounds. She would criticize her staff on a daily basis. She puts people down so she could feel better about herself and her life.

The Ice Queen

Empathy is an important trait because it allows you to fully understand the people around you. It allows you to step into other people's shoes and really feel what they are going through on a daily basis. It helps you build amazing relationships.

Ice queens are cold people who do not have empathy and compassion. They are disrespectful, disinterested, and unresponsive. They make you feel like you are not worthy of their attention and they often minimize your pain, sufferings, and even your needs.

How Negative Energy Directly Affects An Empath?

As mentioned many times in this book, empaths are highly sensitive beings. This means that they feel emotions more intensely than others do. When they are happy, they feel like they are floating in the air. They feel like they are on cloud nine. Every cell in their being exudes joy and excitement.

However, when they are sad, they feel like they are carrying the world on their shoulders. It feels like you are drowning in the sea of sadness and hopelessness. They cannot concentrate.

Empaths experience intense emotional contagion. This means that other people's negative energy affects them strongly.

Let us take Emma and Camille's case as an example. These women work as customer service representatives in a huge telecommunication company. They entertain difficult customers day in and day out.

Camille is a great customer representative. She is empathetic, but she is not an empath. When she talks to a difficult customer, she would sometimes feel bad or angry. However, after the conversation is over, she can easily shake the negative energy off.

Like Camille, Emma is also a great customer service representative. However, she is an empath. Whenever she talks to irate customers, she would feel their stress, anger, and pain. She soon developed depression and anxiety. Being regularly exposed to negative energy can lead to nightmares, lethargy, and extreme fatigue. It can even lead to suicide ideation. This is why empaths should always try to stay away from toxic people and learn how to block off negative energy.

How to Block Negative Energy and Protect Yourself from Toxic People

Constant exposure to toxic people can lead to a plethora of mental health issues including depression and anxiety.

To protect yourself from toxic people and block negative energy, you have to follow these tips:

Stay away from negative energy.

Distance yourself from toxic people. However, you have to stay at least twenty feet away from an energy vampire.

Create a foolproof plan in dealing with stressful situations.

You must address your empathic needs and honor your sensitivities. Create a plan that you can use in handling emotionally rattling situations.

For example, let us say that you become disoriented and drained whenever your boss questions or belittles your work. You can address this problem in many ways. You can improve the quality of your work to avoid criticism. You can also leave your job and get another one. Alternatively, you can start your own business so you become your own boss.

Creating a solid stress management plan can help you protect your energy and easily handle challenging and draining situations.

Listen to your heart and your gut.

Remember that folks aren't always, what they appear to be. We are now living in a world where folks wear all kinds of masks. Lots of people pretend to be someone they're not only to get what they desire.

In order to protect the energy of yours, you should listen to your heart and gut. Be slow to fall into friendship. Before you open yourself up to someone, try to check his/her energy. Stay away in case he has/she is giving you bad vibes.

Respect yourself enough to walk from anything that drains the energy of yours and also can make you sad.

Don't take things personally.

One of the greatest methods to defend yourself from toxic energy is to numb yourself. You've to stop taking things personally. Remember that hurt folks hurt other folks. Various other people's unhealthy and toxic behavior has absolutely nothing to do with you.

When you stop taking things individually, you're saving yourself from needless suffering.

Practice guerilla meditation.

Meditation has become one of probably the biggest buzzwords in the "new age" industry. Nevertheless, it's more than that.

Meditation is an old practice of focusing on a certain word, object, vision, and even person. It has a number of benefits, can strengthen your mind, and help improve your focus.

If you do not have a lot of time for regular meditation practice, you can try guerilla meditation.

This is how you do it: Whenever you feel exposed to an energy vampire, take a step back and close your eyes. Focus your energy on positive experiences.

You can think about a goal or a happy memory. You can also think about the things that you are grateful for.

This practice increases your vibrational frequency, blocking negative emotions and energies.

Use healing crystals.

Healing crystals do not only protect you from narcissists. It also protects you from other types of toxic people – the complainers, the manipulators, the pessimists, and the drama queens. We will discuss these stones in the next part of this book.

Set healthy boundaries.

Limit your time with stressful people. If a toxic person asks you to spend a little time with her/him, just say "no". Be clear about what you will and will not tolerate.

Visualize.

Before you leave your house, close your eyes and imagine that you are covered with a protective cloak. This can help you feel secure and protected. Remember that your imagination is powerful. It could instantly raise your vibrational frequency.

Say a powerful mantra.

To avoid getting caught up with someone else's drama, say this mantra "what's yours is yours and what's mine is mine". You can also use the mantra "I do not accept energies that are not mine".

Take the time to be close to nature

Go for a walk. Be close with nature. You do not have to go to the beach or a forest. You can just go to the nearest park and enjoy your local scenic views.

Rub your palms together for 30 seconds to one minute.

Rubbing your palms together creates warmth and friction. This helps switch your moods and ward off negative energy.

Stay away from negativity.

Distance yourself from pessimistic people and surround yourself with people who radiate hope, happiness, and positivity.

Put your foot down.

You have to get clear with people about what you will and will not tolerate. This helps you stay in control of your energy and your life in general. You have to teach other people how to treat you.

Do not react to other people's negativity.

Disarm negative people with a positive response. When someone is putting you down, smile and say "thank you for your opinion" and then walk away.

Don't feed the beast.

Even when you're surrounded with negativity, make a choice to maintain the positivity of yours. The most effective way to accomplish this's to practice detachment.

Whenever you're feeling down, near the eyes of yours and think about happy memories.. Think about your goals. Think about all the things that you are grateful for.

Negativity has no space in your life if you keep feeding yourself with positive thoughts.

Visualize a bubble.

Every morning, close your eyes and focus on your breath. Block out any distracting thoughts and just observe how your chest goes up and down as you breathe.

Concentrate on your breathing. Remove any distracting thought that enters your mind.

Now, imagine that you are in a sacred bubble. This energetic bubble recharges your energetic field, surrounding you with positive energy. This bubble helps you block off negative energy.

This bubble helps you remain calm even when someone is freaking out or you are in a highly stressful environment.

Do an aerobic exercise.

Aerobic exercises such as running, walking, dancing, swimming, and cycling help you shake off excess energy. It helps you stay grounded and ward off unwanted energies and emotions.

Lastly, make a daily choice to adopt a positive attitude. Fill your days with joy and gratitude. Always choose to look at the brighter side of things.

CHPATER 5: SELF-LOVE

Before we proceed with the book and take you through the different steps of how to excel in the art of self-love, you need to be well-versed with some of the key dynamics about what self-love is all about. If you don't have the first clue what self-love is and have no idea why you are looking to achieve it, you have no hope of ever arriving at that destination. If you understand exactly what the topic is about, you are opening up your mind to achieving it yourself.

What is self-love?

Self-love is essentially the regard that someone has for themselves, basically the kind of feeling and affection you share for yourself. To be able to enable you to ascertain if you like yourself and in case it's adequate, I'm going to share a questionnaire with you. It' s worth noting at this point that there isn't one person on this planet who is completely and utterly in love with themselves, and that is probably a good thing – there is a fine line between loving yourself most naturally and healthily, and arrogantly loving yourself; every single person has something about themselves which they don't like, and while that is normal, it's important to balance all of that out with the things you love about yourself too, e.g. your shining plus points.

Your job here is to dutifully and honestly answer the different questions, as this short survey will act like a real assessment of how much you truly love yourself and the kind of improvement that you need. If you can identify your trouble hotspots, you can get to work on them much easier than if you have no clue where to start.

- Do you hold yourself responsible for the troubles you often face?

- Do you loathe who you are as a person?

- Do you regret who you are?

- If you were given a chance to be born again, would you like to be born as yourself?

- What is your definition of self-love?

- Do you tend to love others ways more than how you love yourself?

- Do you suffer from body image issues?

- Are you short on confidence?

- Do you take good care of yourself?

- Do you approve of yourself? Is the approval of others more important to you?

- Do you give yourself credit when you do well?

- Does the thought of failure make you feel less worthy?

- How would you rate your self-esteem?

- In terms of priority, how far down the list do you place yourself?

- Do you do everything for other people, and not much for yourself?

- Have any of your past relationships been extremely successful? If not, why not?

• How many things about your personality do you love?

• How many things about your appearance do you love?

• If someone gives you a compliment, do you take it, or do you bat back with a deflecting comment? E.g., if someone says "oh you look slim in that dress", do you say "thanks", or do you say "oh it's because it's black, black is slimming"?

• Do others treat you the way you wish they would?

These are some questions which will give you a fair idea of whether or not

you love your self. You do not need me to explain to you what the answers mean, because these are part of your journey; generally speaking, negative is bad, and positive is good, you don't need to be a brain surgeon to figure that out. The questions in themselves are self-explanatory and they will help you have a clear idea regarding how much work needs to be put in for the sake of loving who you are as a person. This is a journey which is worth every single step, so make sure you do it justice and be as honest as you can be, even if it is down to being painfully honest.

Basically, self-love is mainly about being honest about who you are and to be happy with your choices. You should not loathe your personality, you should be accepting of who you are and with the right kind of changes, you will be able to enjoy your personality, and allow others to appreciate it too.

Self-Ranking and Self Love

It's very common for man to rank themselves based on numerous factors. In the modern world, a sense of competitiveness is often seen as a path to doing well. When you perceive yourself as low on the social hierarchy, self-love suffers. Nobody wants to feel that they are inferior or worth less than other people. When we make the mistake of ranking ourselves on a low level, it sabotages your sense of self love.

However, this innate instinct to compare ourselves to one another can help or hinder, depending on the context. We often rank ourselves based on our professions, economic statuses, looks and appearance, and several achievements in a broad amount of areas, among many factors. In the animal kingdom, ranking determines the pack's leader, the chosen hunters and gatherers, the outcasts, and even the servants among the masses of different species on Earth.

When people also say that they have poor self-worth or low self-esteem because it implies that you can move higher on the ladder of self-love. Although accomplishments in these areas can boost one's ego, it should never be the lifeline source of your self-love.

Why do you need self-love?

Now that you know what self-love is, the next thing you need to be familiar with is the importance of self-love. Until and unless, you have a clear understanding of why self-love is so important, you will not be willing to put in too much effort for the sake of loving yourself, after all, if you don't understand the point of something, you're really not going to give it 100% time and effort.

It'sBecause of this, I'm going to talk about several of the major reasons you have to indulge in self-love. When you are going to have the best reasons to follow, it'll provide the incentives which are likely to guide you in an apt manner towards the spot we're targeting.

Improve your confidence

When you are willing to love who you are, it will give you the right confidence to excel. There are a lot of different challenges which life will throw in your way. In order to make sure that you can handle these challenges in an apt manner, you will have to be confident in yourself and in your ability. Confidence doesn't have to be about arrogance, gentle confidence is about being sure in yourself, and this shines through to other people, be it in a relationship, a friendship, or in a working situation. A confident person is happier person, and a happier person is a more attractive person overall.

Confidence arises from loving yourself. When you are happy with who you are as a person and you love yourself, you will be a whole lot more confident in your abilities. Confidence is needed in all walks of life and by choosing to love yourself, you will be able to enjoy the benefits of confidence in the long run. It's right that many situations in life can knock our confidence down a little, and this is perfectly normal, but it should only be a short-term process which is recovered from after a little time.

Feel better

It is important that people come to understand the fact that beauty comes in all shapes and sizes. There are so many people who are battling body issues day in and day out. They are so stressed about their own body type that it becomes really hard to love their own body. This is why you need to learn how to love yourself and you will begin to feel the change.

Modern day media doesn't help us in this regard, we are constantly being bombarded with pictures of the 'perfect' beach body, or the 'perfect' size 10 figure, but the bottom line is that nobody is perfect, and those images you seen in magazines and on the TV have probably been air-brushed to within an inch of their life! On top of this, just because someone has a so-called 'perfect' body, it doesn't mean they are happy with who they are on the inside – you never know how someone is feeling or what they are going through until you have walked in their shoes. Avoid comparisons at all costs!

Better productivity

There is no doubt about the fact that when you choose to love yourself, you will find better productivity. Those who are comfortable in their own skin are likely to offer full focus and concentration to their work, which can help them enjoy improved and better productivity.

Look at it this way, if you are hampered down with confidence issues, body issues, self-esteem issues, and you basically don't like yourself very much, are you going to wake up every day with a spring in your step and a will to tick off every item on your to do list? Probably not. If you can learn to love yourself then you are happier, and happier people are focused, productive, and they achieve success in various parts of their lives.

Harmonious life

Some too many people are battling issues of self-destruction and depression. When you can love yourself, you will feel how harmonious life will be. These little changes can trigger the right kind of reaction in your body and this is likely to bring in the much-needed difference as well. We all need peace and harmony and in order to attain that, you will have to look out for ways by which your inner mind is at peace. This is why you need to ensure that you can fall in love with yourself.

Feeling content is a wonderful feeling; you don't have to a high powered entrepreneur to be successful, you can simply be happy in your own life and in your own skin, and feeling content is a harmonious way to live. Battling issues in your own mind about how you feel and trying to fight with your emotions every single hour does not make you feel balanced or happy; however, if you can attain a self-love level, you won't have these issues to fight.

Happiness

In the end, we all know how each one of us craves for happiness. If you cannot enjoy happiness in your life, nothing is ever going to work out and this will create a lot of ruckus for you. Put simply, you have to choose happiness, because it isn't going to fall into your lap without a little work and a change of mindset. Happiness emanates from your inner-self and you have to make sure that you can love your own self in order to give you the best possible chance to feel happy overall.

When you are in love with who you are, it will help you choose happiness and this, in turn, can bring you a lot of joy as well. No individual can be happy unless they are pleased with who they are as a person, otherwise those dangerous comparisons can

81

come into play, which breeds negative emotions, such as anger, greed, jealousy, and unhappiness. This is not a pleasant or helpful road to go down.

Self Approval

When you have a stronger sense of self live, you learn to approve of yourself. What used to bother you and make you feel uneasy evaporates in the face of true self compassion and acceptance. Seeking the approval and live if others to make your world go round no longer becomes a priority or a prerequisite to happiness. In a world where many people forsake joy based on what others think of them, you will be free and much more illumined by the uplifting spirit of self love. Self-love will give you a lifelong advantage and higher self-esteem that is not dependent upon the approval and praise of others.

These are some of the key incentives to put you on the right path towards achieving self-love, as well as helping you to understand the core concepts of self-love too. Until, and unless, you are willing to do your bit and you have the fire to hone your skills in the field of self-love, it will be very hard for you to grasp the lesson. You are reading this book and you have got this far, so you must be determined to achieve that destination mark! You are Not Alone

One of the most important things that you must remember on your journey to developing greater self-love is that "You are not alone". There are people all around you, some you may interact with every day, and others that you may simply pass by, who are struggling to love themselves more and treat themselves as worthy individuals deserving of happiness.

82

Interestingly, when two individuals who lack self-love enter into a closer relationship of any kind (romantic, social, and business) those feelings of inadequacy tend to seep out and affect circumstances. Spouses that do not love themselves may find it hard to show affection, and are more likely to

argue or become angry when the other person doesn't meet their expectations in any way. In the workplace, employees who lack self-love may underperform regularly, or choose to doggedly undermine and compete with others to validate themselves through success. In a social environment, friends and associates with a lack of self-love may constantly seek approval from each other to lift and strengthen their secretly bruised egos.

This can be a difficult concept to understand when you are engrossed in your feelings, but if you can grasp it, you can change your entire life and positively affect others' lives.

It all starts by learning to love yourself.

At the end of the day, you must realize that there is no escaping yourself. You can change the way you look, alter your environment, raise your socioeconomic status or income, and even trade in your old buddies for a new crowd, but you will still have to live with yourself.

There is no escaping You as long as you are alive. Learning to have self-love and compassion takes time to build, especially if you have judged yourself harshly or accepted the negative words and ridicule of others as law. Fear not, for you can demolish the negative words and imprints of others from the past to start loving yourself today and creating a future that supports your well being and essence in every way possible.

So, before proceeding with this book, my advice to you is to first make your mind up that you need to indulge in self-love. You have to understand that until and unless your desire to love yourself is intact, nothing will happen. If however you are determined and you put in the work, determined to overcome your obstacles, there does lie a pot of gold at the end of that metaphorical rainbow.

It isn't rocket science, although learning to change your mind-set can feel difficult at the start. With some simple tips we will be listing here, you will be able to hone your skills and you should succeed in loving yourself lot more than what you are used to doing.

CHAPTER 6: INTROVERSION AND FRIENDS

People dislike being lonely, and if they sense that they can feel less alone by engaging another person in a simple conversation, they will. Many shy people tend to feel alone because they cannot find the courage to talk to another person, even if they are sharing the same space. However, certain social conventions might be the cause of anxiety, which prompts one to think that it is difficult to deal with other people and that one is much safer without inviting a new person into one's life. After all, most shy people have been let down by others at some point, and it is an act of self-preservation to be anxious around strangers.

Strangers

Solitude can be unhealthy for some, and it can even make one feel that he or she is unprepared for "battle." When shy kids enter school, they are forced into social interaction at a level that is unprecedented for most children at that age, making them engage in a battle armed with a gun, but no bullets. Some children can become cynically shy. In other words, they may feel so disconnected from the rest of the world that they become hostile towards others. In a world where everybody seems to want to make connections, being left out can be utterly frustrating. Many shy people try to connect with those around them, contrary to the belief that shyness is equivalent to passiveness. Those who are shy are excited to be invited to events. Still, they often feel depressed due to their perception that their preparation is incomplete, since after all, they cannot muster the courage to start a conversation. Some seek the courage to connect by lowering their inhibitions with alcohol and drugs, a temporary solution, not to mention potentially fatal.

People are encouraged to talk to others to prevent feelings of hate and hatred towards others who belong in social groups. After the day, everybody desires to feel acceptance and belongingness, and also to feel the planet is a safe place.

When you make it past the introductions and the first couple of generic conversational lines, you have to find a means to differentiate yourself from others who might, initially, seem quite similar.

Suppose your newfound potential friends learn anything distinctive about you, due either to your shyness or conversations simply never getting passed the most mundane of topics. In that case, it is unlikely that you will ever develop a deeper connection with them. There would simply be no way for them to know if the two of you have anything in common worth pursuing, any shared interests that you may want to delve into a deeper conversation about one day. They will be unaware of your strengths, your weaknesses, your quirks and your charms. Of course, this is hardly information you need to display openly to anyone. Some traits might very well be best kept firmly under wraps until true intimacy is established but revealing select tidbits that might prove interesting can allow you to build and enhance new friendships by opening up about yourself. In turn, your new companions will be more inclined to do the same, possibly revealing shared eccentricities, interests or lifestyle choices that you can enjoy and/or discuss together in more detail.

Often, the biggest detriment to letting others see glimpses of our personality and interests is due to shame. What if they dislike those features or interests, and we simply embarrass ourselves? What if they consider the information we share out of place or too forward and everything is awkward between them and us forever? Others won't like all too often we convince ourselves

86

that the stuff we want and our personalities, but the sole method to find out should be to let potential friends know about these issues. If you hide them, you will be rather bland since none of your best personality features or fun interests will be shown at all. You will also eliminate the chance of learning if they might enjoy similar pastimes or share your quirks. That would be a shame because shared interests and features are a surefire way to trigger bonding and a memorable impression.

As for technique on how to accomplish this, it is fairly straightforward. If something comes up that interests or excites you, simply mention it. Ask your acquaintance their thoughts on it and share yours. In this way, you can discuss skills, hobbies, even qualities you possess or value in others in a relatively organic way. Be careful not to force your viewpoints upon your chat companion. Express yourself in an enthusiastic but non-judgmental manner. You might discover that you have a lot in common, but the reverse could also happen. Even if you discover that you have little in common with the person who was so recently a stranger, it will do you little good to burn bridges or create an enemy. If you discover that your opinions diverge in a manner too significant to move past pleasantly, change the topic or if you must, politely end the conversation. If on occasion someone does hold different values or simply does not seem to share any of your interests, do not take it personally. In many cases, if you approach such people with flexibility and genuine interest, you might find that you have more in common than you thought or at the very least you will gain an interesting new perspective. Ultimately, no harm is likely to befall you from making your own interests and personality traits apparent, the worst case scenario, you simply both move on, leaving your own mentalities firmly intact. In other scenarios, you may be able to enjoy conversing with even someone with very different viewpoints from your own once you understand the reasoning behind them. Do not let fears of shame, judgment or rejection keep you from letting others see who you really are. It is the only way you can have valid and legitimate conversations with others, and that is worth the relatively minor risk incurred.

Colleagues

When running into a long-lost friend, colleague, or acquaintance, you can be more informal. Even a simple, "Hello! How are you? It's been a long time" will start the conversation, perhaps even lead to a longer conversation or a future hookup. Still, it doesn't hurt to know these tips to ensure that an accidental meeting can become productive and pleasant.

- Show your enthusiasm for the meeting. You can say, "It's beenforever! How are you?" or "I haven't seen you for so long! What's up?"
- Smile and make eye contact, too. You may either shake hands or hug each other depending on your past relationship, although a physical touch isn't mandatory in all cases.
- Listen to the information shared by your friend and offer your ownpersonal information, too. But keep it brief since there's little need to go into the gory details of your life. Ask about other members of the family, if you're familiar with them, too, since it shows your concern and extends the conversation.

You don't have to share details if you aren't comfortable with it. Just say, "Oh, nothing special, just the usual work-study-home routine" or "Same old, same old." You may, nonetheless, have to offer just a little bit more if the other person graciously offered a tidbit of information about what's up with his/her life.

End the small talk with an invitation to spend time in the future, which may or may not be definite. You can say, "Let's get together for coffee sometime," but you don't necessarily have to ask for the other person's contact details or give yours unless you're being asked for it. You can give your social media account, or your cellphone number, or your email address, whichever suits your mood at the moment.

Being introverted is more of a personal characteristic that is based on inner emotions rather than focusing on outer stimuli. Being an introvert does not make you fretful and shy. On the contrary, introverts are quiet but bold as a lion. They are not easily tossed around by others because most of the time, they are stern and smart – they know what they want and would stop at nothing to get it. To be shy is to be afraid of people and the situation at hand. One's inability to deliver a composed speech at a social or official gathering due to shyness isn't an indication that such a fellow is an introvert; it is a sign of fear. Although introverted people typically do not like moving close to others, they do appreciate it when they are around intimate people.

Quite a handful of people have mistaken shyness for introversion and have received the most shocking surprise ever. Some extroverts wish to have an introvert as a spouse. Because they cannot differentiate between introversion and shyness, they are caught in the middle. Most of them ended up getting the extroverted, shy partner or the ones with the personality that is neither introverted nor extroverted. These are the ones we earlier discussed to fall between the line.

Kayla was an easy-going, beautiful woman. One day, she was trying to get a shower after the day's work when she heard her next-door neighbor screaming at the top of her voice. It was a hotel room, so, she had every right to ignore the noise and mind her business. She went to the hotel every time she had business to settle out of town. This was one of her trips, and she had worked all day. Nothing was more important to her than her rest and a quiet environment at the moment. She had always chosen that particular hotel for its serenity over a period of time.; but that day made her want to regret her choice of hotel. She just needed a sound sleep and then this brouhaha. When the chattering wouldn't stop, she angrily left her room to find out what the problem was. On getting to the entrance of the door, she overheard the lady screaming, "How dare you treat me like trash? You don't care about anyone but you" and the ranting continued. Kayla had no choice but to knock. No way was she going to have a sound sleep with this woman been left alone. The door was opened, and she got in. After all said and done, Kayla discovered that Nora had misjudged Steeve. She thought he was just been shy when they met when in actual sense, Steeve was an introvert. He liked been left alone. He was not the outgoing type and didn't seem to be interested in things that caught Nora's fancy. Nora thought Steeve might be having an affair. Steeve on the other hand, when asked why he chose to shut Nora out of his world, replied by saying "I thought she was like me." Steeve had mistaken Nora's shyness for introversion on their first meeting. It wasn't too long that he found out that she was directly opposite of him. Nora always wanted to go shopping, hang around with friends, and get Steeve to talk about everything!

Kayla who was an introvert like Steeve had to seat Nora down and advised she either work on making the relationship work by accepting Steeve for who he truly was or just quit and walk away. For the first time in hours, there was peace in the vicinity.

From the story above, we see how most people mistake shyness for introversion. Although Steeve and Nora have been living peacefully with each other by learning to respect each other's personality, Nora must have gone through a lot to bring serenity into her home. When asked how she managed the saga, she said "to fall and stay in love with an introvert you must understand the following;"

Don't demand too much.

Introverts do not like it when people ask for too much of them. They don't want to be that seat filler that fills every empty seat in your life. He loves to be a part of your life but not you choking him with too much of you.

Don't be in haste.

Due to his quiet nature, an introvert would always like to take things slow, be it physically or emotionally. Rushing things up might piss him off and send him off.

Be original.

Introverted people are thrilled when they meet people who are original. He has enough in his head to analyze, do not add to the list with a bogus life.

Love silence

Sometimes, the introverts do not want to talk or be talked to. All he wants is to enjoy silence. Do not try to break that chain of fun. Respect his choice and pull back by giving him the space he needs.

Grow listening ears.

Introverts are though quiet people, but sometimes they want to talk too. They want to have that assurance that someone cares enough to hear them out.

Be sincere.

Nothing thrills an introvert more than other people's sincerity. Introverts understand how difficult it is to have people who can be trusted. People who say things the way they are without mincing words. Once you are tested and trusted, you can get them to open up to you at a cost next to nothing.

CHAPTER 7: HOW EXPERIENCES SOLVE FEARS AND INSECURITIES

Are you afraid of being in a large group of people? Do you feel anxious when you are about to meet new people?

Understanding the Problem

If this is the case, you need to find out why. You also need to identify the specific aspects of being in a crowd and meeting new people that make you anxious. There is a pattern of how fear or anxiety builds up. For most people, it starts with a trigger. Your concern may begin when you hear that you need to attend social events. Some introverts only hate social events when they did not expect it. Others become fearful when they need to take part in a social activity that focuses attention on them. This fear is usually related to performance in the social setting.

Fear is normal. It is a natural way for our bodies to warn us of danger. However, it can be socially debilitating, especially if fear creates a habit of preventing us from doing our duties.

Let's take Mike, for example. Mike is about to spend his 3rd Christmas in the company. He did not attend the two first Christmas parties because there are always activities where he can get embarrassed. He tries to talk himself into going to the activity, but his fear always wins. In the past two years, he ever decides, on the last minute, to stay home and make up some excuse on why he can't make it.

In the past two holiday parties, Mike did not understand why he does not want to go. However, as he analyzed the pattern of fear, he realized that it was performing in the crowd that made him anxious. He enjoyed the idea of having a good time with his colleagues, and he even looks forward to talking to some of the people. However, whenever the idea of performing in front of his coworkers pops in his mind, he begins to feel anxious. He starts imagining scenarios wherein he becomes embarrassed.

By knowing the specific part of the party that Mike fears, he may be able to avoid the performance part instead of avoiding the whole event altogether.

Triggers are thoughts of social activities that start the fear in your mind. When the fear begins, a socially anxious person begins a series of activities that will lead him to avoid certain social activities. In the professional world, missing certain events and activities may be interpreted as not being a team player.

To prevent your social fear from stopping you from doing something, you need to identify the specific cause of your fear. Here are some of the common social activities that people fear:

• Speaking in public

• Doing something while a huge crowd is watching

• Being teased or laughed at

• Presenting in front of people with authority

• Being on a date or meeting someone you are romantically interested in

• Performing on stage

• Starting a casual conversation

In most cases, most people realize that the things they fear the most are unimportant and can fight it. However, some introverts never find the willpower to fight their fears even when they know that the scenario they fear may not happen. Here are some of the things that you can do to prevent your fear from taking over your actions:

Control How you Think to Deal with your Fears

There are certain thinking patterns that socially anxious individuals often use. Here are some of them:

• Assumptions and predictions

Anxious people assume that there are always opportunities in events for them to become embarrassed. They make a lot of assumptions that lead to their fears. They also make predictions on how things will happen. For people with social anxiety, this becomes a habit.

When you begin assuming and predicting fearful scenarios, it is a signal that you need to distract your mind from the fear. People have different coping mechanisms against fear. If you are in the office when the fear happens, for example, you can occupy your mind with work to prevent it from ruling over your thoughts.

• Extreme negative thinking

Their extreme negativity usually worsens the assumptions and predictions of introverts who have social anxiety. When thinking of these events, they focus on the worst things that may happen.

• Personalizing

When thinking of the things that can go wrong in the social events, they also focus on how the people in the party will react towards them. They think that people are out to make fun of them. They imagine that the bosses are there to humiliate them.

95

• The flight or fight response

When the fear starts, stress hormones will then activate their flight or fight response. For socially anxious introverts, the automatic response is to avoid the event. They may have made a choice not to attend the event in the past, and they turned out all right. Whenever they faced the same type of stress after that, they decided to use the same response to the stress.

Over time, these patterns of thinking become automatic when they are

required to attend events that they are not familiar with. Continued use of these patterns of thinking and behavior prevents a person from enjoying social success.

How to Prevent Social Fears? Breathing exercises

Breathing is one of the few functions that our body performs with both the conscious and subconscious mind. Being able to control the subconscious acts of breathing by being conscious of them is a powerful tool. One of the first signs of anxiety is an increased pace of shallow breaths. This may happen when you are about to go to the event. It may also happen even when thinking of the event. When you feel this happening, you should try to take bacK your control of your breathing. For example, when you feel that you are becoming nervous or fearful about a certain social situation, you should find a chair and do the following breathing exercise:

Sit and relax on the chair with your back straight and your face forward. Put your right hand on your right lap and your left hand on the surface of your stomach.

Slowly take a deep breath through your nose while expanding your stomach as the air comes in. Take at least 4 seconds to inhale. Hold the air in for 2 seconds before you slowly exhale it. Exhale through your mouth. It should take more than 4 seconds for you to exhale all the air out.

You should do this for 2 minutes or until you feel relaxed. By the time you are done, any fast-paced shallow breathing should be gone.

Change anxiety-related behavior with actions related to countering your fear For most people, the flight response becomes a habit after the trigger. In the beginning, a socially anxious introvert may still try to convince himself to go to the event. Over time, the person no longer considers going. Every time an idea of attending an event makes him feel uncomfortable, he automatically decides not to go.

You can change such habit even if you have been practicing it for years. All you have to do is to identify the trigger of your fear and explain in detail the behavior that follows it. You should then identify the rewarding feeling that you get when you decide not to attend an event because of fear.

Now that you have identified that cycle of your habit, you need to associate bad feelings towards the habit. Think of the negative effects of the habit. Make a list of it so that you can remind yourself of the negative effects that the habit has done for you. This will convince your subconscious mind that the habit is not doing any good for you.

Next, you need to think of a behavior change in response to the trigger. As mentioned above, first comes the trigger. It is then followed by the routine of the habit. The trigger feeling and the fear will always be there. You cannot change that. You can change the behavior that follows the fear. Let's say you always avoid your family holiday dinners because of some embarrassing experience. Every time you think of the event, you feel embarrassed inside. Over time, this feeling has developed into fear that the same experience will happen in the future.

You need to decide to go. You must not argue with yourself or waiver between the decision of going or not. When you have decided that you will go to the next one, your next challenge will be the thoughts that will bring back memories of your dreaded embarrassing experience. To prevent it from affecting your decision, you should look for a way to change your behavior every time memories of the experiences enter your mind.

Instead of thinking too much about it, you can say the phrase "I'm going" and think of another thought. Every time your fear of social events creeps in, you should say this phrase. Verbalizing it creates a sense of strength in most people. It symbolizes the change in habit that will bring them back to attending social events for good.

Lastly, you should identify the trigger as it happens. Every time you feel the fear, start anticipating the behavior that follows. You should then use the phrase used above or any variation of it to prevent your mind from going into the habit.

Expose your mind to your fear

One of the best ways to deal with fear is to face it. You may feel overwhelmed if you face all of your fears all at once. A better strategy is to face them one at a time. Instead of going to all the social events that you are invited to, you should focus your mind to only one. Once you have attended that event, you should think of the next one that you will attend. You should assure yourself that the worse case scenario that you think up in your head is always your irrational fear speaking and will probably not happen.

After attending dozens of social events, you will begin to enjoy the experience. You will start to develop courage when you fear something about an event. As you go to more events, the habit of going to them begins to develop. Once that habit develops that's when the magic happens and your confidence take a noticeable turn for the best. The key is changing your habits.

Set Achievable Goals

Goals are important to add clarity and focus to our efforts. However, we mustn't set impractical goals. When we set unrealistic goals, you are bound to fail. Nothing can dampen our confidence, like a failure. Hence it is important that you set only achievable goals. For instance, you are bound to fail if you have set a goal of losing twenty pounds in a week. There is no point in feeling disappointed in not achieving these goals.

On the other hand, when you have achievable goals, you feel happy when you accomplish them. You feel positive that your efforts have yielded fruitful results. This, in turn, will improve your confidence and self-esteem. You will start believing in yourself more when you achieve more goals. You will feel confident when you take up more work and responsibilities as opposed to feeling scared.

Learn To Embrace The Unknown

Despite the best efforts of ours, we can never predict what'll happen next. Being prepared for everything is going to improve our self-esteem and confidence. When we expect only certain results, we're not emotionally ready for other things. This way, when anything unexpected happens, we fail miserably. We're not equipped mentally to deal with this unpredictability. On the flip side, if you make room for the unknown, you're ready for probably the worst. This way, you are going to be ready to handle anything that's thrown at you. Understand it's not in our hands to manage everything about the lives of ours. Some things are certain to be out of the power of ours. The secret is to be ready to deal with them.

Address Your Weaknesses

Sometimes, it is our weaknesses that hurt our self- esteem. For instance, one of our weaknesses could be our social awkwardness. When you are socially awkward, people shun your company. You start believing that people don't like your company. This, in turn, results in very low self-esteem. Hence you must overcome this weakness.

List the weaknesses that can be changed into your strengths. Do not include physical attributes such as your height or skin tone as a weakness as they cannot be altered. When you've identified the weaknesses of yours, think about how you can overcome them. When you overcome each weakness, you feel far more confident. You start off loving yourself better than previously. Your self-esteem is improved to a much better extent this way.

These are the various pointers to increase your self-esteem and self- confidence. Follow these religiously, and you will find your confidence improving tremendously.

CHAPTER 8: STRENGHTS OF INTROVERTS

Lifestyle Changes for Empaths

Aside from incorporating meditative practices into your daily routine, you can also opt to make lifestyle modifications that can help you maximize your gifts, while minimizing the energy draining effects it has on you. Here are a few simple ideas to help you get started:

Start with avoiding people whose energies are toxic to yours. Some will purposely manufacture drama in their lives and these are the people you need to stay away from. Try to keep your circle filled with upbeat friends and people who are stable and optimistic.

Another thing you should avoid would be any form of media that affects you adversely. Unfortunately, this includes books, as certain ones can trigger ill feelings in many empaths.

It would be god to do a bit of research before purchasing a book or watching a movie this would help you avoid wasting money on something that you won't end up enjoying. Reviews would be very useful for this purpose.

As much as you can, spend plenty of time in nature. Plants are great buffers for your emotions and the environment immediately puts you in a more relaxed mood. Treat yourself to getaways a bit more often, even if it's just a quick trip to the country or a garden close to your home.

Do not be afraid of doing things on your own. Most empaths recover better whenever they spend time by themselves.

However, not everyone is very comfortable with this solitude. Think about why you're not comfortable and do your best to get better acquainted with this side of you. Your mind will be thanking you for it.

Be more aware of the places you frequent that aren't good for your overall energy. This differs for every empath so a need to be more observant is needed. If you can, avoid these places. Explain to your friends why you cannot stay very long in that area, and suggest other ones that they might enjoy more.

If you explain your needs well enough, they should be able to easily understand the discomfort you are in that environment.

Be better at handling conflict. Conflict is inevitable chances are, you will never grow to like it. However, you can start managing it better. A counselor would be helpful for this purpose, but if you would rather try and provide a solution to the matter on your own, there are plenty of self-help books that could give you more insight. Just research, you'll find exactly what you need in time.

Most empaths tend to choose professions where they can help other people think teaching, counseling, coaching, and healing. For empaths who are in these particular fields, you must remember self-care.

Learn how to use your energy for yourself. You'll be better at your job too! Look around your personal space. Is everything organized? Is it clutter-free? A clean environment breeds a clear mind. If you can, always keep your surroundings organized. This lessens the amount of things you need to be anxious about and provides you with a calm place to restrain your mind.

Remember, your home must be your sanctuary so treat it as such.

Here's a fact: Despite an empath's efforts to create limits between themselves and energy vampires, there will always be an "emotional hangover".

Negative energy tends to linger a lot longer than others, often leaving an empath feeling ill or lacking clarity. In some cases, especially if an empath deals with energy vampires daily, it would take them a lot of time to recuperate.

So, what can they do in this situation? Well, cleanse themselves of the bad energy is a start. There are many different ways of curing emotional hangovers it depends on the situation and what the person needs as well. To help you better understand this and give you an idea about how to cure emotional hangovers, here are a few strategies to get you started:

Tips for Curing Emotional Hangovers

Shower meditation

If you have enough time during the mornings or the weekends, use your time in the shower to cleanse you of any negative energy that might linger. Stay under the shower head and the let water stream from the top of your head to your feet; as this happens, recite the affirmation: "This water will cleanse all the negative energy from my body, my mind, and my spirit." As you repeat it, visualize that bad energy leaving you. Repeat it until you start feeling lighter. By the end of it, you will feel a lot more rejuvenated.

In continuing with cleansing and adjusting your space to meet your needs, try using salt lamps and negative ion generators. These would produce negative ions, which then clears the environment of different pollutants such as mold spores, dust, pollen, odors, viruses, cigarette smoke, and different types of bacteria.

Light a white-colored candle.

This is especially useful when you're meditation or simply unwinding after a long day. This creates a calming mood and also helps in removing negativity your surroundings.

Aromatherapy

Take advantage of the soothing effects that aromatherapy has. Rosewater is a favorite among many people, but choose the scent you feel most comfortable with. You can use sprays or synthetic oils which you'll need to add to diffusers to spread the aroma around. You can even choose purifying scents such as frankincense, myrrh and sage.

Nature

We've already established how effective being in nature can be if you want to ground yourself. Earthing takes this one step further and connects you to the ground first, take your shoes off and stand barefoot on the ground. Do this while your practice both visual and breathing meditation.

You'll find that focusing on nothing but your breath helps clear the mind of any negative thoughts. The earth, with its natural energy, will replenish yours the longer you stay grounded to it.

Create your sanctuary.

If you live with other people, it is important to create a safe space for yourself. You'll need this if you want to properly meditate and keep any distractions at bay. It need not be an entire room. Even a corner of your bedroom would work just as fine as long as it has the basics: incense, candles, flowers, and a totem that you can focus your gaze on while you meditate.

Now, when should you practice some of these tips? There need not be a "time" for it. These are small lifestyle changes you can add to your everyday life. Things that you can turn to whenever the emotional hangover becomes a little too burdensome for you.

As an empath, you'll find that this will happen a lot. So, instead of only acting when the problem arises, always be one step ahead and prepare for the situation.

Empaths have a great deal of strengths that support them in living complete, wonderful lives. When you begin to come to terms with your identity as an Empath and integrate protection and self-care measures into your life, working in alignment with your empathic gift will become easier. This means that you can begin to enjoy the many benefits and strengths of being an Empath.

Here are some of the wonderful strengths you can look forward to developing and embodying when you awaken to your empathic abilities and begin to take control over them:

A Great Power

Empaths are extremely powerful. This is one of the reasons society puts them down so much. They are afraid of their power. As individuals who can sense things about people that they may not be willing to share or deeply connect to plants and animals around them, you possess clear differences from the average person. In modern society, many individuals are deeply disconnected from the world around them. They struggle to tune in on basic levels, never mind as deeply as you do. You may see it as a weakness, but that is only because you have been conditioned to. In reality, you possess a great power. Once you learn to embrace it and use it to your advantage, you will be unstoppable in creating positive change.

An Amazing Friend

Anyone who has an Empath as a friend should be incredibly grateful. Empaths are amazing friends. Empaths truly cherish the people they love and will go to extreme lengths to help and protect them. They give great advice to their friends. When a friend has a problem or some sort of difficulty, Empaths are happy to use their beautiful gift of empathizing and putting themselves in their friend's shoes to understand the particular situation and figure out what the best possible decision is.

Ability to Detect Red Flags

Because of your ability to see what is going on beneath the surface, you have an uncanny ability to detect red flags in any person or situation. You do this by empathizing with the other person, essentially allowing you to step into their shoes. This means that you can detect the harmony between the person's words, actions and feelings. There, you can determine whether they are acting in alignment with the truth or lying or being dishonest in any way. By sensing any signs of incongruence, you can detect possible ulterior motives.

Whether you choose to recognize and act on these is a completely different story, but your ability to detect them and become aware of them is extremely powerful. You are capable of knowing any time there is something inherently wrong about a situation, making it easy for you to avoid danger and energetic attacks if you are tuned in and capable of acting on this information. If you are not yet, do not worry. As an Empath, you are capable of tapping into this ability at any time. It is not too late for you.

Detecting Compulsive Liars

Another great ability you have with telling what is truly going on under the surface of others is that you can easily detect compulsive liars. When people are lying, you know it almost instantly. Like the red flags, you can detect the harmony between the person's words, actions and feelings. By recognizing any signs of disharmony, it can be easy for you to suspect lying. This often comes as just a "knowingness" within. This encourages you to refrain from believing them and can help you prevent yourself from getting drawn in and trapped in their web of lies. The more you practice this, the better you will become at using this gift.

If you are a wounded healer and cannot utilize your gift efficiently, you may find yourself getting trapped into a person's web of lies. This is something important to address in the process of healing this archetype, if you have it.

Strong Creative Talents

Individuals who are gifted Empaths are known to be very strong in their creative talents. As we have already discussed, they are skilled artists, singers, poets, writers and creators in general. Empaths view the world in a poetic way that enables them to create unique art pieces highlighting their unique view on the world. Their ability to visualize something in their head and bring it into the material world with their creativity is simply amazing. The challenge for most Empaths is first eliminating all the negativity they

have absorbed growing up. This negativity could be in the form of doubt, insecurity, fear of failure, and lack of confidence.

Virtually every Empath can be creative, though how they express or use the trait may vary. Not every Empath will be great at the same thing, but they all will have some degree of creativity that they can use to express themselves and serve the world. This is incredibly satisfying and fulfilling for the Empath.

Excellent Problem Solvers

When an Empath has developed their empathic gift, they can be excellent problem solvers. Using their empathetic ability, they can analyze the wants and needs of different parties from multiple perspectives. Being able to analyze a certain situation and see many different points of view, gives the Empath a great edge to be able to come up with the best possible solution that will be beneficial for both parties.

Great Entrepreneurship Abilities

Because of their intuitive abilities and their superb ability to solve problems, Empaths make great entrepreneurs. They are highly focused on delivering the best results to their clients, no matter their line of work. Furthermore, they are heavily driven by a desire to have freedom and escape from the toxic, overwhelming, and greedy environments of traditional 9 - 5 jobs.

Empath entrepreneurs are great at coming up with creative companies that reach their clients' needs in ways that larger companies tend to overlook completely. They typically find themselves in their own companies that offer some form of healing or shifting modern society. Counselors, life and business coaches, alternative healers, artists, writers, and other career paths are extremely common for Empaths to choose. Fortunately, each of these can be done on an entrepreneurial basis. They are also excellent choices as they cater to the unique strengths and weaknesses of the Empath, allowing them to shine their brightest and serve in the way that their soul needs to shine.

If you are an Empath and you are not presently on the path of being an entrepreneur, you may find great joy and benefit in beginning this life path. With your gifts and abilities, you have the capacity to begin your life as an entrepreneur and create great success in doing so. There are many great benefits to choosing this career path. Some of these benefits include:

You are able to experience much more flexibility and freedom in your life compared to working a job

You can control your own working schedule and holidays

You do not have to deal with the draining and toxic environments of a 9-5 job You can choose the people you want to work with or work solely online. You can work from home. You have the potential to earn much more than what a job can offer you You can put your creative ability to good use

Become more fulfilled and happy in what you do

More travel opportunities may present themselves to you

General health and happiness will improve when you remove yourself from negative, toxic work environments

Many people believe that empathic entrepreneurship is the way of the future. As more and more people seek to lead a more socially conscious and responsible life, many are avoiding large businesses and corporations that are typically known for being irresponsible, unkind, and savage in their business dealings. These exact same people are seeking entrepreneurs running their own socially responsible businesses in a way that genuinely serves their needs on a personal level. As an Empath, you have exactly what it takes to serve in this way, meaning that you and your gifts are exactly what these people are looking for.

Strong Relation to Animals and Plants

Another great strength possessed by Empaths is their connection to animals and plants. As you know from animal Empaths and plant Empaths, these individuals have incredible talents when it comes to communicating with animals and plants. This is a breath of fresh air in a world where very little concern has been shown to the environment and those who inhabit it. Many humans in the modern world rarely consider other humans, let alone other species or life forms. As an Empath, you may have a powerful ability to relate to these life forms and protect them from the destruction of humans who experience little to no empathy in their lives.

Animals and plants are also believed to be Empathic, meaning that you may find that animals and plants respond well to you, also. You may find yourself attracting animals into your life and having an uncanny ability to help plants thrive in a way that others may struggle to do. This is because they are intuitive and can sense that you are kind. This allows them to automatically trust in you and feel safe, protected and nourished in your presence. They sense your energy, and it supports them in thriving.

CHAPTER 9: RELATIONSHIPS AND SELF-ESTEEM

As earlier illustrated in the book, we were opened up to the importance of ideal self-esteem and self-confidence in one's life. Likewise, we can practically see that the two factors can determine the level of achievement. That is why this section will unveil various ways you can enhance your self-esteem and self-confidence. Also, due to the close similarity between these two factors, the enhancement option below will boost both factors.

Here we go:

Have the "Can do" Spirit: Exhibiting the "can do' spirit is an essential quality in every trace blazer. It simply means you should believe in yourself about achieving specific things. According to the common saying, if you don't help yourself, nobody can help you". This doesn't literally mean no one will try to help you in some ways; they would. But the desired change still lies with the action you will take personally. Quite a lot of successful people have faced various hurdles to get to the point they are now. And what makes them different is their capacity to infuse themselves with the 'Can do' mentality, assuring themselves that no matter what the constraints ahead of them maybe, they will face it and actualize their goal.

Build capacity (Self-development): Unpreparedness has also been a significant cause of low self-esteem and self-confidence. In light of this, you should ensure grooming yourself in any way possible. Are you going for a presentation, exam, tutoring, or deliberation? Equipping yourself with relevant information ahead of time will undoubtedly enhance your confidence and self-esteem beyond your expectations.

Know your strengths and weakness: A mistake some people do commit is by thinking every trace blazer out there is perfect in all ways. Unlike what you might be thinking, those world shakers also have their weaknesses deeply buried in them. But what they are doing differently is realizing and leveraging their strengths to stand out of the crowd. This is why it becomes vital to take a moment, think deep in identifying your strength, then work around it to make the difference you desire. Nonetheless, no weakness can't be worked upon; aside from leveraging your strength, attending to your weakness to convert it to advantage will help boost your self-esteem and confidence.

Discard negative thoughts from your mind: If care is not taken, negative thoughts can make you fail where you have 100% capacity to win. Negativity is also a major player in reducing one's self-esteem and confidence; however, you have the key to make its power do not affect your life. And the key is countering the thoughts with positive thoughts.

Think about your achievements: There are specific situations or moments in life where we tend to feel intimidated, querying our inner consciousness, or challenge the belief that we are ever capable of overcoming a hurdle.At this point, if one is not careful, the rush of negative thoughts through your mind might adversely affect one's confidence and self-esteem. But a quick and alternative cause of action needed in eliminating the adverse is by thinking about the achievement you have also bagged in the past. This does encourage you that if you achieve a specific goal in the past, you are capable of overcoming the challenge ahead of you.

Go slow on your communication with others: Some people may think that the need to talk a bit slower will not in any way boost one's self-esteem and confidence. The fact is that how you present your conversation greatly determines the level of accolade you attract from your audience. For some, they have the in-depth knowledge of what they are talking about, but talking too fast as the thought rushes through their brain might prevent them from clearly illustrating their point; this might decrease their confidence and esteem, probably for not being able to meet expectation on the discussion or presentation. But don't you think going slow and steady in rolling your speeches out will make your audience want to listen to you more?

So, if you are the type that experiences some difficulties when passing verbal information across to others, it will do you a great deal of good to take it slowly. This will boost people's eagerness to listen to what you have to say, and this, in turn, will boost your morale for a more excellent experience. Therefore, you must understand that presenting your thought slowly doesn't make you less capable of having the right impact on your audience.

Facing a challenge is a must for successful people

Many people out there still believe challenges must be avoided at all costs. Do you fall among this category of people? The fact here is that, without challenges in life, we will remain in the same spot, and our situation can further get worse. Challenge is that hurdle one must successfully scale through to experience not only the next phase of life but greater height. Imagine someone that doesn't want to sit for a promotional exam due to the fear of failing. Imagine an individual that doesn't want to work but desires to earn sustainable income. What of an athlete that always dreams of winning without wanting to go through the challenges of rigorous training? The simple ideology here is that challenges are steps to greater height. And aside from scaling to them, your self-esteem and confidence are also developing, with the capacity to handle subsequent challenges.

Aside from the above hints to improving your self-esteem and confidence, the followings will also come in handy and should also be added to your rule of engagement:

consider change as a constant factor in life, and always be ready for it. strive to create solutions to peoples' needs around you.

always exhibiting friendly gestures like smiling, responding to greeting among others.

appreciate the people around you. keep yourself physically fit. manage your time well.

avoid idleness

take small strides toward your desired goals; slow and steady have the potential of winning the race.

don't procrastinate.

Knowledge gives access to power. With all the above-listed arsenal in your weaponry, it becomes vital to add one more thing: discipline. This makes you stick to your plan irrespective of the situation. never forget to keep yourself motivated.

"Treasure your relationships, not your possessions."

As much as we'd like to believe that our self-esteem shouldn't be dependent on relationships, the truth of the matter is that it is to a great extent. Chances are, our self-esteem level is highly correlated to the quality of relationships we enjoy. While it's true that many lonely narcissists are extremely self- confident, they are far and few in between.

Consider that a lot of times, the way others view us is the way we view ourselves. As such, we should also practice mindfulness and being deliberate in our social relationships.

Speaking of being deliberate in our relationships, here are some ways to make our key relationships work.

EVALUATE RELATIONSHIPS

Are our social relationships conducive for a healthy self-esteem or are they destructive? Often, we aren't aware that they are either way. By taking the time to pay attention to how we feel about ourselves and how our key relationships affect that, we will become aware and put ourselves in the position to act accordingly.

How do we know? In practical ways, we can ask ourselves:

-Is this person always putting me down?

-Does this person complement me regularly?

-Does this person make light of my dreams and aspirations?

-Is this person supportive of my goals in life?

-Does this person take me seriously at all?

-Is this person genuinely concerned about me?

Questions like these can help us evaluate if our key relationships with particular people or groups are conducive to healthy self-esteem. SELF EVALUATION

It would be unfair to blame, if the relationship is destructive to our self-esteem, on other people all the time. If after evaluating that our key relationships with certain people aren't conducive to a healthy self-esteem, let's ask ourselves why they treat us like that? For example, it's possible that certain key people in our lives are critical of us because we are critical of them first – that they merely react in defense or retaliation. Sometimes, being aware that we are first attacking their self-esteem can help us make our key relationships better by being more affirming, supportive, and encouraging to other people. As they respond similarly to our change in behavior in the relationship, we also reap the benefit of being encouraged, affirmed and supported. For self-esteem, that's all good.

BLAME NO ONE

This can be very hard at first, especially when you know that the other party is at fault. But by ditching the tendency or the habit of putting blame on the other party or parties, we can start fostering a mutually beneficial relationship for our and others' self-esteems. By starving the "blame game" beast, it becomes weaker until it dies and gives our key relationships a chance to flourish.

I find this one to be a very helpful approach to fostering a self-esteem friendly relationship. When stopped blaming my spouse for many mistakes, I was blamed less and less until it stopped. That helped me start seeing myself in a better light as a spouse.

LOOK FOR SOMETHING BETTER

Sadly, there may be situations where some key relationships are just self- esteem dead-ends. If after we've exhausted all options the key relationship is still affecting our self-esteem significantly, then it's simply time to move on. Nothing in this world is permanent except for change and it can apply to our key relationships. Let's just move on to greener self-esteem pastures.

Benefit from Your Relationships

According to the longest study on happiness - a 75-year old study on adult life -the key to a happier and healthier life is having good relationships. This may seem bad news for an introvert who barely keeps in touch with one or two of his friends. Fortunately, it is not about the number of our friends we have, but about the quality of our relationships. With this, we are actually at an advantage. Introverts are experts in cultivating deep and lasting relationships.

However, though we possess traits advantageous to a good relationship, we also have those that harm it. We have to discern whether we are strengthening our relationships or destroying them.

Which traits benefit your relationships?

Being a good listener—People normally want to talk about themselves, even introverts, but rarely find someone who really listens. That is why good listeners are valued friends, especially for an introvert who always does the listening.

Youraptitude for deep conversations—Deeper conversations leads to deeper connections. Even an extrovert appreciates a meaningful conversation. They can open up about serious topics because they know they will be taken seriously. Researchers also found that the happiest people are those who have more meaningful conversations over small talk.

Your contemplative nature– Because you think before you speak, you rarely

regret what you say. Continue to be cautious of your words because careless words can heavily damage even the closest relationships.

Your preference for a smaller group of friends –Fewer friends guarantees intimacy and loyalty. Besides, humans are only capable of maintaining a few intimate relationships. That is why some friendships end when new ones begin. The fewer you friends you have, the longer you keep them and the more valuable they become. Introverts are also naturally loyal to the few friends they have.

Which traits harm your relationships?

Passive listening–Sometimes, when we get so wrapped up in listening or contemplation, we forget to respond to the person talking. Add some interjections to show that you are listening.

Reticent nature–Being reserved is not a bad thing, but sometimes, we leave too many things unsaid, even words that show our affection. Get out of your comfort zone. There are times when you should compromise for the sake of the people important to you.

Avoiding confrontations–This may keep the peace for a while, but it is silently corroding your relationship. This is another occasion where you have to step out of your comfort zone. Confrontations can always be done calmly and rationally.

Tendency to be too critical and judgmental–Our judgmental tendencies and reluctance to open up hinder us from making new friends. Remember that not all our judgements are accurate. Give people the benefit of the doubt. Most of the time, we end up befriending the least person we expect.

Being suddenly out of reach–Give your friends a heads-up whenever you plan on recharging your batteries. Your extroverted friends may not understand if you don't explain the need for it because for extroverts, being alone give the opposite effects.

Enjoy casual socializing

It is true that introverts are drained by socializing, but it is also true that we enjoy the time spent with others. A conversation with a nice stranger or a cheerful cashier can liven up our mood. Researchers found that acting assertive or being more talkative can result to positive emotions, even for an introvert.

Just like everyone else, we become happier when we socialize. The only difference is we are drained of energy whereas extroverts are recharged. So how can we benefit from socializing? Do we have to be drained every time we want to feel happy?

Here are some ways you can be socially connected without the compromise: Find like-minded individuals - Spending time with another introvert is less taxing because you understand each other's limitations and sensitivities.

Strike-up short but meaningful conversations - Walk up to the store clerk and ask about her day. Initiating the conversation is being assertive.

Make time and effort for the people closest to you - Their presence can make you comfortable and confident of who you are. Since they have accepted the way you naturally are, so should you.

Read a blog or a book - Though this is a solitary activity, you get the social connection you need. It can even be more intimate than a short conversation. Through reading, you get to see a person's inner thoughts and feelings.

Go out this weekend and spend some time with that friend whom you haven't seen for some time.

Strike up a conversation with someone you don't know. He can be the cab driver or your favorite barista. Practice having short but meaningful conversations.

Do You Have Low Self–Esteem?

Low self–esteem usually results from deep–rooted childhood experiences. For example, if a parent mistreats a child, the child will believe they deserve it, and if a parent abandons a child, the child will see view themselves as insignificant. If a parent withholds love and affection, the child will automatically deem themselves unlovable. As they grow older, they subconsciously continue holding onto these beliefs that they were molded in, and see themselves through unrealistically negative and distorted lenses, and generally assume that people see them in the same negative way they view themselves, which of course translates to low self–esteem.

However, there are other factors that can play into the development of low self–esteem. Being bullied as a child by classmates at an early age can also contribute. A child who is berated by her peers for being fat, for example, may develop a negative relationship with her body. If a young girl is ostracized from the other girls in her class, she might think she is not worthy of love.

Similarly, low self–esteem can develop from abusive relationships with partners or friends. We've all had "toxic people" in our lives at one point or another, and often these people prey on those they perceive as not being confident. They may constantly tell their partner, "No one else will ever love you", or criticize her appearance or hobbies. A common tactic with abusers is to make their loved one feel useless and unlovable in an attempt to gain control of them. This can greatly increase low self–esteem and form a deep– rooted dislike of one self, even if the abusive relationship has ended.

These are, of course, just a few examples of where self–esteem issues stem from. You may find some of these situations familiar, or you may not. It can be incredibly helpful to deeply reflect and try to uncover the exact source of your low self–esteem. Sometimes, it can be painful to think back to times when we were mistreated, like opening an old wound, but your low self–esteem is the result of the wound never healing properly. You can't break a bone and leave it without medical attention in hopes that it'll be good as new. Instead, the bone needs to be set. Your low self–esteem is like a bone that healed the wrong way––the wound is no longer fresh, but it will continue to give you trouble until it is taken care of properly. Once you are aware of where it is coming from, you can begin to heal.

Common Characteristics Of People With Low Self- Esteem:

Irrational and Distorted Inner Self Statements

People with low self–esteem carry on an inner dialogue with themselves in which they make untrue or unproven statements about themselves. They will also inwardly agree with others' negative feedback, even if they initially choose to argue against the criticism.

People with low self–esteem may think to themselves, "I'll never be good enough" or "I can't change my situation." Their self–esteem may not even be linked to their physical appearance, but an overall sense of inadequacy. It may keep her from applying to a job, asking a love interest out, or reaching out to make a friend. Low self–esteem can be debilitating and prevent development.

Even overachievers with low self–esteem share a similar thought pattern, as they hold a belief that their success will eventually evaporate.

Any success achieved may feel short lived. Those with low self–esteem will undercut their achievements with statements like, "I could have done better" or "It's not a big deal". They often view their success as something anyone could accomplish. When they are not successful, they are much harder on themselves than they need to be.

Prone to obsessive–compulsive or addictive behaviors

People with self–esteem will often attempt to make themselves feel better by becoming involved in over–spending, overeating, alcohol–use, perfectionism, drug use and sexual promiscuity.

123

These behaviors can often become unhealthy, and in some cases, dangerous, life–threatening addictions.

Overreact or become easily offended in situations where others do not

Filled with negative thoughts about themselves, those with low self–esteem are generally prone to emotionally overreact in situations in which a person with healthy self–esteem would not. For example, they may overreact at a comment they feel is offensive or inappropriate.

They may also take things more personally than others might. While someone with healthy self–esteem may be able to remove themselves from a situation and see that the result of something is circumstantial, a person with low self–esteem may take the actions and words of others as a criticism of themselves. It can lead to irrational outbursts and unnecessary arguments that can strain relationships.

Indecisive

People with low self–esteem have a very difficult time in making decisions – even when it comes to small, insignificant things, like what they're going to wear that day. This is because people with low self–esteem are extremely concerned (and in some cases obsessed) with what others think of them, and how they perceive them. That being said, simple actions like getting dressed for the day can often be very stressful and demanding tasks for those with low self–esteem.

Experience a great deal of shame

People with low self–esteem often feel a great deal of shame from past and present situations. Instead of lightheartedly laughing off an embarrassing situation and moving on, people with low self–esteem continuously beat themselves up over something embarrassing they experienced, and feel immensely shameful about it for extended periods of time.

They may not be able to let go of past experiences, no matter how inconsequential. They may go over the same conversation over and over again, thinking of what they should have said. They may return mentally to something that has happened many years in the past and regret their decisions. They may lie awake at night, unable to sleep, worrying about the past. For example, a waitress might say to you, "Have a nice meal", after serving food. You may respond, "You too". It's a silly little mistake that everyone makes at some point, but someone suffering from intense low self– esteem may feel excessively embarrassed by the event. They may worry that the waitress thinks they're stupid. Instead of letting the mishap go, they might bring it up to the waitress, who likely forgot it ever occurred.

Constant worrying about the future

Those with low self–esteem live in constant worry and fear over what the future may bring. They don't believe they have what it takes to establish a promising future for themselves.

Similarly, this can affect sleep and make their own head a difficult one to inhabit. They may worry that they will never be good enough to obtain any of their goals or to proceed in life. They might be concerned that they'll always be alone or that their family and friends will leave them. They might also be concerned about being in poverty or not being able to afford medical expenses should the need arise.

Difficulties, Practical Tips to Improve your Relationships (With Friends and Your Partner for Men and Women)

This situation then means that the introvert may be compelled to move out of their comfort zones so that they maintain the relationships that they have formed and that they value.

The thing with introverts is that, for the most part, they will often form relationships that they want to establish. The people that they keep around, the people that they hang around are usually people that the introvert wants to have around.

Now, as with any relationship out there, you will come across relationship problems as an introvert. In your case, though, your introversion makes things a little more complicated. For example;

Differing Communications Styles

How many times have you and the people in your life fought? If we are honest, it is a couple of times, if it's a healthy relationship.

Now, when you look at things from your perspective, you often take the time just after a bit of confrontation to get lost in your thoughts momentarily. Because of this, the person in your life may come to take this as a sign that you are avoiding them when in reality, you are accepting the time, as you are wont to do, to comb through your thoughts.

Extroverts often find that they are more responsive in a fast-paced scenario. If you are an introvert and you begin dating an extrovert, the different ways that you communicate could create some friction between the two of you.

Communication is an integral part of a healthy relationship. Therefore, as an introvert, your desire to be in your own world and make worlds out of your own thoughts will often mean that you will place little value and emphasis on the real-world relationships that you have, leading to a nasty breakdown in communication, which is only the first step in a decreasing value of the connection.

As stated, a few introverts may also suffer from shyness, which would then mean that they will have an even harder time communicating effectively due to their low confidence and social anxiety. This situation can crumble the relationship.

Being Quiet Can be Read Wrong in A Conflict

How many events of conflict have you found yourself in? Probably more than a few times, right?

The thing is that, because of their quiet and calm demeanor, introverts will often not display their full range of emotions. When they are angry, they will often talk will composure, and when things indeed do get to a head, rather than explode (unless really pushed), an introvert will sit back quietly and ruminate. You have done it, right?

Now, many people out here are extroverts. They understand that conflict is an exchange that has both people going at each other. However, in your case, your silence and calmness can be looked at as a lack of concern or as a show that you do not value what the other person is saying. If you are at work and it is your boss confronting you, you may inexplicably be giving off the vibe that you do not take what they are saying seriously.

If you disagree with your significant other, you may come off as being arrogant towards them, as uncaring, even when this is not true. When you do not take care, this situation can lead to a breakdown in communication, which could adversely affect your relationships, which means so much to you.

Conflicting Needs with Your Partner/Friends

When you date someone o is more outgoing, the chances are that your personalities may overlap and cross paths.

So, there you are, having gotten used to spending your quality time alone, curled up on a sofa with a book perhaps, or a movie. Then you get into a relationship and suddenly, you need to make plans to go out with your partner.

While these kinds of differences can be ironed out with communication, there is still often that feeling of dissatisfaction when you push yourself to get out more and become more outgoing, which can result in frequent problems between you and your spouse.

When you and your partner go out, and they need to take a picture, you will have to do it, even when you are uncomfortable with it. These kinds of situations always arise and may lead to conflicts.

You Don't Like Talking About Yourself.

Imagine yourself going out on a first date. Wow! Butterflies and all! But then you get there, and immediately you realize that you may not be too keen to talk about yourself to this new person. Even after a few dates, you may still not be comfortable.

This desire to not reveal too much about themselves will often cost many introverts relationships.

To build relationships requires that we become comfortable in being vulnerable with the other person. This helps foster trust and allows people to bond more deeply.

While an introvert will cherish the chance to form deep bonds with others, the thing is that they will often do that in the hopes that they do not get to reveal too much about themselves. It is usually not because they have something to hide. Perhaps it is because they may feel overwhelmed then or probably may not be too deep in the relationship yet. Introverts take their time to build relationships, which then, can make a frustrating experience for the extroverted friend or partner.

Because of your lack of desire to talk about yourself, you may then come off as disinterested, and perhaps the partner may interpret this as a sign that you do not value them.

Over-Thinking

Hey, thinking is great! You sure do know that. But then, as with anything else, it can become problematic when overdone.

The natural tendency of an introvert to become obsessed with details and planning and observing and decoding will often mean that they approach almost everything from a thinker's perspective.

In shopping, you obsess over the choices you are to make. The jam is too sugary, but the marmalade that you want has run out. The alternative jelly looks good, but it is from a brand you don't know, but the third option looks promising. The fourth option appears like a cheap knock-off of your fave. The fifth option is far down, and so on.

This issue can be frustrating to the people that are in your life. Because of your desire to make the right decision, your obsession with details might create a wedge between you and the people around you.

In this case, this scenario could lead to your friends and partners avoiding you as you begin to become dull.

While it may appear superficial and vain, overthinking may be counterproductive in the long-term as this will mean that you get caught in

the paradox of choice, and you may end up choosing the worse option. You Struggle in A Group Setting

As we have stated, as an introvert, you find great solace in your own company. In that alone time, that is often most of the time, you brainstorm ideas, create stories and drawn art. You toy around with thoughts and ideas and concepts. Essentially, you become your biggest library.

But then, when you go out with your friends, you find yourself as part of a group. Suddenly, doors close shut in your mind. The stories you wanted to tell are locked inside. With all the people around, the interactions drain all your energy. Unable to access your inner thoughts, you become quiet in the group, and you come off as just a hanger-on. Your friends begin to think that you do not value the relationship, even when you reassure them that you do. Your actions seem not to match your words.

Being an introvert means that it is hard to survive in situations that acknowledges extroversion.

What this does then is, it can create friction between you and your friends. You will appear stuck-up and unwilling to take part in the interactions, even though the truth is that you are not really able to access your best thoughts in a group setting. This is also frustrating to you as an introvert too. You can't adequately explain why you do not know how to think well when with others. As such, it becomes hard to create a connection with others.

If it is in your romantic relationship when your partner begins to take note that you enjoy being on your own, perhaps more than you enjoy being with them, they will distance themselves too, in the knowledge that you do not need them.

So, to avoid these scenarios, what could be the solutions? Ways to Build Better Relationships as an Introvert Embrace Yourself

 Because of the cynical view that people attach to the introvert, it might be easy then for some introverts to go to extreme lengths to create a fake extroverted exterior so that they can obtain other people's approval.

The obvious thing here is that you are already setting up the relationship for failure by pretending to be someone you are not, which is dishonesty. Aside from this, though, you will be unable to communicate well how you feel about things and thus, will be forced to double down so that you do not sell yourself out. This occurrence goes on and on until it gets to a point where you can't take it any longer, and you snap. Things change suddenly, and now, your relationships stand on the brink of collapse, balancing precariously on the edge of a precipice

You can avoid this. To build better relationships, many relationship experts will advise that you first begin by loving yourself. As an introvert, this will mean coming to terms with your introversion and understanding how you communicate and how you want others to communicate with you. What is your love language? How do you show your displeasure? What words of affirmation do you use, and which ones do you appreciate when someone tells you? How do you like to be touched? What gestures do you want? Gifts? Words?

Only through becoming comfortable with yourself will you then be able to move on to the other steps.

Use Your Knack for Listening to Your Advantage

This skill is one of your key strengths as an introvert. As such, it can be a powerful tool to use to create a better rapport with the people that you come into contact with or interact with.

But now, to build from this, rather than just listening, take time after the other person is done talking to say back what they have said to you. This active strategy will allow you to gauge how well you listen while also letting the other person know that someone is listening to them. People often will feel closer to other people that make them feel worthy. By repeating back what the other person has said (not in the exact words obviously) you tell them indirectly that you value them and want to interact more with them. You will find that you will create better relationships without having to pretend to be outgoing or loud.

Also, listen to learn about the other person. You will be amazed at how this will quickly allow you to bond with them.

Accept Invitations to Parties Sometimes

Yes, I know this freaks you out, but social circles are often built and maintained by frequent time spent together. When you have friends, and they make the point to include you to events, you could work with them in how you will accept the invitations.

To create strong bonds with them, being honest with them will create a situation where they can extend an invitation to you, and you can accept some and reject others, or maybe even accept all of them but them come to an agreement with them that you leave early.

We all thrive on social bonds, so don't isolate yourself too much. Say yes to going out sometimes, but of course, not at the expense of your mental state. Your friends should be able to respect the boundaries that you agree on, and you do the same.

Be Kind to Strangers

Well, mainly we should be kind to everyone. But, for the most part, many people are often rude to strangers when it is undeserved. Because of this, it is in many of us a habit to treat strangers with indifference and disdain in some instances.

As an introvert trying to build better relationships, try by being the opposite - be kind to strangers. What this does is that it helps you acknowledge the humanity of the other person. by being thankful to the cashier, you begin to tell them that they matter. By pardoning the person that stepped on your toes, you tell them that you acknowledge that to err is human.

When you are with your friends, this will help them feel more connected to you and want to associate with you. You will win their admiration, and they will most likely want to associate more with you.

133

On the other hand, you will create a vast pool of potential friends with the people that you are kind towards and will have something going. Since you will be making this gesture from your own volition, and not under the pressure of making friends, you will enjoy it, and it will allow you to gain a better perspective of what people want and what they need. Even when your actions do not have the desired effect, you still know that you did your best.

Create Small Talk Around Topics You Enjoy

Small talks are a bore. That much we have established. Often used as a filler for awkward silences, it is often more awkward and bland and often superficial and without direction. For an introvert, who chooses their words carefully, and takes time to think, these kinds of thoughts, of course, makes them want to tear their hair out.

However, while it is indeed true that small talks are mostly terrible, most of it is usually not because of the very concept of small talk, but because very many people out here, both introverts and extroverts, are very terrible communicators. As such, you will find that you are not exactly opposed to small talks as you are to the fact that it will be forced and unnatural.

Therefore, take the time to think of how you would like someone to make small talk with you and where and how. If you are in a position to approach, do it. This approach could be easy to achieve if you attend a function on something you enjoy or consider meaningful.

To do this, take your time. Do not rush into it just because you want to get through it. Give yourself room to grow more comfortable with the idea of going out to strike a conversation.

This point is not to say that you will become someone who will go out and talk to others, but you will know when and how you approach this, thus, still ensuring that you are comfortable with the interaction.

CHAPTER 10: LAW OF ATTRACTION AND PRACTICAL EXERCISE

The Law of Attraction Exercises are realistic tools designed to oil the wheels of the Law of Attraction principles to achieve the anticipated positive results. The Law of Attraction exercises help you cultivate positive mentality, beliefs, positive approach, and positive models that propel you to achieve your positive ambition. The use of the exercises enhances your swiftness and precision to attract and obtain your targeted desire. The Law of Attraction resonates around the positivity level of the mind to achieve what you want. The Law of Attraction Exercises is the actionable pathway to achieving your dream and aspiration in life. They are the authentic roadmap to guide during your craving time to reach your destination. No traveler gets to his or her intended destination without knowing how to get there. A clear understanding of these exercises backed up with focus and positive energies make your dream easily achievable. No matter how efficient the engine of a gasoline-powered car may be, it will not come to life without gasoline. The Law of Attraction Exercises is the gasoline that the law relies upon to perform for the manifestation of your dream.

Benefits of Using The Law Of Attraction Exercises

There are several benefits for using the Law of Attraction Exercises. Knowing the benefits of these exercises will make them more attractive and enticing, particularly to achieve the best you desired for your life.

The first target of the Law of Attraction is YOU. Yes you, you, and you. The attitude of You in YOU determines what YOU achieve from the Exercises of the Law of Attraction.

Check out the benefits of the Law of Attraction Exercises as expatiated below.

The Law of Attraction exercises encourages you to create a positive mindset and focus on positive energies. They help you to eliminate negative thoughts and negative habits.

Steer you to create a positive dreamland and roadmap to achieving your dream

Exercises of the Law of Attraction help you focus on what you desire, want, or where you want to be.

The exercises help you discover where you are and where you desire to be after that.

They prompt you to dispel clouds of self-doubt Build self-confidence and self-determination Propel you to take positive actions

It creates an aura of 'POSSIBILITY' around you with a thick field of positive energies.

They build a clear focus program that eliminates distractions for the manifestation of your dream

Helps you from unnecessary dissipating of energies on speculation, thereby focusing your real dream.

25 Laws Of Attraction Exercises To Benefit You

To manifest anything positive in life, you need to engage and apply the Law of Attraction exercises, consciously or otherwise. These exercises as relating to the Law of Attraction principles to give you a step-by-step 'must-do' routine to achieve your life dream.

Unarguably, everyone emits a vibration which can be either positive or negative.

As provided by the Law of Attraction, your thoughts and feelings determine the type of vibration you emit. Whatever type of feelings you harbor in your mind determines the type of vibration you send out which in return the establishment of what is attracted to your life.

To achieve positive vibration and the attraction of positive aura, you need to implement these '25 Laws of Attraction Exercises to Benefit You'.

Discover the 'Real You' in you:

Since the major player in the theatre of life is you, the first exercise, in this case, is to truly discover who you are in reality. Since you are looking forward to achieving your dream, the first task before you is to be sincere and fair in accessing your true YOU in you. Know where you are in the present moment and your immediate and long-term destination. Without this true assessment of yourself, you may string unfair chains of failing and aborted dreams; just beating about the bush. A sincere and well-coordinated sense of self is a vital exercise to embark on to achieve your dream.

Start to Think Positively for Positive Outcomes:

Done your self-assessment exercise, proceed to cultivate a habit of 'positive thoughts' to attract 'positive outcome' to your mind. Whatever you 'package' in your mind resonates on what the outcome of your dream delivers. A new computer cannot deliver more programs than what the manufacturer had packaged in it. Think positively to

avoid 'viruses' from corrupting   your mind. Here, you need to install a 'mind-and thoughts-anti-virus' device in your mind to protect the 'security identity of your mind'. Watch what you think about, what you say, and the company you keep and where you go.

Treat Your Mind with Fairness and Kindness:

This may sound odd to you but it's true. Some people are brutally unfair and unkind to their minds. If you need to consult a physician for treatment for an ailment you have, you are handed a list of drugs. If you don't believe in the competence of the physician or the efficacy of them, I'm afraid you get no healing. This means if you doubt your dream, aspirations, and goals, you may not experience any manifestation.

Visualize a Creative Dream:

Don't be a bland blank dreamer. Know what you want and tie it to your belief. You need to be precise about your dream and be brave about what you desire in life. This is the basic roadmap to know where you are going. No guesswork.

Affirm and Confirm Who You Want to be:

This has to be with your belief. If you load your mind with positive thoughts about your dream, nothing can hold you back confessing it to yourself every time. You can only speak from the abundance of what is in your mind. Confess and affirm that belief to manifest your dream.

Design and Follow a Roadmap:

You need to prepare a checklist of the activities you need to carry out to achieve your dream. The checklist will guide you about what to do, when to do it and how to do it. Since your dream is personal to you, prepare your checklist (you may need some guidance and input from someone who has manifested in your area of pursuit). You can consistently revisit your checklist to know if you are doing things right.

Don't Expect a Robotic Manifestation:

The Law of Attraction is not robotic. You may desire to up your annual income from $120,000 to $800,000. Your belief and constant affirmation will happen, but it may not be directly from your current work. The manifestation of your dream could come from an unexpected job opening you can try some other vocation. But the truth is that you can achieve what you'd planted in your mind, somehow, anyhow. When pursuing your dream, don't limit your scope or expectation of the manifestation to one rigid platform.

Increase Your Faith:

Nothing fires the embers of the Law of Attraction like faith. I am talking about faith in your dream, your ability, capability, vision, and creative consciousness backed with total belief in the workability of the Law of Attraction. Maintaining a constant and unwavering faith fires your dream to fruition. Stand on a faith-platform that affirms that "I can fly higher," "I can do it," "It shall come to pass," and "I'm a winner." Constantly repeating and believing this faith stratum will make your dream to come to full manifestation.

Slaughter Doubt:

No winner is a doubter, and no doubter is a winner. Doubt is a killer of dreams. If you don't murder doubt, doubt will murder your beautiful dream. Doubt is an enemy, no warrior spares an enemy, doesn't spare doubt. Doubt resurges from time to time, knocking on the door of your dream. Yours is to resist opening the door. Confront every element of doubt with your positive confessions, and it shall let you go. Imagine, if Abraham Lincoln had doubted his intrinsic ability, he wouldn't have ever become the President of the United States of America after so many failures. Doubt strangles dreams.

Constant Meditation:

To see your dream come to manifestation and obtain your desired goal, you need to create time for constant meditation. This is a time you engage your mind-eyes and your creative visualization for better focus. Stand in a quiet place as often as you can to ruminate on your dream. Focus your mind-eyes with positive energies at work to see, savor, and 'enjoy' the future you desired. This exercise is complemented with a positive declaration of the positive things you ever want to achieve. Meditation builds the peace of your mind and happiness. It enhances a better perspective on life.

Be Happy:

Cultivate treating yourself with happiness. Happiness is the product of a positive mind. As you continually focus on your dream, let happiness surrounds you every time and in everything. Ensure that you are happy inside and outside. When your mind is filled with happiness, it emits positive energies which will consequently and constantly attract happy and positive energies around you. Nothing and nobody can create

141

happiness for you until you train and condition your mind to remain happy. A mind filled with positive energies will exude happiness to your environment and attracts positive cosmic elements that will facilitate the delivery of your dream. Remember that in the platform of the Law of Attraction, 'like attracts like'. Happiness attracts happy occurrences.

Be Thankful:

Rather than nursing regrets, always be thankful to the universe for who you are, what you have, where you are, and the expected future manifestation. A mind full of regrets never shows appreciation. If you are not appreciative and thankful for who you are, you are likely not to appreciate and be thankful for any future achievement. Thankfulness to the cosmic elements around you prompts greater positive cosmic interaction in your daily life. This makes the Law of Attraction to be more effectively operational in the manifestation of your dream.

Discover your Intention Point:

Your intention is what you work, drive, and aim at achieving. When it is discovered, you must solidly plant it in your heart. Your heart is the defining meeting point between your mind and your intention. This gives your dream a quick correlation with your manifestation.

Shun All Existing Limiting Factors:

The fear of existing limiting factors runs in the mind mostly trying to frighten you with the belief of impossibilities It constantly reminds you why it's impossible, why it is unachievable, and why it won't work. But suppose your heart is well tuned, emitting superior positive energies. In that case, it will help you to filter out the impossibility syndrome from your belief system resolution, leaving you with only the possibility mentality. The possibility mentality is what fires the Law of Attraction to deliver that life you so much desire.

Create and Expand a Positive List:

It is your life, and there is no limit to what you can aspire to. Make up a positive list of all you want in life, and you can constantly expand the list. Your positive list emboldens your focus and enriches your belief system if backed-up with positive energies.

Constantly Declare your Dream:

Share your dream and your goal with people. As you constantly talk about it, the universal elements and the positive energies will begin to manifest what you talk about. This will make you more resolute about your goals as you want people to see the manifestation in your life. Some may mock you in the beginning but go ahead with your declaration.

Use a Vision or Dream Board:

You can create a 'dream board' or chart that helps you keep your dream in focus. Spell out your dream and make a beautiful design of it on a board or poster. Place it in a very conspicuous place where you can see it when you wake up, on your way out of the house and immediately when you arrive to your house and see it before you retire to bed at night. You can also include some of your positive affirmation on this board and recite it to yourself, possibly in front of a large mirror. This exercise has the creative power to send out positive energies which your mind will aptly magnetize. Repeating this every day will re-tune your mind to the new reality of your new YOU in you.

Wear Memorabilia:

Nothing helps keep you constantly in tune with your dream and aspiration like wearing a 'reminding body tag'. Wearing memorabilia has almost the same effect as using the 'visual dream board'. This can be in the form of a precious pendant, necklace, a wristband or wristwatch, or a special gift from a loved one or a friend. The essential thing here is that you need to 'tag-link' the memorabilia with your dream or desire which will always remind you of the tenets of your dream. The connection here is that when you see it, your mind eyes automatically switch to your dream and the principles of achieving it. This will help you a great deal.

Perceive and Savor your Success Story:

Remember this is your dream and life and your manifestations are purely yours. It is worth celebration even ahead of its attainment. Take time to envision the glamour, the glory and the celebration that the fulfillment your dream will generate. Focus and see the reality of the positive transformation you will garner to yourself at the end of the exercises. This alone will serve as a driving force to push forward until you achieve your desire. Your dream house, car, vacation holidays with your loved ones, getting all, you ever wanted. Seeing the reality and the fulfillment of your desire ahead is like roller skate to your dreamland.

Be Driven by your Dream:

Make your dream and aspirations your focal-point of your life at this time to

144

get what you want. Remember, there is no easy road to wear a crown without carrying a cross. Challenges, obstacles, insecurities, lack, and bundles of thorns usually lay in wait of every dream actualization. It's your responsibility to focus and be driven by your dream. Device personal techniques as enshrined in the Law of Attraction to maneuver your steps to safely navigate through the thorny pathways to your promised land.

Watch and Weigh your Actions:

It is may be impossible to remain flawless in life, but it is important to always submit oneself to a critical 'checks and balances' to analyze how we fair in our relationship to others; be it neighbors, coworkers, colleagues, superiors, subordinates, and people in authority. There are guiding rules and laws in every facet of our lives. Your attitude towards others and every known 'law' determines the level of interactions you enjoy receiving from all the Universe elements. Constantly weigh your actions and reactions at every situation.

Share Positive Thoughts:

In your everyday life, you come across different people of different personalities with different characters, habits and beliefs. It's always good to share your gains from a deep heart that exudes cheerfulness, kindness, happiness, smiles and laughter. Demonstrate what you have acquired; the profits of the Law of Attraction. In your journey forward to actualizing your dream, constantly remember that, "The luxury of doing good to others surpasses every other personal gain." Share the smile, share the laughter, and share the happiness. A. Neilsen was right when he said, "Happiness adds and multiplies, as we divide it with others." You cannot lack light when you bring sunshine to others.

Think and Act in a Certain Way:

In a class of 20 students in a college under the same tutorship, orientation, and study environment, you discover that some students excel above others. Surprisingly, the cleverest student may not be the most excellent student in terms of academic performance. Still, the most excellent student in college may not become the most successful person in later life. This may sound odd, but it is the reality of life. This is as a result of doing things differently and 'in a certain way.' Doing things differently and in a certain way is what matters and what distinguishes one person from the other. What separate success and failure is just a thin silver strand and the thin strand is hinged on the basics of 'think and act in a certain way.' One of the wonderful and vital ingredients of life and getting what you need is doing things in a certain way; differently from others. To achieve your desire, don't stick to the old norms or the general belief; act in a certain way, do it differently. It quickens your journey to manifestation and stands you out amid the crowd.

Read and Explore:

No matter your destination, aspiration, need and want, you need wisdom empowerment. Wisdom, understanding, enlightenment, and insight are bundled and derived through an exploration of books' power. Go for books of proven manifestation in your areas of interest. Go for books written by authors with proven track records of success in your desired area of interest.

Guide and Maintain a Healthy State of the Physical and Spiritual: Health is wealth. Spiritual health nurtures and enriches your life which is needed to be in tune to acquire, maintain and sustain all the interaction of positive elements and the Universal elements needed to actualize your dream. Don't neglect the aspect of your physical health for you need physical energy to combat daily demand. Health is wealth! You need moderate physical

exercise, relaxation, and good diet plan are absolutely needed to maintain a great healthy lifestyle.

Quick Takes:

The Law of Attraction is not magic but a scientific system that has changed the lives of many people across the globe. The application of the exercises of the law is not a hoax. The transformation effects of the exercises are concise and real, giving rise to positive manifestation realities in the lives of uncountable people. The law of transformation has succeeded in bringing people to realize who they are truly are and cautiously guided them in realizing their life ambitions and dreams. There is no gainsaying that if you guardedly follow the rules and principles of the law, you too will enjoy the wonderful change of life which other ardent users had enjoyed.

CHAPTER 11: BOOSTING YOUR SELF-ESTEEM AND CREATE A NEW SELF

Introverts are unique, although many people just don't know what to make of them. You'll usually find them on the perimeter of most parties. People will perceive them as shy, although that's pretty much a mistaken belief. It's just that introverts can only expend so much social energy, and then they need to withdraw and re-energize.

In a world of extroverts, it may be more difficult for introverts to be considered for a promotion or make new friends. But they should stay in their introverted lane, because trying to portray themselves as anything else is too hard and would imply not being true to oneself.

Many introverts need to have their self-esteem boosted so that they can shine as exactly who they are. Although this can be a difficult process, it is not impossible.

Being an introvert isn't a character flaw, it's a personality trait, just like being an extrovert. Western society is the more extroverted gung-ho, while Eastern societies have been more accepting of introverts.

Countries like China, Korea, and Thailand are a haven where introverts are not made to feel inferior; instead, they are perceived as ideal individuals. The inhabitants of such countries believe that being reserved and thoughtful is commendable and indicates good character.

There are Many Ways for Introverts to Shine

Have a positive view of your personality – Don't be ashamed of being an introvert! It's not a flaw, it's a personality trait. Introverts are not alone. Actually, there are more of you than you realize.

Don't be self-critical, and accept the fact that you may find certain things difficult to do. Perhaps talking with strangers is not your strong suit, and speaking in public, in front of an audience, is scarier than the tour of a haunted house. Whatever your weakness is, acknowledge it; don't pile on self-judgement.

Understand your introverted personality – Introverts come in different personality types. The most basic element of introversion is being re-energized by spending time alone or with a close friend who shows you support.

Another fundamental facet is absorbing information before you respond. You want to contemplate what's being told to you. For instance, an extrovert may read an article online and immediately respond and give their opinion about the content. You, on the other hand, want to go away and think about what was in the article before you respond with your opinion. That is, if you decide to give any opinion at all. There's the privacy issue that you enjoy coveting, so sharing what you think may not happen. (Boyes, 2013)

Every introvert is different. You can therefore extract the advice you find helpful and ignore whatever doesn't relate to you.

Don't compare yourself to extroverts – As an introvert, you've probably dreamed and imagined that you're the center of attention, the life of the party. You're the one that everyone listens to as you regale them with your latest adventures about your vacation in Australia, where you went, what you did and who you met.

Even though it seems that being the life of the party wherever you go is great, you should know that being an introvert also has its advantages.

For instance, suppose you published a best-selling novel that turns out to be a hit nationwide, and your publisher informs you that you're going on a book tour. will you enjoy the endless interviews and the spotlight being on you?

If you're an introvert, the previous scenario is not necessarily something you wish to be presented with. If you're an introvert, you would rather receive the recognition you deserve from a safe distance.

Accept who you are – namely, the person who can read between the lines more carefully than those who get more attention. (Hayward, 2018)

The difference between a lack of confidence and being introverted

Confident people have confidence in what they do and how they do it; they also believe that most people will like them. If either of these elements is missing from your confidence bag, it's time to work on it.

Write a blog – Introverts enjoy time alone to ponder their thoughts and jot them down. Today's online blogging world is perfect for introverts to express themselves.

Extroverts are frequently touted for getting out there, but introverts can be impactful through social media, too.

Having a reserved nature can help to build credibility. Our world is where the people shouting the loudest tend to get noticed, while introverts take the time to be observant and make the effort to listen. Their observations can therefore be translated into pieces of writing that truly touch the audience.

Get creative – Introverts spend quite a bit of time in their heads, thinking about things they've heard or seen. As previously mentioned, this creativity is great for writing a blog, and it can also unlock other facets of one's personality.

Introverts tend to be more creative. Studies have proved that introverts can work on their creative projects more thoughtfully than others.

The same studies noted that introverts can work well with others, meaning that you may not necessarily be an artistic spirit. Still, you'll be able to share good ideas without drowning out the other people involved.

Be a leader and set an example – The notable Forbes magazine points out that some of the best leaders in business, ranging from Bill Gates, the founder of Microsoft, to the super-wealthy investor Warren Buffet, find their time alone to be extremely valuable. The question Forbes addressed is: can the quiet, more reserved businesspeople become illustrious business heads in their own right?

The answer - and the reasons behind it – are as follows: introverted leaders 'think before they speak' and consider what the others are saying. Introverts also react more calmly during a crisis, which can set the example for how the staff will react.

A business leader who takes time to re-energize can be more responsive to difficult scenarios and step in rationally rather than reactively.

Avoid the small talk – Introverts are not big talkers when making new friends or developing romantic interests. This can be misinterpreted as a sign of disinterest. We suppose we have to be friendly and talkative to get the ball rolling with someone new, but you can also get to what you want to talk about without the small talk.

It isn't that you don't have to practice your small talk skills to make communication easier, but you can also get right to the point and talk about what you have on your mind.

There isn't any real need to talk about the headline of the day, or whether it's going to rain. You can just acknowledge the person by saying "Hi." The conversation will take off from there. No fear, no huge amount of effort to get the conversation going.

Love interests need attention – Introverts have a difficult time when meeting people for the first time. They're quiet and thus project what appears to be disinterest. To counteract this perception, you can let the other person know that you're an introvert. They might turn out to be an introvert themselves, which could help you feel more relaxed during the date.

Another way to get the date to flow is to ask questions like where they've traveled or what books they like to read. Ask the same questions you've been asked by your date as well.

The date is not all about impressing the other party. You're looking to see if you're interested in your date, not if they're interested in you. Remember, the date is a two-way street.

Learn what overstimulates you – Here are a few examples: being asked for an answer and decision while you're focusing on what you want to answer, being interrupted (that's a fan favorite), noisy surroundings, the back and forth of being social, group meetings, and social media – all of it.

Minimize and find ways to work around whatever it is that specifically overstimulates you. Learn physiological self-regulation tactics. (Boyes, 2013)

Physiological Self-Regulation Tactics

These self-regulation tactics can help with stress relief. Psychology experts confirm Their efficiency.

You don't have to be exceptional at everything. However, making strides to improve can still be useful. Perfection is not required, and we all know there is no such thing as perfection!

Don't "act extroverted" - Seek ways to team up with others who don't overwhelm and overstimulate you. Understand your tendency to think things through for longer than most other people.

Be conscious of when it's okay to go with your natural propensity versus when you need to supersede it, try to understand when it's best to decide a situation you've been considering for a while. (Boyes, 2013)

Stop the negative self-talk – Don't look at yourself through other people's eyes. Become aware whenever you're comparing yourself with others and stop it.

Develop a positive attitude with positive thinking. Recognize the positive traits you have, develop them further and acquire new ones.

Take note of the negative traits you have (like negative talk about yourself) and eliminate them. That may not be easy at first, so learn to take control of the situation and don't let negative thoughts you back.

Write a list of your positive skills and traits. Remind yourself of these skills by re-reading the list from time to time.

Do positive self-talk once a day, every day. Drown out any negative self-talk you catch yourself doing.

Think about it: Introverts have more opportunities to build healthy self- esteem than extroverts.

Introverts get their mental energy from their inner self – having alone time and contemplating their thoughts and ideas. By contrast, extroverts are driven by outside energy, by connecting with other people.

That being said, extroverts depend on other people for their mental energy, while introverts only depend on themselves. The latter also love to delve into self-understanding and self-analysis, thus getting to know themselves better and improving their personality.

The better you know yourself, the more you will have an opportunity to improve yourself and gain self-esteem.

There are many extroverts who are good at social networking and use this to their advantage. In today's society, it's important to meet people who studyand/or work in your field.

Introverts are extremely self-aware. When they're around people they know well, they're more sociable, thoughtful and gregarious.

Meanwhile, some extroverts waste their time gossiping instead of using the opportunity to build networks to make progress. Extroverts may have social and interpersonal skills, but that doesn't necessarily mean they hold all the cards to be confident.

Self-esteem versus Self-Confidence – Sometimes introverts get confused as to what is self-confidence and what is self-esteem.

Self-confidence refers to the feelings you have about your abilities. These feelings can differ from one situation to the next. For instance, you may have healthy self-esteem and still experience low confidence concerning your math and science skills at school. When you have love for yourself, your self-esteem grows, and that, in turn, makes you more confident.

Someone you know may tell you they don't feel they're good enough and display low self-esteem. They may have been in career positions where they didn't advance or may have been belittled by their supervisor; they may have had toxic personal relationships which ended badly. They're always saying things like "I'm not worth anything."

Acknowledging that this is a negative script is the first step toward changing one's attitude.

As for self-confidence, these people may be wonderful, caring friends, who volunteer at animal shelters, adopt pets and ride the neighborhood in search of abandoned and injured animals.

They may have submitted their application to study at a top veterinary school, so they can get their degree and work towards opening another animal shelter to save and treat more animals. They are confident in their goals and will work hard to achieve them.

As it is, this friend focuses on the things that they are confident in and working to change their negative self-talk. They are striving to improve both their self-esteem and self-confidence. (Ahmed, 2017)

Adopting a positive attitude and spending time in an environment where you feel positive, with people who are supportive and cheering you on achieving the goals you've set for yourself will increase your self-esteem and self-confidence.

How to Keep Your Self-Esteem in an Extroverted Society

Introverts do have self-esteem. They are simply less likely to obtain their self-esteem from socializing. They are more apt to get their self-worth from within. This is not true of all introverts, however. (Gaut, 2016)

There are introverts who feel happy knowing that there are no videos of them being drunk and doing stupid things out there; they also take pride in having a small group of trusted friends rather than a big group of acquaintances.

Introverts are usually happy to stay in the background and show little interest in impressing people. However, if they're creative, they are proud to have people notice their creation. That is because their artwork speaks for itself, without requiring any words from the artist.

By comparison, extroverts crave social approval. They want people to like them and some get pretty bothered if someone doesn't like them. Their work is how they display and connect to their personality, and they want their success to be noticed.

Extroverts usually aim at having a large social group, frequently taking pride in being friendly towards wide varieties of people or having the respect of the people within an organization. The persona they display is the foundation of their self-esteem how they are recognized.

Neither personality is right or wrong. Many introverts are proud of the fact

they don't need much approval from outside forces, and they have a sense of true self. Extroverts pride themselves in being too self-focused to have rapport with other people and can adapt to the demands of society.

Both personality types have their place, and both need to take care that they don't begin to believe that their side is the only right one.

Creating a New self

It's not about how others perceive and judge you. It's about how you see and evaluate yourself. It's your discovery of your own self, which will eventually lead you to creating a new, better self. A self that is more confident, more comfortable in the knowledge of his own worth, and much more ready to take on the challenges that obstruct his journey towards greater success in life. What this entails, then, is discovering the inner you, which, in turn, requires scraping away the upper layers of your individuality and finding the core of your true personality.

This process of discovery begins by asking oneself a few questions. Do you love yourself? Do you respect yourself the way you want others to respect you? Do you see a confident, happy and likeable person when you look into the mirror? Or are you so overwhelmed by your little imperfections that you're unable to see the brighter side of your personality, allowing it, in fact, to remain suppressed and hidden under layers of your own sense of inadequacy?

It is a process that involves much introspection, but at the same time taking care not to allow such introspection to trigger a sense of depression at your inadequacies. This would naturally require a kind of tight-rope walking, necessitating a sense of balance between accepting your imperfections and allowing them to overcome your strengths. It would also require an acknowledgement of the fact that, unfortunately, imperfections are a part and parcel of human personality.

So perhaps you're one such person, suffering under the burden of low self- esteem, yet unwilling to take on the cudgels to get creative with your imperfections and utilize them to bring your strengths to the fore. Yes, it's

actually possible to utilize imperfections to build self-esteem. Now you're probably thinking that it's easier said than done. No, getting creative with your imperfections is not a difficult task, once you get down to it. Fortunately for you, it's quite possible to get creative with your imperfections by following just a few easy steps. This creativity will, in turn, facilitate the creation of a new and better you - one that's more self-confident with a much higher degree of self-esteem. It will, thus, help you get back your lost belief in your own worth. And once you start believing in your own value, it will become easier for you to get creative with all those imperfections that you've so far been looking at as flaws in your personality.

With creativity comes a new perception, enabling you to look at your imperfections as mere blobs on the canvas of life. Creativity inspires change, and change leads to transformation in the overall persona you carry and present to the world. Once you get creative with yourself, you'll see the world look differently at you, as friends and strangers begin to see a person with a lot more self-esteem and much more confidence. This may seem somewhat far-fetched to a person wallowing in self pity and low self-esteem but is actually quite an achievable goal. All it requires is focused and concerted efforts, backed by a strong will and intent to change.

Unfortunately, however, self-esteem, like almost everything else in life, has a flip side to it too. So you can actually have too much of it. Excessive self- esteem, mind you, can be as bad as no self-esteem. Some say it can be worse, and it's actually better to err on the side of less than too much. Now that's a debatable subject which you shouldn't waste time in thinking about. The fact is that excess of anything is bad, and it's important to strike a fine balance between too much and too little.

The problem is to figure out just how much self-esteem is too much? And how do you rate your level of self-esteem on a scale of, say, 0 to 10? This issubjective, and hence contentious. Let's assume, for the sake of understanding, that anything less than 5 is definitely not enough. So if you feel that you're level of self-esteem is definitely lower than this magic figure, it's time for you to start working on your self confidence. Because one thing is certain - self-esteem is critical to the process of creating a new and better you!

But do remember, however, that there's a difference between self-esteem and perfection. The point we're trying to make is that self-esteem will not make you a different person; it will only make you a better human being, who takes pride in his strengths and doesn't get discouraged by his weaknesses. So the inner you need not really change in order to make you a stronger and more assertive personality. All you need to do is to be creative with your own imperfections and make them work for you as you strive to become a more evolved human being. That's the new you which you need to develop if you want to appear to be a better person, who evokes a sense of respect and admiration in all those you come across.

So is self-esteem all about leveraging your imperfections to deliver creative solutions to your own problems, as well as the problems of others? Well, that's actually a very prosaic way of putting it. Self-esteem runs much deeper than that. But creativity is definitely the first step towards garnering self-esteem, and emerging a more holistic individual.

As a French artist once said, creativity takes courage. And courage, according to psychologists, is a sign of self-esteem. A 20th century American inventor chose to define it somewhat differently. In his view, an essential aspect of creativity is not being afraid to fail. Despite their different approaches, the basic premise for both these definitions, as you can see, is more or less the same. If you have courage and are not afraid of failure, you can't possibly be lacking in self-esteem.

So if you think you're suffering from low self-esteem, it's time to tighten your creative belt and to gather the courage - not to fight your imperfections but to innovate upon them. Once you start improvising on your imperfections and start utilizing them creatively you'll find your self-esteem getting gradually elevated, till you reach a point where you're no longer shy about facing the world and taking on the challenges in your progressive journey with courage, without fear of failure.

CHAPTER 12: WHAT IS ANXIETY AND ITS CAUSES

Anxiety can be entirely debilitating for the individual that suffers from it. It can make it difficult to function in school, at work, in social interactions, and more. When you are anxious, you are constantly in survival mode acting as though your death or demise is imminent. It is something that comes on suddenly when you least expect it to and can cause a myriad of problems. You can be entirely fine one minute and then suddenly shift over to a full-blown panic attack. People around you may feel as though you are losing your mind, or you may be convinced that you have something seriously wrong with you.

The good news is that anxiety disorders are incredibly common. In fact, anxiety is the most common mental health disorder that you can have. It is estimated that upwards of 285,000,000 people worldwide suffer from some sort of anxiety disorder, and it may be easy to understand why surviving is hard. It is tough to live in a world that largely does not care about you when you understand that that is the case.

While the exact cause of anxiety is not yet definitively known, there is plenty of information that we do already know about anxiety. We can define what it is and identify several different kinds of anxiety disorders that people can suffer from. We understand how to treat the symptoms and make sure that those who suffer no longer have to. We understand that there are certain people that are predisposed, and we understand the risks of not treating the disorder altogether.

Often, certain markers make someone more or less predisposed to developing anxiety in the first place. While it is not guaranteed that anyone that suffers from any, or even all, of these risk factors will develop anxiety in the future, they are at a higher rate of developing them. First and foremost, women tend to develop anxiety disorders more frequently than men for reasons that are currently unknown. A family history of people having anxiety can also be indicative of an increased risk, such as having a parent, grandparent, or sibling that has suffered from anxiety in any form. A major trauma can also cause an increased rate of anxiety if you have lost loved one unexpectedly, such as a child oR spouse, or been the victim of some sort of traumatic event like an assault, you are more likely to develop anxiety at some point. Changes to your life, such as divorcing unexpectedly or having children can also bring about anxiety, particularly right around when it has happened. Lifestyles can also impact the risk of anxiety, with those who smoke or consume caffeine in excessive amounts at an elevated risk. Lastly, those who endured abuse or trauma in childhood are also likely to show higher results of anxiety.

What is Anxiety?

On its own, anxiety is a very normal emotion that was likely developed evolutionarily to keep those who feel it alive. Anxiety is often accompanied by behaviors that people identify as largely nervous, such as pacing, biting nails, shaking, or otherwise appearing uncertain. It most often presents with an imminent fear that something is coming or that death will happen soon. The key difference between anxiety and fear is that fear is a response to an immediate presence of a threat you know that there is something dangerous right in front of you and that you are at risk of being hurt or killed. In comparison, anxiety is a reaction to a threat that is not guaranteed it is the possibility of a threat or the fear of a future threat.

The feeling itself is meant to keep you alive when you feel it legitimately, such as when you are walking through a dark alley at night, it cues to your body that you need higher levels of vigilance. That vigilance will keep you more aware of your surroundings, and when you are more aware of those surroundings, you are better prepared in case something does go wrong. For example, if you know that people often get robbed when walking through alleys, it makes sense that you would be hyper-vigilant in that setting. You know that you are in a dangerous situation, and that discomfort you feel and the anticipation that the worst is about to happen will keep you ready to respond accordingly. That is normal and even healthy.

However, sometimes, anxiety becomes abnormal. You are feeling threatened or terrified in situations that are largely considered safe or low-risk for danger, such as when you are walking through the local park in broad daylight, making a phone call, or even seeing a small spider on the outside of your window. When your anxiety starts to arise in situations in which you know that it is illogical or unrealistic, when it becomes a regular state for you in which you are constantly or frequently feeling anxious, or it starts to distract from your life, it is time to reevaluate it to see whether it is an anxiety disorder.

Self-Esteem Issues Related to Anxiety

Unsurprisingly, those who report feeling largely anxious also report having lower self-esteem than their non-anxious peers. Those who are anxious may feel as though their anxiety makes them flawed or incapable, or they assume that their anxiety makes them unlikeable, and that can lead to plummeting levels of self-esteem.

Consider the fact that humans are social animalS we have developed emotional responses to being included or excluded as a result of being social, and the self-esteem that humans develop is directly related to whether or not you have been accepted or rejected in the world. When other people react dismissively toward you, as they are likely to do when you behave irrationally anxiously and have your anxious tendencies waved away, you will feel rejected and invalidated, which has a direct impact on your self-esteem.

The more frequently you feel rejected or discounted, the lower your self- esteem will fall. Coincidentally, having low self-esteem can also make your anxiety worse. This, of course, then makes your cycle of feeling invalidated and can directly impact your self-esteem, which will then impact your anxiety levels.

Looking at that cycle, you may realize that your anxiety going unchallenged and untreated is only exacerbating the situation, resulting in worsening symptoms. No matter the kind of anxiety you have, it is likely to go through that cycle, resulting in worsening self-esteem.

Generalized Anxiety Disorder

Perhaps one of the most common kinds of anxiety disorders, and the one that most people mean when they say they have anxiety is a generalized anxiety disorder. When you have this disorder, you likely have worry that becomes excessive and is recurring or persistent, and those worries extend to several areas in your life. There is no specific trigger for your anxiety, and you are likely to feel anxious in many different situations, regardless of whether you feel like it is legitimate or not.

Those who suffer from GAD often find themselves suffering from symptoms that are both mental and physical. The mental symptoms can range from constant or persistent worries disproportionate to the subject, a tendency to overthink, and struggle to relax or cope with problematic thoughts, feelings, or behaviors, and struggling to concentrate. This, of course, then leads to indecisiveness in a wide range of situations.

Physically, the individual suffering from GAD will frequently suffer from fatigue, insomnia, tension, feeling shaky, being persistently nervous in a wide range of situations, gastrointestinal distress, or discomfort, and being vaguely irritable regardless of the situation. These physical symptoms can become quite problematic, leading to stress, and even disrupting life if you are permanently exhausted but unable to sleep, or struggling with stomach issues.

GAD is not constant you may frequently have periods in which you feel largely capable of controlling your symptoms, or when your anxiety is not nearly as bad as in other situations. Other times, you may feel as though your anxiety is debilitating to the point that you cannot function. The intense fear and dread you are feeling could lead to you struggling to make any real progress in your daily life, crippling your work production and making it difficult to maintain social relationships.

Obsessive-Compulsive Disorder

Many people do not assume that obsessive-compulsive disorder (OCD) is actually an anxiety disorder, but it does fall under that umbrella. When you have OCD, you suffer from obsessions or uncontrollable thoughts that are recurring or repeated despite being unwanted, and then compulsions or behaviors that are designed to help alleviate the thought. You feel powerless to the cycle of obsessions and compulsions, and it often becomes repeated endlessly. The obsessions and compulsions are frequently irrational and something that many people may think are over the top, but you cannot help engaging in them.

These obsessions and compulsions can interfere with your life, particularly as

they get more and more pervasive and begin to crop up in areas of your life that they were not present before. Nevertheless, you can target these behaviors and learn to overcome them.

Obsessions can take on many different forms, ranging from thoughts and images that are intrusive, and they are frequently a source of shame. The most common forms that these take include being afraid of dirt or contamination, struggling with intrusive thoughts about harm, sex, or other taboos, thoughts that are aggressive toward other people or yourself despite the fact that you would never act upon them, or even making sure that things are exactly right. Those obsessions frequently lead to compulsions.

Compulsions are behaviors that are repeated in an attempt to respond to an obsessive thought. For example, if you are afraid of being contaminated by germs, you will frequently engage in repeated handwashing beyond what is considered normal or rational. You may have to wash your hands after touching anything at all, or you may feel the need to carry gloves to touch things in public. If you have a problem with order and symmetry, you may feel the need to rearrange items in order to ensure that each and everyone is perfectly in place. You may even insist on having certain items or activities done in a certain pattern or number.

While some of the compulsions people may have may seem somewhat normal, such as double-checking that doors are locked before bed, those with OCD are entirely unable to control the thoughts or behaviors. They know that their thoughts and behaviors are likely excessive, but they have no real control over the situations. The thoughts typically have to consume at least an hour a day, and the behaviors are likely not pleasurable in general. Perhaps the most important part is that there are significant problems developed as a direct result of the problematic behaviors.

Anxiety is an adaptive feature that is inborn in all of us. It is only the anxiety that happens when there is no apparent danger that is a problem. This one is caused by a variety of environmental, lifestyle, and genetic factors. These conditions make people susceptible to anxiety attacks. The actual manifestation of anxiety, however, happens when a specific event or emotion triggers or worsens symptoms of anxiety. In this section, we will discuss both the causes and triggers of anxiety. Keep in mind that triggers and causes bear close similarities. A cause may just as easily act as a trigger in one person but require an extra trigger in another. The way anxiety occurs and manifests is very specific to the person experiencing it.

Causes

The causes of anxiety are those conditions that make you susceptible to anxiety. They result in latent anxiety that may actually remain inactive if you have an effective coping mechanism, but that is activated by the triggers discussed later to result in the signs discussed in the section above.

Health Concerns

Anxiety occurs as a side effect of some types of sicknesses and accompanies most serious ailments. Health issues result in nervous system hyperactivity as the mind attempts to adjust to the consequences of a disease. Diseases with a

high mortality rate such as cancer and heart problems are especially stressful because they force the sufferer to deal with possible mortality.

Heart problems are especially anxiety-inducing because they have the same effects as anxiety attacks; uncontrollable pounding, shortness of breath, etc. After a heart attack, many people will experience symptoms of a heart attack caused by their anxiety and often end up in the emergency room.

Drugs

Drug use, addiction, and recovery are among the biggest cause of anxiety. Panic and social disorders are especially common among alcohol-dependent individuals. The fact that it is impossible to function without alcohol is what makes one fearful. Hard drugs also cause anxiety, but because of their high price, it is more of financial anxiety. Drug use is especially anxiety-inducing when it is not appropriate, such as during working hours, among minors, and illegally.

Drug addiction is another thing about drugs that induces anxiety. You get anxious because you are partially or completely dependent on the drug even though you are aware of the harmful effects. The anxiety is simply the fight- flight-freeze response of the body to a harmful substance that you are admitting into the body willingly, even eagerly. As long as you continue fighting and losing against alcohol, cigarettes, marijuana, or other drug addiction, you will continue experiencing anxiety attacks.

Finally, the recovery period is also characterized by immense anxiety as well. When you go into acute withdrawal, your levels of anxiety shoot right up. The anxiety of withdrawal may last for up to two years after quitting.

Financial stress

Money problems affect a substantial portion of the world's population. And in a world that is very materialistic, the financial pressure of having no money can be very stressful. From rent to food, education, transport, and healthcare, you need money to enjoy many of the basic survival needs. Financial difficulty makes you more susceptible to anxiety in and of itself, but it also makes it easier for you to fall prey to other forms of anxiety caused by poor body image and social inferiority complex caused by comparisons.

Genetics

General anxiety disorder is a condition that runs in families. Children of parents with GAD are six times more likely to come down with it than others. This is mostly because of the actions of parents, such as overprotectiveness and parenting styles that predispose children to a particular way of thinking or looking at the world. So, a parent who sees the world as a dangerous, risky place is likely to teach his or her children the same thing. They will thus grow up looking at the world as an unfriendly place to be anxious about as a way of avoiding getting hurt. This translates to anxiety being passed on from generation to generation.

Body image

Body image is a big contributor to personal well-being among all population groups. For people who are overweight, this is an even bigger problem because there is a clear preference for slimmer body types in modern society. Bodyweight is a double threat in anxiety because over the counter weight loss medicines contain anxiety-producing chemicals as well. So, not only will you feel the social anxiety of having a body type that most people consider to be 'inferior,' but any attempts to bring the weight down will also expose you to even more anxiety.

Triggers

Now that we know the things that make you susceptible to anxiety, let us discuss the exact causes of anxiety. The following specific triggers set off anxious behavior.

Caffeine

Caffeine is one of the most popular morning beverages, guaranteed to give you a jolt of delight and push you into action early in the morning. But it also contains some anxiety-inducing components that might be harmful to people with panic and social anxiety disorders. So, if you have been diagnosed or self-diagnosed with these two, be very wary of that morning mug of steaming coffee.

Skipped meals

Have you ever noticed that you feel more irritable when you are hungry? It is true that food affects your mood in a big way. Failing to eat or skipping a meal causes more than just a drop in blood sugar content. It can be a trigger for anxiety as well. Not only does a balanced diet provide you with vital nutrients and fill your body with energy, it also produces enough energy for

your brain to avoid sliding into anxiety. So, the lunch break you failed to have so that you could prepare for the presentation you will be giving in the afternoon could very well be the thing that makes you flunk. Rather than skipping a meal altogether, it is much better to have a healthy snack to fill up on the nutrients you need.

Negative thoughts

The mind is the control panel for the whole body. This makes it very easy for you to influence the rest of your body. The mind is an effective communication tool, so in moments when you are frustrated or sad, the things you say to yourself can turn out to be triggers for anxiety. People who think about themselves in a negative way only succeed in increasing their levels of anxiety every time a negative thought pops into the mind. It is entirely possible that as you let a negative thought fester inside your head, the level of your anxiety increases until you are experiencing a full-on anxiety attack.

Social events

For someone with social anxiety, a social event in which one is obligated to participate turns out to be a trigger. So, at the very mention of a party in which your attendance is expected or an event where you are expected to say a few words in front of people, the fear or flight response kicks in. The dread of attending and/or talking to the gathering increases as the event draws nearer, so that one may be battling a panic attack when the social event actually arrives. The reason for this is usually a perceived threat from the social obligation accompanied by a deep-seated fear of rejection that causes one to expect a negative reactive from others. Changing your view of social gatherings from threatening to friendly and dealing with the fear of rejection could be a very effective way to take care of it all.

Conflict

A dispute is another trigger for anxiety. Whether it be arguments with strangers (or friends), problems in a relationship or disagreements with significant partners (boss, colleague, etc.) conflict raises the levels of anxiety significantly. This is mostly because conflict is tension inducing in nature. The heightened levels of awareness and threat expectancy make your body go into fight or flight mode. Depending on your dominant reaction between fight and flight, you will either get more aggressive or withdraw into yourself. Both of these are flawed techniques of dealing with conflict. A more proactive method is necessary to ensure that one deals with conflict in a productive and mature manner.

Environmental triggers

For people who experience PTSD-induced anxiety, environmental triggers are the most common prompt for their anxiousness. A person who survived a kidnapping may get very anxious when a car pulls up close to them on the road, someone who has been through a battle may react more dramatically to random loud voices, especially if they are unexpected. From a song to a smell, environmental factors can arouse anxiety at the unconscious level, leading to manifestation consciously. In some instances, you may not even be aware that a particular environmental trigger prompts your anxiety because they register on the subconscious level.

CHAPTER 14: WHAT INFLUENCES OUR THOUGHTS

When thinking, two processes are launched: we either recall (that is, repeat) the thoughts that we have ever had, or create new ideas. In both cases, our senses play an important role. Hearing, sight, touch, smell, taste, and balance are needed not only to navigate the outside world but in order to carry out the process of thinking. We use the memory of "the different reactions of our senses" to think. Remembering something pleasant, such as a summer vacation, we mentally see a beach in front of us, hear sounds that were there, smells, etc. Remembering, we recreate the experiences that were at that moment and sensations. But the senses play a role in the creation of new thoughts. Read this text, passing images through your mind.

Imagine walking along the beach. You feel the soft sand under your bare feet. It is evening now, and the sand has cooled a little. The sun is low, and you have to squint so that it does not blind the eyes. You hear only the sound of the waves rushing to the shore and the rare cries of seagulls over the sea. You stop and breathe in the air, smelling algae. You have a shell in your hand, and you run your finger over its rough surface. You put the shell in your pocket and move on. Now voices of people are heard. Far ahead, you see a cafe, and your nostrils catch the aroma of food. You feel hungry. You are drooling. You speed up the step. The voices of people are getting louder, and the smells are stronger.

If you really felt the content, then you could mentally hear the sound of the waves, feel the sand under your feet and the smell of algae. Maybe by the end of the text, you even drooled. And while you are sitting at home on your couch. You didn't recall what was described in the text, and you only recreated what you had to collect a whole picture from pieces of different mosaic memories of the past years. You were holding a shell, and you know how it feels. You know how algae smell. But it is quite possible that you never walked along the beach at sunset and you didn't have such memories. You just collected a picture from what was in your memory, from the stories of other people, scenes from films, everything that helped you mentally recreate an evening walk along the beach. So, you created something new, as real as if this happened to you really. That is how we use our senses in the process of thinking. Sometimes we do it only in our head, sometimes in reality. We alternately use our senses mentally and in practice (perceiving the world around us). The more we are immersed in the text, the more our thought works. But at the same time, the brain doesn't really care if something happens around us or only in our consciousness. Both brain areas are responsible for both.

We prefer different feelings.

I want to emphasize: the senses affect our thoughts. At the same time, we can choose which feelings are more important to us. Most people prefer vision; these are so-called visuals. Some others prefer not to see, but to hear. The third group of people chooses touch: they like to feel the surface, the temperature, the shape of the object. Such people are called kinesthetic. The inner reflection of touch is found in the senses. The question "What do you feel?" It can concern both pain in the leg and the emotional state of a person. The smallest group of people prefer to taste and smell.

Finally, there is a group of people who prefer logic and rationalism to feelings. Such people are called digital or binary. For them, there are no intermediate states, and everything is limited to the categories "on / off", "yes/no," "black/white". I prefer to call such people neutral because they are less dependent on external stimuli.

To a greater or lesser extent, we use those senses that dominate our worldview, that is, are the main ones. Other sensations we use to confirm the information obtained through the main.

Different people set priorities in different ways: some people rely on vision, almost without using the sense of hearing or touch (visuals); someone can equally well use hearing, and vision; someone may belong to the visuals, but at the same time enjoy hearing and touch, etc.

Different Sensations – Different Thoughts

An interesting fact: depending on which of the sensations we prefer, we develop one or another view of the world. We communicate in different ways and pay attention to different things. Having determined which group of people your interlocutor belongs to, you will understand how he looks at the world, how he thinks, how he prefers to communicate and what he may be interested in. This ability to identify several times increases your chances to analyze the thoughts of another person, not to mention the fact that it helps to establish rapport.

Sour Exercise

Imagine that you have a peeled lemon in your hand. Feel it in your hand, how soft, heavy and wet it is from lemon juice. Do you smell strong? Now imagine that you bite off a piece of lemon. Sour juice fills the mouth.

If you have done this exercise qualitatively, then you will have a physical reaction involuntary salivation. And this is despite the fact that you ate a lemon only in your imagination. Your brain responded and sent signals to your body as if a sour lemon actually hit your mouth.

An interesting question: if it is so difficult for our brain to distinguish our fantasies and reality, how can we be sure that everything that happens is not a hallucination? Think about it at your leisure.

Look at Me – What Does Eye Movement Mean?

Researchers note that in the process of thinking, people use different parts of the brain, and depending on this, their eyes look in one

direction or another. This link is called LEM Lateral Eye Movement (Method of lateral eye movements). In the late seventies, a psychology student, Richard Bandler, and linguist John Grinder formulated the EAC theory, Eye Accessing Cues. They were the first to declare that by eye movement one can determine what a person is thinking about.

Do not forget that this model is common and does not work in all cases. Also, do not forget the wise words of Erickson that if something does not work, it is necessary to stop this activity. I cannot say that this model is true. But you must admit, in the words that the eyes are a mirror of the soul, there is a grain of truth.

According to the model presented, people who think in images look left up when they remember something, and right up when they create new thoughts, construct them. When a person

179

remembers sounds, he looks to the left (for example, when you think about what someone told you), when he comes up with new sounds to the right (for example, when he thinks out what to say to you). Remembering the physical sensations, the man looks right down. Unfortunately, for this kind of thoughts, here is no division into memories and new constructions. When a person speaks to himself and solves logical problems (a neutral person), his gaze is directed down to the left.

Creating a Picture

If you ask a friend how he spent his vacation, and he will first look to the left and then to the right, it means he remembers how it looked, and then checks the information with the help of the memory of what he felt. American specialist in body language Kevin Hogan recently expressed doubts that this model is true. He conducted a series of experiments, which resulted in the conclusion that our thoughts do not affect eye movement. I myself can only say one thing: I often used this model, and always with brilliant results. And Hogan is right that it doesn't matter whether it's a true model or not, it's important what results it gives.

Strategies for Anxiety Relief

When you are suffering from anxiety, it can become easy to get so caught up in the negative that you feel as though there is no hope for survival or freedom from the negativity. You get so stuck in that negative mindset that you fear that you will be there forever. However, that could not be further from the truth.

You can, in fact, achieve anxiety relief. This section will offer you four more ways that you may find relief in your life from anxiety. Hopefully, some of these strategies will be beneficial to you in some way.

Realistic Thinking

This is one more method of controlling your emotions and thinking in a reasonable manner when you engage in realistic thinking, you are identifying which thoughts are realistic, and if you find unrealistic thoughts, you are making them become reasonable in some way. When you do this, you are essentially ensuring that you can correct thoughts on the go.

The first step to this process is knowing what you are thinking about in the first place. This is where your mindfulness tools come in when you utilize those skills, you can identify where your mind goes, and that can help you locate all sorts of loose ends and thoughts that are unrealistic. Identify which of those thoughts make you feel bad somehow, and target those. For example, if you feel devastated that your date night, that you get weekly fell through, you have an unrealistic thought. Pay attention to how that makes you feel and identify the thought behind it. Why do you care about why you were unable to attend your date? Yes, this is similar to identifying negative automatic thoughts. In fact, that is exactly what you are doing here you want to identify that negative thought so you can simply correct it with one short sentence.

Your answer to being upset about the date night maybe that you do not want your partner to feel like you no longer love him because your partner always leaves you and you really want to

181

make sure this one is the one. When you stop and look at that thought, you may recognize that the thought is quite the overreaction for missing a single date night, and you remind yourself of that: You tell yourself that if a relationship were destroyed over a single date, then it was not a worthwhile relationship in the first place. By correcting that thought and making it more positive, you essentially fix the problem in your mind. You are able to calm yourself down a bit because you see the truth.

Seeking out a Therapist

Sometimes, the best thing you can do for persistent anxiety is seeking out a therapist. This is far easier said than done, but even if you feel like you do not need one, it may be worthwhile to consider. Therapists are not evil or a waste of money they are actually quite useful. They can help you navigate through all sorts of negative thoughts and ensure that you are able to better handle yourself no matter what the situation at hand. Through these processes, you will get customized content that a book cannot provide for you. You will get real-time feedback, telling you how you are doing and whether you are making a mistake in the execution of something that you are doing.

If you think that actively seeking out a therapist may be useful to you, you should make an appointment with your primary care provider to get advice or a referral. Sometimes, insurance will not cover any therapy without a referral, so this is one way to skip that step. As a bonus, your doctor will also be able to ensure that there are no physical causes to the symptoms you are having, particularly surrounding your heart. You only have one of those, after all.

When you have gotten a referral for therapy, you can then begin to consider what kind of therapy would work best for you. Would you want a cognitive behavioral therapist? Traditional talk therapy? Some other kind? There are several different forms of therapy for anxiety, and ultimately, the one you pursue will be your own choice. When you have made your decision, you should then check out any in your area that accepts your insurance, or if they do not, that is affordable to you.

When you do eventually meet your therapist, keep an open mind, but also keep in mind that you need to click with the individual. You want to make sure you feel comfortable with the person that you are talking to. However, it is hard to judge that after a single session in many instances. Try to meet with a therapist at least twice before deciding that he or she is not right for you. Finding the right match for you is essential if you want to make sure that your therapeutic process is actually effective.

Worst Case Scenario Roleplay

Another technique some people find useful in managing anxiety is to engage in what is known as a worst-case scenario roleplay. In this case, you are challenged to imagine the worst possible ending to whatever you are anxious about. For example, if you are anxious over getting a divorce, you may then stop and consider what the worst-case scenario would look like you plan out exactly what would happen. Perhaps you fear that your soon-to-be-ex will get full custody of the kids and get to keep possession of the house, leaving you with a massive child support bill for children you never see, and your children are quickly alienated against you so they no longer want to interact with you at all. Maybe this goes a step further and you lose all contact with your children, and all you become is a wallet for all of the activities, medical insurance, and everything else the children need while your ex marries someone else who gets to be the parent to your child that you wish you could be.

Stop and play out that situation. Then, you need to consider how realistic that is. How often do parents lose all contact with their children unless they are doing something that is bad for the children? How often do you hear about people who do drugs retaining custody of their children, or people who abuse their children retaining custody? How likely is your ex to stop, take the kids, and run? Why would your ex want to do something that is so bad for your children, who would benefit from having both parents present, barring any abuse or neglect?

As you dismantle the situation, you start to realize that the chances of your worst-case scenario actually happening are exceedingly slim, and that gives you some of the comforts you need to move on without further anxiety over the subject.

Play out a Situation to the End

The last of the methods to cope with anxiety that you will learn is to play out a situation until the end. In this case, you will be thinking about considering your fear and allowing yourself to think through what will really happen in that particular situation. For example, perhaps your fear is that you will lose your job when you go to work tomorrow because you were sick for a week and missed a lot of work. Your anxiety is keeping you up and you know you need to sleep, but you just cannot manage to do so.

In this case, what you should do is stop, think about that fear, and then play out how you think the situation will go. If you are afraid that you will be fired when you show up, imagine what you think will realistically happen. Perhaps you imagine that you will arrive, and your boss will come over. Rather than telling you that you need to talk in private, however, your boss asks you if you are doing better and says that you were missed. He does not say a word about you being sick because he is a good boss and he understands that people get sick sometimes.

Because you play out the realistic ending, you are able to contrast it with the worst-case scenario that you may have also developed for that particular situation. You are able to look at the two and realize that you will be okay. You know that being fired is a possibility, but it is always a possibility. There is always a chance of being fired at any job for any reason. You are then able to relax a bit and tell yourself that things will be fine, which enables you to finally fall asleep and get the rest that you need.

Strategies for Improving Quality of Life

Now, you are going to be walked through several steps to improve the quality of life you have. These are other ways that can benefit you that are not necessarily directly designed for anxiety in particular but can help you find more enjoyment and value in the life that you have. As you go through this process and read through these four different activities, imagine how you could apply any of these possibilities to your own life to develop the life you want to lead. You may realize that there are several different ways you could implement more positivity into your life that may have a pleasant side-effect of lessening your anxiety.

Understanding Body Language

In learning to better read other people's body language, you do two things you teach yourself how to read others so you know what they are thinking at any given moment in time. You also ensure that you are able to develop the skills to get yourself acting in ways that are directly related to the mood that you would like to be in. Remember fake it until you make it when you engage in learning to read other people's body language, you are able to better engage in the body language that you, yourself would need to get your mind thinking in certain mindsets. Further, you also develop the idea to recognize your own body language, learning what your own body language means, and in doing so, you are able to better understand your own moods when you are struggling to read them.

Studying Emotional Intelligence

The last piece of advice you will receive in this book is to learn how to become a more emotionally intelligent individual. In doing so, you are making yourself more capable in social settings. You are ensuring that you know how to control yourself and your own behaviors. You are ensuring that you can always behave properly because you know how best to regulate yourself. You also are developing the self-confidence that you need to get the skills desired to keep your own anxiety at bay. By learning to be emotionally intelligent, you are saying that you want to better yourself, recognizing that you can always improve and that you can always find a light in a dark situation, no matter how small that light may be. That light can guide you to a learning experience that you may find is incredibly beneficial to you.

186

As you go through CBT to change negative self-talk, your emphasis should be on realistic thoughts. While it is okay to think positively, you should focus on practical ideas. If you do not address them carefully, positive thoughts can cause you to set insane standards you might not be able to meet.

CBT should help you understand your current predicament. You must realize and accept the negative things happening in your life and address them in a realistic and balanced way. You will be retraining yourself, learning new habits that eventually help you move in the right direction. Progress in CBT is gradual and might take time. However, the benefits when you complete the therapy sessions can change your life.

Significant Causes of Anxiety Disorder

Scientists have done multiple research studies on the causes of anxiety and still do not have a simple answer for why someone might have one of these disorders. All we know is that multiple things can cause it. Sometimes only one of these factors is the cause and sometimes, all of them. Everyone is different and how anxiety affects people can drastically change from person to person. Anxiety can be a significant problem in your life. If you have extreme anxiety levels where it affects your everyday life, you might have an anxiety disorder. Feeling fearful, worried, or apprehensive are completely normal reactions to stressful situations, but people with anxiety disorders excessively experience them.

Many things can cause anxiety disorders. Speaking to a mental health professional will be very helpful if you would like to determine the root cause of your anxiety. CBT focuses on solutions rather than the problem but your therapist will still need to hear the history behind your anxiety. They will be able to determine why and how your anxiety got to the extreme level.

External Factors

An individual can develop an anxiety disorder if the environment they are in is highly stressful. Your personal or work relationships, job, education, or financial problems can affect your anxiety levels to a great extent. A toxic relationship with no boundaries can force you to feel like you have to take care of the whole house and family by yourself. If your partner is not helpful with the physical chores in the relationship, you are more likely to think they will not be useful with your emotions either. Same goes for friendships and family members. Sometimes, manipulative people can cause anxiety in the people around them, pushing some so much that they develop anxiety disorders.

External factors are not limited to other people. Your surroundings can also trigger your anxiety. Things like a dirty or untidy room can cause you to feel anxious since there is so much going on in a small amount of space, and you might not feel comfortable with how many germs there might be in there. The sense of smell is one of of our most reliable senses and we often connect smells to memories. Lastly, it is possible for low oxygen levels to also trigger your anxiety. We are human and we are meant to breathe in and out. when we are breathing in, we need a certain amount of oxygen to fill up our lungs. Your brain knows that and can throw you into fight or flight mode when it feels there is not enough oxygen for your lungs to fill. If you don't exclude yourself from these stressful environments, your anxiety will grow and become worse over time.

Exercise 1: Think about your daily life. During what time do you usually feel the most anxious? Who is around you when you are feeling overwhelming amounts of anxiety? Do you feel unsafe and unusually anxious when you are at a particular place? Take some time out and think about a day you felt crippled by your anxiety. Analyze that day and consider the external factors that might have caused your anxiety.

Family and Genetics

Does one of your parents have a cleaning obsession or hoard things? When you were younger, did you always think that your mom's reactions to things were too high? Could you have inherited a behavioral pattern since you seem to react like one of your parents to stressful situations? The answer to that question is that it is very possible. Our families can have a lot to do with our anxiety levels. Anxiety disorders can be inherited through genes and learning. A person who has a parent with an anxiety disorder can inherit an anxious brain from that parent. People can also learn to respond to stressful situations with anxiety if that is how their parents met.

Everyone is at least a little like their parents. That does not mean they have to keep passing down the anxiety they inherited or learned from their parents. Once you realize that your anxiety is getting in your daily functioning, it is time to take action. You don't want your children to experience the same anxiety as you, and the anxiety does not need to be a part of you.

Exercise 2: Evaluate how you and your parents (or whoever raised you) react to certain stressful situations and see if one or more of them also have anxious responses to small things. You can have anxiety about different things so think about a scenario that stresses you out and compare it to a scenario that stresses them. If you find that your anxiety might be inherited, you might want to suggest therapy to your parents.

Medications for Other Conditions

It is not unusual to feel anxious when you are sick. Since we feel more anxious when we are not in a good mood and are hard to come by when we are sick, it is reasonable to catch yourself overthinking and worrying while we are not at our best health. Your anxiety can also be caused by the medication you use for other conditions. Certain medications have anxiety as one of their side effects. It can also be the lack of a medication that is triggering your anxiety, as it can be a symptom of a physical condition. Your anxiety might be caused because of stress due to your medical condition, the pain related to the condition, or the recovery process of the illness. In these situations, your anxiety should be eased once you stop taking those drugs or recover from the illness.

Tip: If you have anxiety problems already, always mention it to your doctor when prescribed with a new type of medication. If you forget to mention it or realize the anxiety after years of using a certain drug, read the side effects on the bottle carefully to make sure it is not the reason you're experiencing so much discomfort.

Dysfunction in the Brain

People used to believe that a dysfunction could only cause anxiety in the brain. While that has been proven to be far from

190

the only cause, it is still one of the possibilities you and your therapist should consider. Trauma from childhood, developmental problems, and trauma while you were an adult can all cause this dysfunction in your brain.

If you've experienced something traumatic, your brain can start to react anxiously to things it would have reacted normally to before. You might suddenly feel claustrophobic when you had no problems with it before, or you might start to overthink and worry when those were not things you would do before. This is because traumatic experiences alter our brains' way, especially the parts of our brains where fear is controlled. Many types of anxiety disorders occur alongside mood disorders, and your mood can change depending on the chemicals your brain releases. Traumatic experiences might slow down the release of dopamine and serotonin, the hormones that make us happy, focused, and calm, while increasing the levels of cortisol, the stress hormone, in the brain.

The fact that a chemical imbalance might cause anxiety does not mean that it has to be a part of you forever. You can very well help yourself with self-help methods and go to therapy to rewire your brain into releasing the right amount of hormones when needed. You are in control of your body and the hormones your brain releases.

Tip: If you have suffered from a traumatic experience in the past or recently, speaking to a therapist or a support group will help significantly. One of the symptoms of PTSD, post-traumatic stress disorder, is experiencing overwhelming anxiety, and one of the symptoms of anxiety is finding ways to suppress that anxiety. It is never a good idea to suppress your anxiety as it can cause more problems in the long run.

Wrong Beliefs Can Slow Down Your Recovery From Anxiety

A lot of small lifestyle changes can alter the way you react to anxious situations. However, if you force yourself to believe that you can't do anything about your condition and that you are bound to feel anxious and suffer from an anxiety disorder your whole life, you might never see the big picture. It is always great to consider multiple possibilities when it comes to your anxiety disorder. If you hear one thing and it makes sense to you, it doesn't mean that it is correct or the only way to do things. Some people have suffered from the uncomfortable symptoms of anxiety for a long time only because they had the wrong information on how to get better. All this time, people who could have been free from anxiety by simply going to therapy, have been popping pills and trying useless things to get rid of their anxiety just because a money-hungry pharmaceutical company once put it in their heads that they only needed medication to fix their problems.

One of the biggest misunderstandings about anxiety is that it is not caused or controlled by behavior but something else. The idea that anxiety is all about not being able to control one's behavior was dispelled many years ago. We are very well able to control, change, and better our behavior by getting therapy from an experienced, licensed mental health professional and by using self-help techniques like meditation. People, like medicine companies and some doctors, who wanted to use anxiety disorders for their own benefit, have spread false information about anxiety for many years and still continue to do so now. While most health specialists care for people who have anxiety disorders, a few are willing to push these agendas just to make more money. It is not only the people who are after the money who are spreading false information. Some people just don't want to acknowledge anxiety disorders and claim that people who have them are just "weird" or "worry-warts", just because they don't have a disorder themselves and can't be sympathetic.

It can be hard to come to terms with the fact that what you learned about anxiety might be wrong. This can be why people often refuse to seek therapy for their anxiety because they think that it is something they cannot control. Therapists often run into this problem as it can be hard for people to change their behavior and beliefs even if there is plenty of evidence proving that doing so will help them in a major way.

Pharmaceutical companies worked hard to make people believe that a chemical imbalance was the only reason why people had anxiety, in order to get people to opt for drugs to fix that imbalance. However, in 2011, it was proven that while anxiety causes an imbalance in the brain, it is not caused by an imbalance itself. Disorders like PTSD can cause the brain to react differently to situations and have anxiety as a side effect but the chemical imbalance is not responsible for the anxiety in any way. Today, a lot of people still believe this myth to be true even if they are told that there is an abundance of evidence that proves that it is wrong.

Controlling your anxiety is in your hands. While it might not be as easy as deciding that you're no longer going to suffer from it, you can still control your anxiety by changing your behavior. Believing that you cannot control your anxiety can cause you to feel like an anxiety victim, but if you believe that a change in your behavior could make your anxiety disappear, you would feel empowered and take the steps to make a healthy change.

Don't feel like there is nothing you can do about it. Your anxiety is an emotional, psychological, and physical mood that happens when you get defensive due to certain situations. You expect danger or discomfort and it stresses you out even before

193

anything happens. So anxiety is what your behavior is like during certain situations, not anything else. When you learn to deal with those situations in a less defensive way, your anxiety will ebb away.

If you believe that you can change your anxious ways, even just that realization can bring you hope. That hope will help eliminate a big part of your anxiety all by itself because it is not about something going wrong, it is about you feeling nervous about things you can't change.

To learn how to change your behavior to react in a better way to certain situations, you must have the right information. You could see an experienced therapist to talk about what anxiety is and isn't if you want to take a step towards becoming a less anxious, happier person. Your anxiety will continue to cause problems until it is deliberately changed.

Your Anxiety Profile

There are different types of anxiety disorders. Many of them are considered to be mood disorders and can affect your life in significant ways. You might have more than one of these disorders as they can overlap with each other like any other psychological condition.

CHAPTER 15: SELF-ESTEEM, ANXIETY AND PRACTICING MEDITATION

Meditation is an amazingly effective way to build your self–esteem. Also, it significantly improves every aspect your physical and emotional health. Many meditation techniques are very helpful, as they involve eliminating every thought that's going through your head. Clearing your mind by getting rid of negative thoughts will help restart your mind and allow it to be more relaxed, which will allow you to think more clearly and rationally.

Instead, focus on not engaging with those thoughts. Instead of allowing anxiety, criticisms, and worries to have any space in your head, simply let those thoughts pass. If you find yourself too fixated on something to meditate, try to re-focus your mind onto your breathing. Focus on the way breathing forces your chest to expand and collapse. Notice how you physically feel doing the meditation. Don't let negativity invade this space for long!

Practicing mindfulness meditation techniques has been shown to have a wide variety of incredible benefits for your overall health and well–being! It has the power to improve your physical and emotional health, benefitting you as a whole. Here are some excellent reasons as to why should start practicing mindfulness meditation today! Meditation has been shown to reduce chronic pain, lower blood pressure, and alleviate a wide array of gastrointestinal issues.

It also improves sleep, decreases insomnia, helps treat heart disease, and stress. Mindfulness meditation also improves an array of mental/emotional aspects of your health. For instance, it helps treat depression, reduce obsessive compulsive behaviors, anxiety, relationship conflicts, stress and irritability and negative thought patterns associated with eating disorders. It also acts as an important element in treating substance abuse.

Meditation has also been shown to increase brain function, as well as the grey matter that is found in areas of the brain associated with self–awareness, empathy, self–control and attention. Another favorable brain–benefit of meditation is that it has also been proven to regulate the part of the brain that produces stress hormones (cortisol), which in turn reduces stress.

Mindfulness meditation has many favorable advantages that lead to a plethora of improvements and enhancements in virtually every aspect of your physical and emotional health. It has the incredible power to improve immunity while creating positive brain changes, lower stress, and assist in coping with chronic health issues such as chronic pain, cancer and heart disease, only to name a few. A recent meta–analysis of 20 empirical reports has shown plenty of evidence that mindfulness meditation drastically increased both physical and mental well–being in patients who were battling with heart disease, chronic pain, cancer and autoimmune disorders.

Meditation Helps You Become a Better Person – Literally!

According to a study in the journal, Psychological Science, mindfulness has a virtuous effect on us, causing us to be more compassionate, which benefits the people who we interact with! Besides, researchers from Harvard and Northwestern Universities discovered that meditation, particularly mindfulness, is very strongly linked with increased patterns of more virtuous, "do–good" behavior. Who would've thought!

Meditation Helps Support Weight–Loss!

In a recent Women's Health study conducted at Harvard Medical School, participants who practiced mindful eating (they ate slowly, while savoring the food and paying attention to the sensations they felt with each bite) consumed a significantly reduced the amount of caloric intake than those who didn't engage in mindful eating, even though they were hungrier than the opposing control groups! This led the mindful–eaters to lose more weight in the long run and a newly gained appreciation for healthier foods. This will also lead to developed long–term healthy eating–patterns, which helps maintain healthy weight in the long run.

Progressive Muscle Relaxation Meditation Technique

Before practicing this exercise, make sure you first consult with your doctor if you suffer from any physical complications including muscle spasms, back or neck problems, or other injuries or muscle conditions that can be potentially aggravated by tensing your muscles.

Start by getting comfortable – remove your shoes and change into comfortable clothing. Now that you're dressed comfortably, take a few minutes to relax and take nice and slow deep breaths. Inhale and exhale. When you feel relaxed enough and are ready to start with the exercise, direct all of your undivided attention to your right foot. Take a few silent, peaceful moments to focus on how it feels, and be aware of every sensation.

197

Next, start to slowly tense your right–foot muscles while squeezing as tightly as you possibly can. Do this for 10 seconds – If you like, you can count to 10 out loud. Now move onto your right foot, relax and direct your full focus on the tension that's flowing away from your foot, and how it feels as it becomes relaxed.

Stay in this peaceful and relaxed state for a few moments, while slowly and calmly taking deep breaths. Inhale and exhale. When you're ready to move on, direct your entire focus onto your left foot. Now repeat the same process of the muscle tension and release, the same way you did on your right foot. Move slowly upwards throughout your whole body, contracting and relaxing the various muscle groups as you go. It may take some practice and discipline at first, but try not to tense your muscles for longer than 10 seconds.

Walking Meditation

This incredibly healthy practice works wonders on clearing your mind and helping you cope with overwhelming emotions, including grief. For this exercise, start by first finding a space outside, and simply begin walking at slow to medium pace, while focusing on your feet. Try to pay close attention to when your toes touch the ground, when your foot is flat and pressing against the ground and when your toe points back in an upward position. Now, feel the roll of your foot, paying close attention to every sensation, and noticing each sensory detail – whether you feel a tingle, a pull of the sock there, and how your foot feels against the ground.

When feel your mind beginning to wander into the chaotic land of scattered thoughts, which it probably will (and it's completely normal), shut off your mind and gently proceed to bring your attention back to your feet after you've eliminated all other thoughts. With this exercise, you're practicing and building the important skill of being aware when your concentration begins drifting into default mode. At the same time, you'll also be training yourself to bring it back into focus. Building and strengthening this skill will effectively help you be more present in the moment, and more in control of your thoughts and attention, every day, and will be particularly useful in times of stress when our minds tend to wander most. With the skill, you'll be more in touch with your thought patterns while knowing your brains. This will help you immediately identify the negative thought patterns associated with low self–esteem, that way you can put a stop to them and shift to a more positive place in your mind.

For this exercise, it can be very helpful and rewarding to dedicate a specific time and chosen location to practice. When you have become more comfortable with walking meditation, try taking it to the next level by practicing as you're walking to the bus stop, office, classroom, grocery store, or anywhere you please.

Not only will engaging mindful–meditation techniques virtually benefit all aspects of your body, both physically and emotionally, it will also offer favorable benefits and improvements to every aspect of your life, including relationships, family situations and work. It will also allow you to view each situation and aspect in your life with a positive perspective. You will realize the positive benefits they offer, rather than the stress, negativity and inconvenience.

Mindfulness and relazation

Why are Meditative Relaxation and Mindfulness Important?

I often ask people what they do during leisure or daily relaxation and the responses I get are such:

"I watch TV every night."

"I relax by reading a book."

"I hang out with friends."

"I like fishing."

"I take a glass of wine."

"I work out at the gym."

"Gardening is relaxing."

All these activities may seem relaxing and even have some element of awareness in them; however, they don't provide the body and brain with the required meditative relaxation. In fact, most of them stimulate the brain and body.

What is Deep Meditative Relaxation?

When I talk about deep meditative relaxation, I refer to the type of meditation that enables our brain to enter a particular state for a period of time known as the "alpha" state.

The "alpha" state is a term for our brain waves, measured using a machine known as the EEG (Electroencephalograph). Electrodes (usually non- invasive) are attached to our heads to measure brain waves and we discover that different types occur in our brains, depending on our degree of alertness. Our normal state of alertness, which is when we're fully awake and active, is depicted as "beta" waves. On the EEG, they are very active, slow, non- uniform and shallow. It just shows that activities are going on in the brain and they include thinking and physical activities directed by the brain. With this, you can easily describe most of the above statements by a "beta wave state."

Lotus Flower

It's a normal phenomenon for our brain to slow down when we're asleep. Our brain waves become slower, deeper, and more rhythmic as we go through deeper sleep stages, including theta and delta brain waves.

Nevertheless, when we go back into REM sleep or dream sleep, our brains slowly approach the state of alertness or wakeful state of the beta waves because at this point of dream sleep, our brains are active.

These brain waves are predominant in people who don't make a practice of deep meditative relaxation. However, with hypnosis, meditation, deep meditative relaxation and mindfulness, people can experience other brain waves like the alpha brain wave state and theta, which have been proven to have major health benefits.

Health Benefits of Practicing Meditative Relaxation

Lowers Anxiety and Stress

Relaxation exercises help reduce the effects of stress and anxiety. As a result, individuals are capable of performing better and functioning effectively in daily tasks, being more focused and productive at their workplace and thus gaining a feeling of satisfaction.

Lowers the rate of Depression and Substance Abuse

Use of routine meditation helps reduce signs and symptoms of depression. Mindfulness meditation helps reduce relapses in depression and substance abuse as well. Although alertness or mindfulness may not be the only form of treatment, it can be used as an adjunct for treating these problems.

Helps Reduce Symptoms of Various Physical Illnesses

In other studies, cognitive impairment or disability as a result of cancer has been reduced by meditation, which has assisted cancer patients with stress, pain, mood, nausea and sleep disorders. In addition to this, it has been shown that meditation is effective for reducing blood pressure and other conditions like epilepsy, menopausal symptoms, premenstrual symptoms, and autoimmune illnesses.

Improves Cognitive Performance

Constant practice of meditation helps improve cognitive ability, flexibility and attention, which contribute a huge sum to the overall well-being and mental balance of the individual.

Reduces Sensitivity to Pain

People who make meditation a habit have been found to have significantly less sensitivity to pain. Another meditative activity, hypnosis stimulates the alpha and theta brain waves and has been shown to help in pain management.

Slow down Aging of Cells

A report has linked mindfulness's practice to a slowing of cellular aging as a result of a reduction in stress arousal and cognitive stress. They question the perception that reduction in stress arousal is associated with telomere length, the protective caps at the end of chromosomes which have a tendency to deteriorate with age. Nevertheless, studies are still being conducted;

therefore we look forward to the outcome in the future. How Do I Perform Deep Meditative Relaxation?

Various methods can be implored to achieve the same result. Below, we have several common ways and methods to help you begin practice:

Deep Relaxation

The best and most effective way to learn the act of deep relaxation is by listening to a taped or recorded exercise. You can download two different free exercises from this site and start practicing.

The exercises are usually 20-25 minutes long, and all you need do is find a comfortable place to lie down or sit and follow the instructions given. As a beginner in deep relaxation, you may make a common mistake by trying so hard to relax that you increase tension rather than relax. Therefore, don't force yourself to relax, just listen to the exercise and flow with it. Don't get worried if your mind wanders, just let yourself refocus on the exercise.

Over time and with constant practice, you become better at experiencing deep relaxation. If at any point you get bored as a result of doing the same exercise, try to create your own imagery.

For example, when you download using this site, the image seen is a description of two doors at the base of the staircase. You walk through one door and find yourself in what looks like a meadow, or a cabin on the mountain in the other exercise and people ask, 'What's behind the second door?' The answer to this is I don't know. This is because the second door is there for you if you choose to go through it and create your own pleasant image.

Practice mindfulness

An excellent way to describe the concept of mindfulness can be when your brain is more focused on immediate experiences rather than distractive thoughts that are irrelevant and add no value, such as 'What do I cook for dinner?' or worries centered on future occurrences such as 'What if I do badly at the seminar tomorrow?' or criticisms centered on past experiences like 'I shouldn't have said that. Was stupid of me'.

Mindfulness takes all these demands and criticisms away, making issues centered on present experiences more enticing and attractive to the brain even if they aren't exactly pleasant. This goes to say that as we make a practice of mindfulness, our brains choose to be in that state of mind more often than not.

An example is this scenario. Let's say I'm running late in the morning, I could try to speed up my daily routine and focus on more pressing thoughts. 'I'm late! I have to hurry!'

But I've made a discovery and have found that this approach not only makes me slower, but also stresses me, and there's a tendency it'll slow me down because I'm likely to drop or misplace things due to lack of focus, making me spin around in circles.

However, a more conscious approach is to acknowledge that there are demanding thoughts but they are not useful. Rather, I tell myself to focus on doing one thing first, don't worry about the time. The outcome is that I'm less stressed and ready as early as I could be. It's a normal thing to experience the mindfulness state, and most of us actually do.

Take an example. If you've ever watched a beautiful sunset for about ten to fifteen minutes, you'll notice that the colors change and you can feel connected to the world around you without getting distracted by thoughts. We can say you were in a mindful state. In some people it is different. They may find themselves more focused when they engage in some types of activities or work.

In sports, the description of someone being in, 'the zone' is a mindful state in which the focus of the athlete is in the activity and thus he or she responds automatically.

If this state of mind can be experienced naturally, why then is it necessary to cultivate the practice of mindfulness?

First, many people don't experience mindfulness in their day. The second reason being that those who experience it have it contained in such a way that it has becomes useless to them throughout the day.

This just means a person may be mindful while fishing but once they get off the lake, they become irritated and agitated with other people because they don't share the mindful state with them.

Therefore, we can experience mindfulness as we go about our daily activities, and it may be necessary during tasks we do not like. For example, I don't like doing dishes and I always think about how much I hated this task and being hurried so I could finish it quickly, and this made the experience more unpleasant.

One day, I discovered that I was in a mindful state spontaneously while doing dishes. I was more focused on wiping the dishes, getting a feel of the water running through my hands and how my muscles moved each time I lifted a plate.

In the end, I thought "That wasn't so bad after all". This took place before I got to learn about the practice of mindfulness, but I also discovered that the impact of my mental state on my experience was more than the actual task I had to do.

A simple and effective method I use frequently to get people started with mindfulness practice is to tell yourself this: "I'm going to focus on being mindful for the next few minutes." The exciting thing about this is that it can be done anywhere, anytime, thus cancelling the common "I don't have time to relax" excuse.

In the state of mindfulness, you are more aware and capable of engaging in other tasks, which means you can do this while driving, waiting in line, working, having a conversation and other things you do during your day.

All you have to do is take a few minutes and focus completely on your present experience, what you feel, hear, see, taste, and smell. I often tell people to start with a few minutes because this practice can be quite difficult at first.

You're likely to get distracted within 5 to 10 seconds of starting the exercise by your present worries, demands or past experiences. It's fine if you feel that way. It's actually allowed because it gives you the opportunity to practice the second and most important part of the exercise, which is learning to acknowledge your thoughts but channeling your focus to your present experience.

It's like telling yourself "That's fine, but my focus right now is on this." At first, you may have to do this many times during a two minute practice. Try hard not to get frustrated by this because your mindful state may be interrupted by frustration as your thoughts are about frustration rather than the main object of your focus. Instead, refocus your mind gently.

Despite the fact that this can be done for only a few minutes, I still encourage people to make it a practice as many times as possible throughout the day. The more you practice, the more your brain becomes receptive and accustomed to mindfulness, thus you'll notice your brain returning to that state voluntarily.

The idea is not just about achieving mindfulness but making it a practice and letting your brain do the rest.

Qi Gong

I have come to discover that most people perform better with an active form of relaxation. Tai Chi, the ancient Chinese practice, assists people to achieve a deep state of relaxation through movement, together with breathing and focus.

However, mastering the art of Tai Chi and becoming sufficient takes years before you can obtain its benefits. I therefore urge beginners to try out Qi Gong (it has varieties of spellings: Qi Chong, Qigong, and Chi Kung).

This simply means using basic Tai Chi movements to get into a state of deep relaxation. You can see examples of these movements and make a daily practice of them or just follow the instructions given for deep meditative Qi Gong, available on this site.

Should I practice every day?

The popular saying goes 'practice makes perfect'. In order to obtain the benefits of deep meditative relaxation, it is ideal to practice daily. However, I often advise and recommend people to try different relaxation styles, especially as first timers, to find out which works best for them and fits into their lifestyle.

The good thing about these methods is that you obtain immediate rewards that come in the form of a sense of calm and well-being and relaxation. The long term benefits as earlier described are more beneficial.

Quick tips for boost self-esteem

Getting started is the most important key to ever achieving anything, including a healthy self-esteem. Unfortunately, 2 things cause people to fail from the get go.

First is laziness. Some people are just to darn lazy to get anything started. Another reason is discouragement.

People get discouraged from even starting because of past failures or because the initial first steps are intimidatingly difficult. We can succeed at getting started by starting with small, easier steps and gradually increase the difficulty and complexity, allowing small successes to build up to bigger ones.

Here are 10 things we can do within the next ten days to help us quickly build our self-esteem momentum that will carry us forward into long term self-esteem success:

-Day 1: Recall something that you did well, even for the first time. By recreating the sensation and feeling of past successes, you release dopamine into your brain.

It can also help you feel more confident when doing something new. By recalling past successes, you objectively establish our ability to get things done, which can boost your self-esteem.

-Day 2: Indulge in something you do well. By doing this, you physically remind yourself that you are capable of doing things well. I love playing the guitar moments before engaging in an unfamiliar activity or learning something new. It makes me feel good about myself, which is a great way to start doing or learning something new.

-Day 3: Finish those long pending items in your to-do-list. Doing this helps you experience a sense of accomplishment that's beneficial for making you feel good. On the other hand, a growing pile of to-do-list items can hamper your self-esteem because it sends the subtle message that you can't get things done.

-Day 4: Think about others for a change. As much as low self-esteem is about thinking lowly, we can also suffer from it by thinking too much about ourselves. When we do that, every little flaw is magnified, making depression and low self worth mountains out of molehills. By thinking about other people for a change, you redirect your attention away from your perceived shortcomings. That can help boost your self-esteem fast.

-Day 5: Relax by getting a massage, sleeping the whole day or enjoying your favorite TV shows – whatever makes you feel rested and refreshed. Often, being to busy and hectic makes stresses us out, making us highly strung and more sensitive to our "shortcomings" more than the usual. By relaxing, we get to breathe and give our selves the chance to let all that stress and tension evaporate. As a result, we become less critical about ourselves and enjoy a healthier self-esteem.

-Day 6: Treat yourself to your favorite food. Trying to eat too healthy can be stressful and make us feel bad about ourselves. Often, eating healthy is due to a desire to lose weight. By overdoing it as in the case of crash and overly restrictive diets, we run the risk of a very strong rebound of binge eating and more weight gain. By giving yourself a break, you minimize that risk and feel better about yourself.

-Day 7: Exercising, particularly aerobic exercises like running and biking release endorphins in our bodies – a happy hormone. Whenever I feel down, I love to go out for a run. It never fails to make me feel much better about myself and my particular situation at the time.

-Day 8: Buying new clothes can instantly make us feel better about ourselves, especially when we buy clothes that look good. To make the most out of this, you should tag a fashion expert friend along to help you pick out clothes that complement your looks.

-Day 9: Going to church can help you feel good about yourself, even if you're not a religious person. In particular, seeker-sensitive churches like Lakewood Church or Hillsong Church preach messages that are primarily meant to encourage people more than giving them a list of moral to do's and not-to-do's. If you're not a Christian or particularly religious, you can listen to or watch podcasts of the best motivational speakers.

-Day 10: Being thankful for all of our blessings regardless of our situations is one way to quickly raise self-esteem. In particular, I find it especially helpful to remember how many other people have it worse than I do, i.e., people dying from famines, people tortured and murdered for their religious beliefs and people living on the cold streets, among others. Nothing makes for a good self-esteem raise than seeing how things can be much worse and how things are much better for us compared to others.

CHAPTER 16 : TEN STEPS FOR SELF-HYPNOSIS

We will go over ten simple and concise steps to perform a successful and fruitful and positively effective session of self-hypnosis. I will list the steps first and follow up with a step-by-step breakdown featuring a brief and easy to understand the description of what each step should entail for you in your journey.

Step 1: Self

Step 2: Time

Step 3: Space

Step 4: Goal and Motive

Step 5: Relaxation of the Physical Body

Step 6: Relaxation of the Soul and the Mind

Step 7: Realization of Trance

Step 8: Repetition of of Script

Step 9: Exiting the Trance State

Step 10: Returning to Earth

As you read those steps, I'm sure they bring forth images in your mind. It may seem apparent already what you have to do, and ideas for how to guide yourself through this self-hypnosis you are preparing for are blossoming like wildfire in your mind. Let us go in-depth to further prepare and become aware of all that you can do to make your self-hypnosis as easy and effective as your soul will wish to better yourself in the most transformative way possible.

Step 1: Self

One of the first and foremost goals is to become as relaxed as possible before, during, and after entering the trance-state. Relaxation is the key that helps us enter the trance-state, and the trance-state further facilitates relaxation of the entire being both during the active self- hypnosis and afterward, for positive benefits of your being. To achieve the most successful self-hypnosis possible, we must first prepare ourselves, our minds and our physical bodies, for what we desire to achieve, a state of heightened relaxation in which we can become hyper-aware of the inner machinations of the mind, to achieve a closer union with them, to bond with them, and to converse with them on the most intimate level. This can mean many things to many people. Go to the used CD store, and you will see an endless section of new age music, monks chanting, flute playing, choirs, and tribal drums. The popularity of this music exists because people desire sounds that will lull them into a more peaceful state. Maybe you would like to try something like this. Some people prefer silence; some prefer peaceful noise, a sort of hypnotizing drone that guides them into a more relaxed state. White noise, be it from a fan, a laundry machine, running water, or a white noise machine made specifically to fill the air with a light white noise, can also be effective for this purpose.

Anything that has the desired effect on you will serve this purpose. Another thing you can do is drink a nice herbal tea of your choosing; find a blend that is relaxing to you as an individual. Some common choices would be lavender-orange teas or chamomile teas. These will set a space internally for you to prepare yourself for entering your trance-state. Another very common tool for the preparation of the self for self-hypnosis is aromatherapy. Many essential oils, either applied directly to the body or dispersed through the air with the use of an essential oil diffuser, readily and commonly available at most grocery stores, can have a relaxing effect on the mind and body, ideal for the preparation of self-hypnosis. Many essential oil manufactures make and sell blends specifically for the purposes of relaxation or stress- relief. Any of these would be a very great choice for a consumer who is feeling anxious about the large selection of essential oils to choose from and would like some advice on which to get. For those who would prefer to buy oils individually, some common choices for the purposes of relaxation would be, again, lavender, a go-to for many people in many situations, clay sage, ylang-ylang, lemon, or jasmine. Most importantly, find a way to put yourself in a good mood and prepare yourself for an inner-journey. Know that many different things work for many different people, and these are all just suggestions. Find what works for you and your inner peace.

Step 2: Time

It goes without saying that if an alarm clock goes on when you are in your trance-state, the effectiveness of your self-hypnosis session will be largely inhibited. It is necessary, if you wish for an effective and transformative session of self-hypnosis, that you make sure a certain amount of time is allotted where you will be safe, secure, at peace, and uninterrupted by your daily responsibilities. Common inhibitors of time include children, chores, spouses, day-to-day noise, and work. If you have children, maybe you can have a relative or a reliable babysitter, watch them for a certain amount of time. Maybe you could ask your spouse to take the children out for an hour or two and explain to them your intentions of performing a transformative inner-journey that requires the utmost relaxation possible. If your kid is of the age where they go to school, maybe you could find the time while they are away at school. There are many possibilities, but they require planning and foresight to make sure you have your time to do what you need to achieve what you plan to achieve through the designated self-hypnosis session. Spouses or other life partners are much easier to deal with as, unlike children, who require constant attention and care, spouses can have the situation explained to them and are generally ready and willing to give you any space you will need to do anything that you feel will make yourself happier and more at peace. If you are in an honest and communicative relationship, they should already be well on your side as far as your self-hypnosis journey is concerned. Day-to-day noise is something that can be accounted for if it is an issue. If you are living in a town where certain times of the day have excessive traffic outside or nearby, either driving traffic or foot traffic, just keep that in mind when allotting time for your self-hypnosis. If you live across the street from a public school, do not plan your self-hypnosis journey when it is just about time for school to get out, as you will be interrupted by and inundated with an unwelcome rush of noise, and possibly loud bells signaling the end of the day. And, lastly, work should be no issue. If work follows you home, by a cell-phone linked to a work line or other such method, send it straight to voice mail for a time, let whoever is in charge know that you are in need of private time and will be away from the line shortly. These things can always be worked out with whomever they need to be worked out with. Responsibilities can be many and growing and overwhelming. Situations in which you have a large burden of responsibility ironically, are the types of situations that can make necessary long and fruitful journeys into self- hypnosis. It takes planning and cares to make sure that, while all responsibilities are met, there is a designated and a specified time for you to go into your journey with the utmost confidence and care that you will be able to do what you need to do, and come out the other end as enlightened as possible.

Step 3: Space

It also should go without saying that a crowded, busy subway station at peak times of the day is no place for you to go about your most effective journeys into self-hypnosis or the trance-like state. The place is of the essence. Just as your body temple must be totally clean and prepped and ready for the ascension, so must your surrounding area be prepared for you to feel as comfortable as possible to allow for the most successful transition into a strong and malleable trance-like state, allowing for the most successful self-hypnosis possible. Depending on your living situation, this one may or may not be so simple. A young man or woman who is living with several roommates to get by might have a hard time finding a place where they can be alone for a certain amount of time, allowing for the relaxation required to fulfill the depths of the trance. It is up to you, both subject and practitioner, to find where you are most comfortable, and make that space available during the time you have allotted for your self-hypnosis session. You have the freedom to get as creative as you wish. Obviously, for those of you who have homes and places where you are able to spend as much personal time with yourself as you could possibly desire, this task will be the easiest. For others, it can involve hiking to a secluded place, going to a library or other place where silence is golden, a public park at a low-trafficked time of day when few people are there, or even renting a motel or hotel room for a specific amount of time. Do what is necessary so you can perform the actions necessary to better yourself. Once space is found, the task moves to the setting or dressing of the space. Find a position where you are comfortable, using whatever tools or accessories are required to make yourself as relaxed as possible—blankets, pillows, tranquil pictures or statues such as of deities,

indoor waterfalls or fountains, zen gardens, rocks, crystals, orgone generators, the aforementioned essential oil diffusers or white noise machines, any external item that will set the scene for your inner-journey. As always, it is different for different people, depending on beliefs, religion, and personal comforts. Feel free to experiment and find what makes you most comfortable. No one knows how to make you as comfortable as possible, like yourself. Trusting yourself is both one of the biggest keys and one of the biggest goals of self-hypnosis in general, so you must trust yourself here.

Step 4: Goal and Motive

One of the critical factors of self-hypnosis is having a plan for what specific change or changes you wish to enact once having entered the trance state, and how you plan to achieve them. This is where the narratives you wish to express, the prayers, or the mantra or mantras you wish to repeat to yourself, come into play. What do you hope to achieve in your self-hypnosis session? It is always different for different people and at different times. But there is always at least one goal, and preparation for achieving that goal is a must when it comes to performing a successful and fruitful and transformative self- hypnosis session. Imagine you are about to have a very important conversation with a very important person in your life. There is something you really need to tell them, and it is of the utmost importance that this conversation goes well and is effective. You will likely have a plan for what you want to say and how you are going to say it. The absolute same thing goes here, where you are about to have a very deep and meaningful conversation with the self. You must know what you are going to tell yourself, and how you are going to say it. Therefore, you must be totally aware of your goal, what you wish to achieve through the act of self- hypnosis. It is imperative that you don't try to fix everything wrong with your entire life at once, you must be focused, and you must be honed in on one specific, changeable thing at a time. The rest will come later. You are crossing a river one stepping stone at a time, putting one foot in front of the other, and you will make it across if you stay steady, attentive, and aware of your surroundings. Be calm, be collected, and be prepared for what you are about to do.

Step 5: Relaxation of the Physical Body

Now we begin. There are many schools of thought on the best ways to relax the body. One very common through-line in all of these is the act of deep, conscious breathing. Breathe in, breathe out, be aware of your breaths, be in control of each one of them. The goal here is mainly to become aware of every single voluntary and involuntary action of the physical body and slow it down. Feel your heartbeat. Be aware of it. Envision, it slowing

218

down. Relax. Expand the space and the length of each breath. Focus on certain areas of the body and watch them become more and more still.

For you, I will share my personal method. First, I put my awareness into my feet. I breathe in and hold my awareness in my feet, then I exhale and feel my feet get heavier and lighter at the same time. Repeat this process about ten times, and it will feel as if your feet have left your body, having floated away down a stream of serenity. Now work up. Do this for every section of your body, all the way up to your head. Now you will feel totally weightless, as if you are suspended in midair, effortlessly. Your awareness now becomes of your entire physical being, holistically. You are aware of no specific part of yourself but your entirety. Float down the river. The deep breaths will have become unconscious, the world and your body have achieved a kind of totally unthinking symbiosis. Each breath sustains and gives power to the relaxed state. Your whole body is more relaxed than you have ever felt it; it is supernatural and, for some, can be kind of intimidating. There are places you can go that you have never been to before, and you can go there without ever leaving the house. Cherish the feeling, and follow it out the door. Now that you have achieved a state of total physical relaxation, you are totally, still, unmoving, and there is nothing but you and your mind. Let us proceed to relax the mind as we have the body.

Step 6: Relaxation of the Soul and the Mind

So to relax the mind, we can perform a series of steps very similar to those shown when relaxing the body but carried over to another plane. Just as in relaxing the physical body our goal was to become totally aware of all oluntary and involuntary

219

actions of the body, so as to slow them down to a point where they are more malleable and understandable, so too here, we must become aware of all the voluntary and involuntary actions of the mind, so as to slow them down to a point where they are more malleable and understandable. It is like slowly zooming in with a microscope, so things that were once small, almost imperceptible, become very large and monolithic. Our goal is to achieve a state of hyper-awareness.

I eschewed the act of visualization from the previous step, although visualization can play a vital role in either step because I feel it is most pertinent here in this step. Visualization, as we know, is primarily mental and, therefore, most effective and necessary in the mental landscape. It is the mental landscape where we see images and things that we know do not exist in the physical world before us. They exist through the power of and only inside of our imagination. Anything can exist there, and it is the realm where we are the ultimate creators of anything we desire. It goes without saying, the things we conjure up in our imagination may not appear before us instantly, manifested by our mere thought, but they do have an extreme and very palpable effect on our physical reality, an effect which the act of self- hypnosis aims to hone and control. So we will explore means of visualization and the effect that this can have upon us as we aim to enter that state of trance necessary for self-hypnosis.

You may or may not have become in your life familiar with guided meditations, where someone, be it a speaker in your vicinity or someone on a CD or audiotape, or even a YouTube video or MP3, recites a narrative that you put yourself in mentally with the intention of guiding yourself into a more peaceful state of being. They will often say things like "Imagine that you are weightless," or "Imagine that you are floating in space," or "Imagine that you are witnessing the most serene sunset in the most beautiful location possible with the love of your life." The key is to imagine yourself either being something that is more relaxed than you are now or being in a time or place, derived from fantasy or personal memory, that facilitates the transition into a more relaxed state than you are in now. You can imagine a time and place when or where you felt as free as you ever have in your life. A loved one who passed away, who you found comfort with as a child, you can imagine they are there with you, in another dimension, feeding you the love you remember. You can imagine that you are flying, effortlessly, through the cosmos. Totally uninhibited, feeling a sense of freedom hitherto unfelt. You can imagine that you are floating in the ocean, totally unattached to anything resembling typical human constructs or society. Your imagination is your own personal canvas, and here you are, free to paint any picture you can imagine. Imagining specific senses and perceptions, especially when your body is hyper-relaxed, can lead to both ecstatic levels of mental peace and real feelings of the senses that you are experiencing what you imagine. This is a tool with unlimited power in the act and journey of self-hypnosis.

Step 7: Realization of Trance

Now you are here, and you have willfully affected the realization of the trance-like state that is the initial aim of a good, effective session of proper self-hypnosis. Let your awareness span out through the eternity of reality as it is, allow your entire being the freedom to seep out through the full bounds of this new state, float there where you are and simply exist for a time as you marvel in the state you have achieved. With or without the added benefit of the active involvement of your will for the specific and guided change that defines self-hypnosis, this state of being you have entered into is medicinal and a very pure, enlightening experience to be in. So be in it. Float, again, down the river. Float down the river of the self, float down the river of life, float down the river of the universe. For a time, allow yourself just to feel what it is to be an inactive agent in the cosmos. Step outside of yourself, float above yourself, and look back, or down, or beside, and see who you are. Does it look familiar? Know yourself. Know yourself, here, and now, as you have never known yourself before. Feel the intimacy you have achieved with yourself. Feel intimate feelings that you may have never felt before, for anyone, yourself or others. This is you.

Don't be afraid to reach out and touch the light. Fully immerse yourself in this experience that you have prepared for. Know that you are achieving a very important and personal goal, and be glad and grateful and ecstatic and proud about where you are. Feel the ball of light at your core, your solar plexus, emanating out like a shining star, like the sun, like the soil. It may be orgasmic. You may be taken aback by the power you have tapped into, the infinite potential. Focus on the awareness of the self and see who you are.

Step 8: Repetition of Script

Now you have journeyed into space. Speak. Your voice echoes into the cosmos with a power you have never felt. You have never heard your voice this loud and powerful and confident. It is incredible. The memories you are creating here, of your own voice, are going to be some of the most powerful memories you've ever had, totally overriding any past traumatic experience, any other voices, the outliers, the negative drones. These were all nothing. This is everything. Even very simple sounds begin to take on their own gravitational pull that is so large. You are the sun, and you are creating planets to orbit you with each word spoken. It is the inner-voice, in preparation for the inner-dialogue. We are about to do it.

Speak the words you wish to speak to yourself. Each repetition of the mantra will completely change the landscape that you have found yourself in seismic waves. You will feel a growing energy completely under your control swarm over your entire being and beyond. You are in charge here. What you say goes. You are the ruler of this land, and you are going to take care of it well and make sure it is a prosperous paradise. Watch the negative thoughts, the images, the shadows, the memories you feared, the people you hate, the guilt, the pain, watch it shrivel into dust and evaporate before your very eyes, melted into oblivion by the sheer overwhelming power you have achieved.

Step 9: Exiting the Trance State

Just as when you fully submersed, take a moment after you are done with your action to appreciate the beauty of what you are witnessing. Just be here now in this state. It is an eternal state. You will leave, and you will go back to the physical world, but this state will stay, untouched, eternal, waiting for you to return. This is heaven. Know that you are about to return, and you are about to feel very different than you have ever felt before. Embrace these differences. It may be odd and imperfect at first, but it is a learning experience. The physical reality still awaits you as always—a different eternal experience. The rest of your life will be spent juxtaposing these two very different and very real planes and finding the perfect balance where you are in absolute control, yet in total surrender and synchronicity. Are you ready? You may wish to take one last look around, soak it all in, but eventually, you must prepare for the journey home. It can be as simple as opening your eyes. It might be something that you don't want to do so you better prepare.

Step 10: Returning to Earth

Open your eyes. Where are you? Who are you? You may feel like this is something equally new as the realm you have just left. But there is a feeling of familiarity. You are awakened to the infinite possibilities of life. You see that your perspective can change in infinite ways, and with that change in perspective leads a portal to infinite different realties experienced through the multi-faceted crystal that is existence. You may be stunned. You will be changed.

Don't get too excited. Don't run into the other room screaming at your spouse, "I've found the meaning of life! " This is something just for you.

 Keep it quiet and sacred. Other people will come when they are ready. Your job is simply to exist—at peace. Maybe you'll want to make some different choices tomorrow, after a nice sleep, an unconscious refresher to the land of dreams, a place that might seem more familiar and close to you than it ever has before.
Maybe tomorrow, while you're on your commute to work, you'll spontaneously hear the loud booming voice of God pouring through your brain, reciting that mantra you envisioned for yourself. It's a memory—a memory you have now; a memory you created. It will feel fantastic, and you will feel more in control of your life than you ever have before.

CHAPTER 17: SELF-HYPNOSIS IN PRACTICE

Do you have a poor diet? Do you wish you didn't? What is the disparity between your actions and your desires? Negative self-talk is usually the culprit. Let us address this and destroy it. We will go through some specific examples, poor diet being the first.

Negative thinking leads to fatalism in your daily life choices. Fatalism is the feeling that nothing will really make a difference. Your fate is predetermined. It is not going to be good, nothing you can do will make a difference, might as well find whatever pleasure you can get. It is this mode of thinking that causes people more often than not to make poor life choices. You know that if you eat poorly, you will not feel good, but if you wouldn't feel good no matter what, why make the positive choice? There is a logical fallacy here, the acceptance of the existence of a possible alternative that could make you feel better but the all-around denial of any possibility of feeling better. This needs to be erased. Tell yourself that all you can control are your own actions, and if you make the choice to act more positively, you will feel better, and that better feeling will grow and grow into something that will take over your life for the better. You can't change the world without changing yourself first. You can't change your life without changing the way you think. You can't make better decisions until you understand why you make poor decisions.

When you wake up in the morning, and you desire for sustenance, what do you crave? You might crave a candy bar. You might crave an entire pizza. You might crave a greasy, artery-clenching breakfast sandwich. Ask yourself if this really what is going to make you feel your best today? If I follow that pathway in my mind if I go down that road towards immediate gratification of my id, my most animalistic desires, will I go into this day feeling the best that I can? Unsurprisingly, if you are honest with yourself, which you always must be if you are to accept the responsibility of change, the answer is no. Ask yourself, "What can I eat right now that will give me the power I need to be the best that I can be today?" You will be lead down the right path. You will create a new path. You will eat a salad. If you do not have the materials available immediately to create that salad, you will go to the grocery store after work and get what you will need to make yourself have the best possible day tomorrow. This self-dialogue is a powerful force. Ask yourself what you need, and you will always find the answer, somewhere down there, but don't be afraid to ask the tough questions.

Then comes the stress. Something happens at work that you didn't plan for. You crave relief. You want the tangible distraction from this insurmountable problem you are being faced with. You ask yourself, what do I want? There's that road that has been paved in your mind, the road towards instant gratification. You want an alcoholic drink. You want to binge-eat fatty foods. But then ask yourself, "Will that make me feel better? Will that make me stronger so that I can tackle the real problem further down the road? Or will it just distract me and make me weaker, so that when the time comes to face this problem, I am lost without any idea of what to do?" You might be surprised about how many of your impulses are dragging you the wrong way, in different, opposing ways, going all over the place. Maybe the road that has been built in your mind is a circle or a road that goes straight over the edge of a cliff. When there's no supervisor on duty, the workers went crazy and didn't know which map to follow so they built a giant mess that leads to nowhere. You are the supervisor. You need to start asking the tough questions and giving the demanding orders to your workers, to yourself, to make this mess right. There are no easy answers at first. It can be a constant struggle and require constant dialogue inside yourself, making sure that every single decision you are making is for the best. But as progress is made, the simple nature of the whole thing becomes more and more apparent, and you start to see how easy it was all along, to make the right choices, to be aware of your needs, to ask yourself what you really need to get what you want, and what to do to make sure you attain your desires.

Or what if you are an alcoholic? The same brand of problem, different vice, similar solution. You have to change the inner-dialogue within yourself that leads to you falling down the rabbit hole of having another drink. The easiest way to change the dialogue is by recognizing it and substituting key phrases that lead down that one specific path with healthier alternatives—alternatives that can be fed to the mind as mantras through the power of our post-hypnotic suggestions.

The first step to recognizing the inner-dialogue is self-awareness. Take some time out of the day to truly reflect on what your "triggers" are, triggers being any outside stimuli that "triggers" internal stimuli, the inner-dialogue phrases that lead down the path of our negative behaviors, a daily cycle which occurs inside our minds. As an alcoholic, you usually wake up in the morning with a terrible hangover, and your first thought is immediate relief. Relief from the hangover, as the alcohol itself provided us with immediate relief the night prior, though we will get to that end of this specific cycle in a minute. So from the pain of the hangover, how do you find relief? Of course, as any seasoned alcoholic can attest, it's by a good helping of some "hair of the dog that bit you," so they say, jumping back in the pool of alcohol you had drowned yourself in the night prior. More often than not, this is the case. If not, then you just take an aspirin. Any quick fix to tide the pain over for the time being so you can go about your daily life, the life that causes you the pain that you run from at night, only to get back at night to perform the ritual in which you run from the pain, towards more pain in the morning. What is needed is to take a step back, the lauded self-awareness we have described. You must find a place to relax, that relaxation will become your trance-like state, and in your trance-like state you will ask yourself those tough questions, and you will give yourself those positing answers. What are you running from? What causes you pain? How do you stop it? How can you make it go away for good? Obviously, the alcohol is causing us more pain than it alleviates in the long-term. We must tell ourselves this. We must eliminate the impulsive appetite for the alcohol, to abide by our immediate desires. We must reprogram our brain not to lust after the highs of alcohol but always to remember the lows, and associate those lows with the thought of alcohol because those lows are the true effect of alcohol consumption. We will find our inner-peace, our self-awareness, we will take a few deep breaths, and we will say, "Alcohol doesn't make me happy, alcohol makes me sick." We will say it until we understand it, we will say it until there is an internal rhythm singing a song along with our entire physiology. We will program the brain to desire a different path; we will, therefore, carve out and lay the path for a new roadway in our psyche. It can expand, as well, from the symptom of alcohol consumption to the root of our problems in life that cause us to seek some kind of external source for pleasure. This is the true power of self-hypnosis. Over time, and through developing the skills of self- awareness, of relaxation, and of positive thinking through mantra and other hypnotic skills, we will change the structure of our entire thought-system. The things that trigger us to turn against ourselves will be turned outwards, so we are immune to them. Take, for example, a typical trigger for much social anxiety. This is an example that we have already talked about to some extent and should be familiar besides to all living creatures. Alcohol is the social lubricant, as they say, consumption of alcohol lowers the inhibitions of the consumer and allows thoughts to come out more freely. But, as with many temptations, this is a double-edged sword. Consumption of alcohol generally only allows you to form closer relationships with other people who are already under the influence of alcohol. Through this understanding, we could begin to change our inner-dialogue to promote social awareness outside of the influence of alcohol. We could tell ourselves that alcohol doesn't make us happy and also doesn't promote positive relationships. The relationships we make under the influence of alcohol only help to further the use of alcohol, which makes us unhappy. Positive social relationships come more often than not from abstinence. Alcohol makes us forget who we are, which frees us up to be more like other people who we would not normally socialize with. We could reevaluate our relationships with those in our lives, those who we consume alcohol with. We could ask ourselves, do our social relationships make us happy? How did they come about? How are they developing? What causes us to keep the company that we keep? The answer to these tough questions might surprise you as is always the case with the inner-dialogue once the inner-dialogue has been mastered and you have taken control of the internal conversation. There is nothing we can learn about ourselves that we can't learn from asking ourselves the tough questions. Imagine, you are your own psychiatrist. You would have no better subject to study than yourself. Through asking the questions about both the root cause and the peripheral effects of our negative behavior, we can totally define the negative behavior as it pertains to our psyche, and then we can vanquish the behavior from our psyche through a re-structuring of our thoughts—a re-structuring which occurs through self-awareness and then self-hypnosis.

Now, the last example we will go through to illustrate the power of hypnosis, and here, specifically, the hypnosis of the self, or self-hypnosis, is the deepest and most pertinent example we will face in this book, is self-esteem—feeling about the self as a whole. While the prior two examples were about external behaviors, choices we make in our daily lives, things outside of ourselves that we let in, this example pertains explicitly to things that are already inside of ourselves that we are keeping in. These are things that have been ingrained into our psyches, overtime, be it as children through narcissistic, unloving parents, from childhood bullies, from mean teachers or other abusers, from bad or abusive partners and other relationships that we have formed throughout our lives, or from a snowball effect of negative perception of the self, from ourselves. These are all forms of trauma, events from our pasts coming back to haunt us, to define us, time, and time again. You can only be told you are something, no matter who is telling it, so many times before a part of you really starts to believe it.

Now, consider, how do you feel about yourself? Is it good? If it is not good, then why is it not good? These are three very simple questions. ou may or may not be surprised to find out that the answers to the first two questions for a lot of people are negative. It's very simple. We, as a society, suffer from low self-esteem, from issues with perceptions of the self. Walk down the road, and you would be hard-pressed not to see a vast majority of people struggling from severe anxiety about their own appearances, the way others perceive them, physically or mentally, their ability to prove their efficiency and value to others in any and every way. Now, for the third question, being why the way you feel about yourself is not good, the answer is more often than not some form of a statement beginning with "I am." You will hear them say. I am ugly, I am fat, I am stupid, or I am an idiot. They are defining themselves for themselves, a definition that is programmed internally in the brain. This is a learned definition, as any definition. Words have meaning because we attribute their meaning through experience, as do people, places, and things. But given the subjective nature of reality, of beauty, of value to and from the self, are we not kidding ourselves severely when we define ourselves in these negative terms? For an ugly person, would it not do them much better to say, "I have been called ugly, but I am beautiful to myself and to those who matter to me," or, more simply, "I am beautiful to those who matter," or, most simply of all, the ultimate deduction, "I am beautiful"? If beauty is in the eye of the beholder, are you not the most important, the most dutiful and the most consistent beholder of your own self? Learn to find the beauty in yourself and learn to express it to yourself. Let it flow freely. The world is a swarm of negativity. Drown it out with a sea of positivity. You are a voice, and you are the loudest voice in your own head.

Of course, this is all well and good for the average person, but, for some, there are very loud voices in the head echoing from the past. Sometimes these voices echo even louder over time, defying all laws of established reality. Our father's voice as a child, telling us we are idiots for leaving the stove on. This is a voice that never leaves. We remember it. Our memory of it hits refresh on itself every time it is remembered, and it is remembered often. It challenges our own inner-voice, dulls it—diminishes us. This is how we are programmed. There is nothing like the mind of a child to be molded. This is the kind of trauma that is the absolute arch-nemesis of self-hypnosis. This is the demon that self-hypnosis as an art form lives to vanquish. Our mind is a battlefield and everything that has ever passed our mind in one way or another, everything that has gone in one end and come out the other, or gone in to stay, is a soldier on that battlefield in some way, shape, or form. The forces of light and dark are in a constant struggle for dominion over our psyche. Self-hypnosis will be our guardian angel; it will be the guiding force that rejuvenates us each and every day that we live. We are our own saviors, and it is that way because nothing matters more than our own perception of ourselves. If we desire to be the hero, the force of shining light, then we become that force of shining light, first by acceptance, then by embracing our own power to define ourselves to ourselves. "I am love; I am light." This is an incredibly powerful mantra that I tell myself in the throes of absolute despair. In the darkness, when every negative thought that has ever been had about me swarms to my being, thoughts I've had about myself, thoughts others have had about me, or blurred lines between the two, I hold my prayer close to my heart in a sea of deep breaths. I am relaxed, and I am at peace. I am the master of my own reality. I will not be pulled and swayed by demons from the past, and the future is tugging at my being, trying to make me their rag doll. I am in control of my body. I stop here, now, apart from all this wretched negativity and give a firm command in the very core of my being, I am love, and I am light.

This is the power of self-hypnosis. It is the power to circumvent all solid form and change it into whatever we desire, from the smallest quark to the entire universe as a whole. It starts with us, internally, and it bleeds outwards for all of eternity. The difference between the person you think you are and who you want to be is an intangibility that can be changed in the blink of an eye. Close your eyes and imagine the culmination of your wildest desires come to complete fruition. How do you feel? Feel that way forever. Feel that way about yourself, now, and the seeds of those desires will blossom before your very eyes in the most beautiful garden that is yours for the taking. There is a school of thought, well established that studies the power positive and negative thoughts have on frozen water crystals. The leading pioneer of this was a man named Dr. Masaru Emoto. He would take water and put it in containers with labels reading different phrases, ranging from positive to negative. When he froze the water, under a microscope, he found that the water in containers labeled with positive messages formed beautiful and pristine, heavenly crystals, while the water in containers labeled with negative messages formed ice crystals that were much more unpleasant, sickly looking, almost reminiscent of tumorous growths. While skeptics still question these experiments to this day, the idea is a great one, and holds true over many schools of thought regardless of the specific merit; thought affects our being. Imagine, if you will, that you are a beautiful, heavenly, pristine crystal, and positive prayer powers you. Your thoughts give you unlimited power; your positive thoughts fuel the universe, like the sun.

The power of hypnosis is to change the way your brain thinks. But, given that all actions in our daily life are inherently the effect of how our brain thinks, the power of hypnosis over our daily lives can be immeasurably gigantic and unbelievable.

Take, for example, our morning coffee routine. 'It's something that many people all over the world do relatively the same. Every day, they will get up and go to work, and on the way to work, they will stop into a coffee shop and grab a cup of coffee or some other drink that will help them get through their days. 'It's a simple process, but one that can go all sorts of different ways and all these ways are directly tied to our modes of thinking. Many people all over the world experience high levels of social anxiety. It is a part of life. We worry about our interactions with other people and how we are perceived. We think about how we are seen, and these thoughts affect how we act, and how we act affects how we are perceived, and how we are perceived affects how we feel about ourselves. It is a vicious cycle. There are a lot of inner monologues tied to it that can drag the whole experience down, make something lightweight and fun seem unbearably heavy, and do a simple chore into an insurmountable challenge, make every day a living hell. We walk into the coffee shop; 'it's filled to the brim with people. We might get angry. We say to ourselves, "I do not have time for this. I am going to be late." We see the people around us. They might glance at us, and we hear them say about us, "That person is ugly." We wait in line, we feel watched, and we feel judged. We make it to the barista. We think the barista is judging our every move. We feel their impatience; they want us to order faster so they can get through this horrible long line of customers waiting to be served. They are comparing us physically with the other customers. They are judging our appearance. When we talk, what if we stutter? Are they judging our capabilities of communication? Something so simple like getting a drink to

234

help you through the day, a cup of coffee to wake you up, a symbol of pleasure, of comfort, a symbol you cling to in your waking life. Suddenly, it has turned on you; it has become something to fear, something that causes pain. When the whole process is over, you breathe a sigh of relief, now onto the next struggle. And the entire process repeats itself.

Think about all I have just said. These feelings that you are having in this mundane and everyday social situation, something we all go through, this perception of others, and how they perceive you, is it factual? Is it based on fact? Or is it based on your own perception, which might be more fallible, open to questioning, than you might be originally thinking? It's all about what you are telling yourself as you perform these actions, your inner monologue. You are filling in the blanks about what other people are thinking when they look at you. This isn't something they are telling you; it's something you are telling yourself.

Absolutely nothing is being said outside of your own head. You are making assumptions about people's thoughts and intentions; you are also making very negative assumptions about yourself and the impact you are having when you walk into a room. We start off by walking into the coffee shop and getting angry at the number of people. Instead, we could be positive. We could tell ourselves, "We can make this work. We can get our coffee and be to work on time, and, if not, we can accept responsibility and wake up earlier tomorrow, so we are not late again". This is positive thinking; this is positive self-talk. When we see the people around us when they look at us, think about what they are feeling might not be negative towards you, but either neutral or positive. Maybe they are just as worried as you about the number of people in the shop, and the effect this might have on their own punctuality. Maybe they are just as anxious as you in social situations, and they are looking at you, fearfully, thinking you are judging them the same way you perceive them to be judging you. Maybe they are thinking about what an attractive person you are and wondering what your story is. The barista, maybe they are anxious to get through the customers, but this is not an attack on you; it is merely a fact of life, of the workplace. They do not have the time to be judging you. Same with the other customers, it is likely they are too preoccupied with their own inefficiency, their own faults. Similar to the old adage, "The spider is more afraid of you than you are of it." Fear is a creation of the mind. Imagine how much smoother every small part of your daily living could be if you 'didn't dwell on the negative aspects that you yourself are creating, projecting, imposing, directing at, and on top of other people who are just trying to live their lives the same as you?

Negativity breeds negativity. Our mind is a global structure of superhighways leading to and from eternally changing landmasses. Our mind is elastic. It changes whether we want it to or not, whether we think about it or not, whether we intentionally affect the changes, or we just sit back and watch the changes occur and feel there is nothing we can do. When we have negative thoughts, it just makes it that much easier to have the same or similar negative thoughts again. The mind is trained. Just as you can have a daily exercise regimen where you start off doing 50 push-ups a day and then work up to 100, you can start off having a few negative thoughts, and they can work their way up to 1,000. Every thought can become negative. We can become negative. It's very easy. But so is affecting change. It is the same process. Reflect, meditate, catch yourself having these negative feelings. Ask yourself constantly, is the way I am feeling positive or negative? If it is negative, ask yourself, "How can I change it to be more positive? Every time, you will grow, and the growth will create a stronger and larger platform for which more positive thoughts can grow. One positive thought becomes a million. A frown becomes a smile. Fear becomes love.

We get to work. We try our best. We worry about how our efficiency is perceived, just like that barista. Did we give that barista our love or our fear? Now, we ask ourselves, should we treat ourselves the same way? Love others, and love yourself. If you are trying your best, applaud yourself. Imagine others are applauding you. Applaud others who are also trying their best. They will praise you. If you make a mistake, you can admit that to yourself. We all make mistakes. We can all do better. Tell yourself that next time, you will not make the same mistake again. You will learn from the mistakes. In this mode, mistakes become not something to fear, but, alas, something to love. We love making mistakes because they show us how to be better. We always want to be better. You never stop growing in life, and if you aren't growing towards being better, then you are growing towards being worse. We must be aware of this.

You get home, and 'it's time to relax. You want to have a snack and sit down, maybe watch a favorite television program. Watch something positive. Eat something healthy. Tell yourself that you are doing this because you want to be the best you can be. Watch love grow. Take a bath and reflect on the day and reflect on the day positively. Did someone say something that made you angry? Are you still thinking about it? Well, they were just having a bad day. They really meant to say that to themselves. Love them. Love yourself. The weakness of other people will become your strength. The weakness of yourself will become your strength. There will become nothing but strength. Did your boss tell you that you did a really great job today? 'That's fantastic! Did he tell you that you could be doing better? Well, fantastic! Think about how you could be doing better, and tomorrow he might tell you how much you are growing. Because you are growing, and if 'you're growing with love and positivity, you are growing for the better. And if you are getting better and there is nothing to fear. Do you have insomnia? Are you dreading going to sleep? Are you worried you will not get enough sleep tonight and therefore will not be prepared for tomorrow? Well, stop worrying and start relaxing. These racing thoughts of negativity are sledgehammers pounding on the ground in your mind, creating noise, and destroying anything positive that you are desperately scrambling to create. Silence them. Become aware. Clear the skies in your inner-world. Use all your energy to breed silence, beautiful, golden silence. Breed love. Imagine yourself in a golden ball of light. In the middle, the ball of light is emanating from your core and your core emanating from the awesome strength of this ball of light—fall right to sleep. The pendulum is swinging in your mind. Watch it. "I am sleepy," you tell yourself. "I am asleep." This is the power of hypnosis.

Now, to the core of the matter, our current state is the love child of both our nature as humans, our genes, our genealogical history, and our nurturing, our development, how we were raised, how we were made to be. Things happen, things are done to us; sometimes they are great things—things that can make us powerful, sometimes they are terrible things, things that can make us weak. We are made to be a certain way, both consciously and unconsciously. But, on top of that, and more importantly, we can make ourselves to be certain ways, both consciously and unconsciously. As children, we have little power. The adults in our lives overpower us, both mentally and physically; they decide what we can be. But as we grow, as we get older, we realize the decision is up to us now. Maybe it really always has been; it just took us a long time to realize, a long time to grow the strength it takes to take control of our own minds. Anything negative in the past, in the psyche, in the soul, it can be overridden. Anything negative in the past can be changed into something positive right now. There is nothing that has ever happened that can prevent us from being happy right here, right now, wherever we are, whatever the situation is. Happiness is always an option—it is always the best option—and it is always the ultimate goal. Happiness is here with you.

We all have experienced some form of trauma. Be it death, be it decay, or be it some unforeseeable accident, a terrible crime, something that has been done to us, something that we have done to another person, something that we have done to ourselves. How many times have you asked yourself, why did I do that? How many times have you asked yourself, why did they do that to me? How many times have you asked yourself, why is the world this way? Why is there so much negativity? Why is there pain? Why do people hurt each other? We become jaded, every terrible thing that happens to us. Someone hurts us. We become fearful that it will happen again. This limits our options; it limits what we feel free to do in our daily lives. Someone hurts us again; we become more fearful. We notice a pattern. We write this pattern into our minds. Our options become more limited. Or say you had a bad day and you've been known to binge drink. You go home, and you go to the bottle. You promised yourself you wouldn't, but you have to, you tell yourself. Notice the self-talk. You drink, and you feel the warmth, the positivity, the firing of the pleasure signals in the brain. But you wake up in severe pain—the hangover. You ask yourself, "Why did I do this to myself? What is wrong with me? Why do I want to hurt myself?" You might reply back to yourself, "I must be a terrible person. I must do wrong. I make the wrong choices. I am bad. Everyone is bad. Life is bad."

Now, imagine if you could take all this data written into your brain, and hit the refresh button. If you could throw out all these old files and start anew, you would like to be born again, like a brand new baby. Imagine if you could forget the experience of the trauma, you could forget what they did to you, you could forget what you did to yourself. Imagine if you could wake up tomorrow and be a different person, a better person, with different memories, different beliefs, different attitudes, and a totally different way of being, of acting, of presenting yourself to others, of viewing yourself in your own perception, inside, where it matters the most. Imagine this is your reality because it is. This change is just one decision away, that being the very decision to make the change itself. It can be no simpler. As I've said, anything can be overridden. You can be whatever you want to be. All you have to do is be it. Tell yourself tonight, while you are alone, at peace, in your sanctuary, in your temple, tell yourself that you are going to change. You are going to change for the better. You are not going to be the thing that hurts you. You are not going to be hurt by others. You will not allow this. You will not continue to make poor decisions. You will not allow poor decisions to be made for you. You are free. You love yourself. You can be whatever you want. You want to be free. Free from the past. You are whatever you choose to be, and you choose infinite freedom, health, wealth, and abundance. You choose love and life. A nuclear bomb goes off over eternity. The past is evaporated. The future ceases to be. You are here, now, and that is all that matters. Anything is possible. The past is a golden sea of light. The future is a golden sea of light. You are a golden sea of light. Anything can emerge from this golden sea of light that you could possibly imagine. This golden sea of light is life itself. You are the creator of your own life. You are the master of your past and the master of your future. You decide what you are going to be. You tell yourself every day that you are doing a great job and you tell yourself that because you are, in fact, doing a great job. You are the best you can be. The past matters not to the master of the present. The future is more beautiful than can ever be imagined. You will grow and grow, and you will not stop growing. You are a tree growing up to heaven. If a branch will fall, it was merely pruned to make way for a healthier branch. There is only room for enlightenment; there is only room for the tree to grow higher, and wider, into the sky, and into space. You are the bridge between the world and the heavens. Tell yourself that every day. You will become stronger. As you grow higher, the world stays at your feet, and your headspace is taken into the cosmos. Whatever will be will be because you decided it. This is the power of will, the power of intention, the power of our thoughts, the power of our beliefs, the power of our actions, the power of our prayers, the power of our communication, the power of our mind, the power of our conscious being, the power of self-hypnosis.

As you can see, there is very little that could possibly be wrong in life that can't be fixed immeasurably by just becoming aware of the way you think and changing it. Our thought patterns dictate so much about how we experience daily life. They can take us so high, and they can bring us down so low. Our mind is racing, always racing to a finish line that doesn't exist. Slow it down, make it look at itself in the mirror, ask it what 'it's doing, and why. Ask it what it wants to be. Ask it how 'it's working towards being that. Figure out where your thoughts are coming from and where they're going, and how they're going to get there. If they are ineffective, change them. If they are negative, make them positive. Nothing is truly negative. All darkness leads to light. There is nothing wrong that 'isn't just a little light in the distance asking for forgiveness, for your attention, for you to look over at it and tell it that everything is going to be okay and that 'you're going to fix the problem. Ignore nothing in your mind. Become totally aware of your thoughts, your feelings, and your emotions. The wild beast in the forest, the one you are so afraid of, the beast of legend, make him your friend. Make him your deity. When you are sick, go to his temple, become relaxed, and feel his power. Everything can be solved. Find your will. Find your mind. Find yourself. Take life by the horns and embrace the infinite power of being.

CHAPTER 18 : HOW SELF-HYPNOSIS CAN CHANGE NEGATIVE ASPECTS OF YOUR SUBCONSCIOUS-MIND

The mind is elastic. There is never a point before death where the mind isn't changing somehow, be it growing, morphing, or decaying. Surprisingly, most people seem not to be aware of this, or, at least, of some of its ramifications. If your mind is constantly changing, what is controlling its change? What is catalyzing its immediate change? It can be either positive or negative. If you are dwelling on negative aspects, the change can be negative, but if you embrace love, and the power to change all negative aspects of life into positive ones, the natural change occurring in your mind with or without your bits of help can take on a life of its own to become its separate force working towards its betterment while you are going about your own business. Here will we work on examining the subconscious mind's habits, the habits we have formed in our thought patterns that are working day-to-day with or without our conscious knowledge. We will sort through our sub- conscious mindscape, and find the things in our way that our keeping our sub-conscious minds from being as productive and positive as possible. We will sort through them and examine how we can benefit them specifically through self-hypnosis to overcome things in our way of thinking that we feel we may or may not have the power to change. We will figure out how to mold our mind into the most productive mind imaginable by weeding out negativity and dead-zones and creating fertile soil for new growth and powerful new gardens of positivity and love energy. Our body is our temple, and our mind is our garden, and we must make sure that the veins flowing through us are coursing with positive energy and love.

It has always been helpful in schools of psychology to envision the mind as a mess of yarn, and all the negative aspects of our way of thinking, the paths of thought that harm us and inhibit us from positive growth, as knots and tangles in this web of string. We can call these strings our mental pathways, the roads on which our thoughts travel from one part of the brain to the other. These roads must not be jammed, they must be clear, and they must be free and connecting so that our brains, holistically, can be working at their highest level to allow us to function in ways that allow more effectively for our positive growth. Through self-hypnosis, and becoming aware of our minds, slowing down the activity and zooming in, as with a microscope, into these pathways, we can start to see what is working and what is not working, internally and mentally. What seems from afar to be an overwhelming mess of knots, up close might start to take on different faces. You will begin to see that these knots can be individually defined and diagnosed, and, with that knowledge, you will be able to untangle each knot at a time. With each untangling you will feel a greater power mentally, each untied knot freeing up a wealth of potential and power inside of you that will have a snowball effect over the whole process, eventually becoming an avalanche of positivity as your brain begins to work in new, previously unfounded ways towards creating its landscape of pure ecstasy.

As you practice all the steps of self-hypnosis and begin further exercise towards honing your skills, you will become more and more aware, zooming in closer and closer to the problem areas in your subconscious mind. These areas will be familiar to you, like old friends, or long-forgotten memories. You will know them when you see them, and they will carry with them, inherently, a vast wealth of information. This is true because all of these problem areas, these knots, were tied at one point or another in your past. We are born with perfect minds and pure hearts, and they become tangled as we walk through life, just as our flowing hair develops knots if we got enough time without combing it. It is best to comb your hair every morning when you wake up, every night before bed, and several times throughout the day. So, too, it is best to be constantly vigilant of newly developing knots and tangles in the psyche, and, if we have not done this for a long time, in some cases many, many years, it is easy to be intimidated by the number of tangles we are to deal with, now, if we wish to become free of them. With your hair, you can just shave it all off and start anew. With your mind, it is not so simple. But it is not so impossible as to feel anxious about. Simply begin the process and let the workflow find its way.

The biggest knots, or the most problematic areas, will become apparent to you first, but it is not always best to go straight away. Sometimes setting them aside and untangling the smaller knots around them can make it that much simpler when it comes time to untangle the big knots themselves. Don't be afraid to take the easy way out here, just be sure always to be working towards those big knots, and know that their time is limited, and they will eventually become untangled. You will untangle these big knots even if it takes a lifetime. Because that is what we are here on this planet to do, take care of ourselves and grow. Big knots always have a series of knots outlying them, and, themselves, are made up of several interconnecting and related knots. One tiny knot can meet another knot and form a bigger, more complicated knot, and this process can continue until it is put in check. So, as with any giant mess of cords or string that needs untangling, find a point, and start untangling. Begin untangling, and keep untangling, and untangle until there is nothing left to untangle. It can be tough, but if you persist, you will be rewarded with a brand new working system.

Let us examine typical problem areas in the sub-conscious mind and where they may have come from. For starters is the impression that many people living have of their perceived inferiority to others. Their worthlessness, their inability to perform in a way that they would like to, that most others feel, can. This, more often than not, comes from being told as children that we are worthless. As any living creature, children are always trying to do something that they see others doing, something that they want to do, something they have not yet done. They are burgeoning. They are just starting. This is something we can all relate to at any stage of our lives. We should all be so forgiving of our selves as we are of children. Regardless of your stage or lot in life, there is always something that you have not done yet, that you have not yet achieved. Being bad at something is just a fact of life. You find what you want to do, and you become good at it, and if you want to become good at it, you have to be accepting of the fact that as you are trying, you will at first fail, often, and possibly be watched and mocked by some negative outliers in the crowd. Have confidence in yourself that you will get better and don't be afraid to be perceived as inferior. So, it is wrong to tell any child that they are worthless, or poor performers because it boxes them in at an age when they have so much potential to be anything that they can imagine and are merely trying their best to learn. With that said, it is wrong to tell someone of any age just the same, because, while children are the most malleable, the idea is that complicated concepts like reading and speaking different languages or reading and writing musical notation are easiest to teach to and learn as children, adults are also capable of great growth and change. It is wrong to box anyone in, including yourself, with labels, especially when the labels are concrete deniers of the ability to learn and grow.

To overcome self-doubt and feelings of worthlessness ingrained in us as children, we must realize that whoever labeled us in such a way, as a child, was wrong. We were not worthless, and we were not inferior, we were just learning at our own pace, at our comfort level, just as is human nature. Whoever told us this must have been feeling some very negative personal feelings of their own, feelings of inferiority in their ability to bear and raise children, in their ability to teach. It is a fact of nature that parents impose and project themselves on their children, and find value in their selves through their children. It is the concept of pride. When our child accomplishes great things, we are proud of them, and, by extension, ourselves. When our child shows any level of weakness or inability to do something we feel they should be able to do, we fear a negative feeling, and we may lash out in our weakness. Sometimes, the adult will apologize later, but it is not the apology that forms the impression in the child's mind, but the initial outburst. In our self-hypnosis, we can change the focus of the memory to the apology manually. We can realize the shortcomings of the perpetrator of the traumatic memory. After all these years, we can stop giving power to them, and we can give a new power to them, the power of agape love. We can view them as the fallible human beings that they are, not capable of labeling or boxing in any other. Our psyche has boxed us in, malleable, at the suggestion of the other weak person, a learned weakness. It is an inherited flaw, inherited by nurture, not by nature. It is so common, and so damaging, and so powerful when kept in the darkness. Yet, it is so weak when exposed to the light. It may grow and fester for years; it is its organism that yearns for its survival, and hence it tries as hard as it can to stay in the dank, darkest pits of the psyche, never to be exposed. Little does it realize that upon being exposed to the love and the light, it will turn into something beautiful; it will turn into an experience of strength. Similar, ironically, to that very child, who is afraid, and burgeoning on an experience of learning at his own pace. The child who is afraid to go in the water, whose parents choose to wait patiently while the child figures themselves out, or push the child out of frustration and create a whole new cycle of trauma and fear and doubt that must be rectified. Darkness begets more darkness, but all darkness comes to light in the end.

So as you realize that you are not worthless, that you were never worthless, that you are a bundle of energy who just happens to be expending a great deal of said energy keeping that very energy from coming out like a snake eating its tail. You will become stronger in ways beyond your imagination. You will feel no regrets for the past, as the muscles built from this struggle prove positive that there is some divine purpose for being and feeling the struggle and going through with the fight. Not only will you no longer feel worthless but also you might feel a greater relationship with yourself and those who have called you worthless in the past. You will pity them for being so weak as to pin a child down in frustration with words echoing from their subconscious. You will see that they were only part of a cycle of negativity, one that they were too weak to break, that you have broken now, and you will want to share that power with them. Share it internally. Share it with their memory, with their image in your mind. It will spread love and understanding.

This same concept can be applied to and spread over all manner of things that have traumatized us in the past, the entire gambit of traumatic memories that are capable of being experienced by the giant rainbow that is humanity. All traumatic memories are instigated by another, given power by us, and grown and boiled over by their existence into the negative force that impedes on our being today. Shine a light on the instigator, understand their wrongness and weakness, understand how that wrongness and weakness latched onto you, and grow under your ignoring eye into the demon on your back today. Turn that demon into an ally. No abuse goes unpunished for eternity. There is no victim that is not capable, by their own volition and will, of being freed from the traumatic memory that has been imprinted upon them by the abuser. No sin warrants eternal damnation, and absolutely no victim of sin deserves it, either. The fires of hell spread, as fires do, from tree to tree, branch to branch, over fields, but we, as human beings, are mostly water.

Replenish your being with the elixir of life, and tend to the burns. New skin will grow over them, stronger than before, and you will have gained great knowledge and power in your ability to transcend your circumstances. There is no victim of abuse that is living a good and happy life that has not reconciled the inherent hate they feel from just having lived through a terrible situation. This hate is a disease, spread from one human to another. It is a terrible disease, unquestionably one of the worst and most affecting and deadly, but also one of the most infinitely curable diseases to have ever been put upon humanity. Hate is so strong, yet so weak. Its strength is its pretending to be something else, its falsehood, its hiding, and its falsified righteousness. Its name is calling its weakness. Never hate, always love. We must yearn towards the agape love of the deities. We must strive to be like the deities of ancient time; we must strive for their wisdom and their understanding. We cannot love ourselves while hating others, regardless of what they have done to us. Hate hurts just to hold. We must also protect ourselves, and take care of ourselves, as we are the keepers of ourselves, and the only ones fit for the job. No one can box you in; only you can box yourself in. Take no heed in the flaws and weaknesses of others, even as they lash out at your through their veil. Exorcise them. Call them by their names, weakness, and hate. Shine the light on their darkness, the light of agape love.

So, we now understand the malleability of the mind, being its capacity for change. We understand the dangers of hate and weakness thoroughly, and how they can be put onto us as a disease from one person to another, and how they can be excised. We understand that we are the ones with the power over our minds, and only we can strengthen either negativity or positivity within, depending on what we choose. And once you have become aware of the choice, and that it is, in fact, a choice, there is almost no chance of choosing negativity over positivity. Once you become aware of the very real struggle, the struggle practically negates itself just by being defined. And that's what we create, a new definition. We take the definitions that have already been established for us, and elongated over our lifetimes by us, internally, by allowing them to occupy the space in our minds. We change them for our benefit. We redefine the traumatic memories as they are encoded into our psyches. Anything inside ourselves that is telling us who we can be, limiting us, we do away with and replace with a new definition of endless possibility and limitless potential. We understand why these definitions are put on us, not out of malicious intent or any real form of understanding but out of weakness, hate, and misunderstanding. They are wrong. We must right them. It is up to us, in our minds, to exercise power to define who we are and to act in our daily lives the way that we most desire to choose. We must circumvent the script, and write a new one. If someone offers up a new task to you, you would love to tackle but feel that you are not up to, do not ever tell yourself that you can't. Tell yourself that you can, and you will, regardless of how long it takes, how hard you have to work for it, how many people will watch you, and laugh and label themselves, in their weak minds, for their instant gratification, to escape from their darkness and hatred by imposing on another.

You are but a child in the eyes of God, in the eyes of the universe. You must never stop learning and reaching towards new heights. Anything holding you back must be dealt with, face forward, and turned on its head to become a strength, propelling you forward with hitherto unfounded momentum. This is our mission on Earth; this is our goal in self-hypnosis. So find a knot, and begin to untangle it. Once you have untangled it, move on to the next one. Never stop untangling the knots. Once you have untangled every knot, check back the next day to see if there are any new ones. Brush your hair multiple times a day because as we go through life, there are many situations in which our hair can become tangled. The more often these knots are dealt with, the easier it will be.

How can it can increases our confidence

It has been stated; the difference between an attractive person and an unattractive person is confidence. A con man is an abbreviation for the term "confidence man," a man with confidence. When applied correctly, confidence is a power that surpasses anything physical, anything passed down by genes, anything you can buy at the mall, and anything you can achieve by toiling away for endless hours at the gym and cutting calories.

You've seen it in action or heard it talked about. You spend so much time working on bettering yourself, watching what you eat, exercising, on progress in your career, social status, and making sure you are the absolute best you can be. You are so hard on yourself, yet you go out in the world and see all these people who have it so much easier than you, getting more with less effort. They just have a way about them. They have a genealogically inherited savvy, if not looks. What makes them so special? Why can't you be like them?

The answer is so very simple. Some call it the law of attraction, making it spiritual, saying that if you manifest the energy of what you desire to be within yourself, then that energy will attract what you desire to you, making you that thing you desire to be. In deduction, positivity is attractive, and negativity is repulsive. We desire to be around people who feel good about themselves because their affability and acceptance of life and love for the universe make us feel good about ourselves. If we are positive, we desire the company of other positive individuals and very much dislike the company of negative individuals impeding our emotional and spiritual freedom with mindless chatter and noise. If you spend all day worrying about yourself and questioning your value, how does that make the people around you feel? Do you care? Because the way you make the people around you feel is very much a part of how effective you are in socialization. Imagine the beautiful person who feels ugly and has no friends or companions because their hatred and scorn for themselves reflects onto others, making them question their beauty. How could they not be ugly when this person is so beautiful? That beautiful person lives inside of us all, as we are all beautiful in our light, the light of love. We all have something to offer, and that thing cannot be offered up uninhibitedly until we accept it for ourselves first. Beauty is absolutely in the eye of the beholder. Vain people, greedy people who spend all day long judging everyone they see by their looks, like a book by its cover, with some predetermined and meticulously defined specific standard that is incidental in the fabric of the cosmos, completely defined by some culture or fad or another mode that will come and go with the tides, have no close or lasting relationships themselves, and completely fail to understand what drives human beings together in love. This failure only further agitates their weakness and hate to continue increasingly to label others. This is a growing, contagious culture of loneliness and negativity and beauty standards that will never be met.

People in legitimate, loving relationships know that such relationships are not built on looks but on intimacy, which is experienced mentally, physically, and spiritually. Two beautiful people do not make a loving relationship just by being two beautiful people. Two people, open and honest, ready and willing to learn together, accepting each other's flaws and their own, yet willing to grow and better themselves together as a unit, make a loving relationship. As such, a relationship can be comprised of an objectively "ugly" person and an objectively "beautiful" person, depending on the circumstance and the perception of the voyeur. If you are out people watching and see such a relationship, realize your fallibility in defining "beautiful" and "ugly." You may say, "she is only with him for his money," and you may be onto something. Wealth is attractive but not only material wealth but also spiritual, emotional, and mental wealth. Smart people are attractive. Funny people are attractive. Easy-going people are attractive. Loving people are attractive. People who are open-minded and not quick to judge are attractive. People that don't go around labeling others "ugly" and "beautiful" are attractive. People that don't box themselves into a certain predetermined standard of beauty are attractive, and they will attract whatever it is that they need, be it in an "ugly" or a "beautiful" person.

Knowing all this, we must stop labeling ourselves. If we have low self- esteem, we must get to the cause of our own negative labeling of ourselves. Do we feel that we are unattractive? What is it that you feel you are incapable of attracting? Because, when we love ourselves and understand our own needs and gifts, we automatically attract whatever it is that the universe feels that we need. No one is "attractive" to everyone. Everyone is "attractive" to the things that they attract. If you are negative, you will attract negativity. If you are positive, you will attract positivity. Both positivity and negativity come in many shapes, sizes, and veneers. An objectively beautiful person can be incredibly negative and only attract negativity. An objectively strange- looking person can be incredibly positive and only attract positivity. If you are negative, you will see this strange looking person on the street, and envy them, and wonder why they have so much more than you, when they are not as objectively "attractive." Maybe you can find another negative person, and the two of you can go back and forth with insults and bond over the shared labeling of another and the negative energy you try to throw at them. But know that whatever negativity you throw at a positive person will only bounce off of them and come back to hurt you tenfold, in a positive ray of light. And by hurt, I just mean that it will shed light on your own darkness, a light which might cause you to self-reflect and see yourself for what you really are, what you have really been, a negative person only attracting negativity.

So we must stop judging ourselves in a negative light, and find the positivity in our own self-perception. We must find the beauty in ourselves, so that other people may see it in us, as well, and be attracted to it for what it offers, a sharing in the light. We must believe and know that we are attractive and that we have something to offer to the right person, whoever that person may be. And we must grant others the same, and stop reveling in a negative culture of shaming. When we hate ourselves, for whatever reason, feeling ugly and insecure, we do not feel free to be ourselves. And if we are not ourselves, how can we attract what it is that our selves desire? We must open up the floodgates and be ourselves above all things, and stop worrying about how we will be perceived by others. When we are who we are, nature has a way of sorting out those that we belong with and those that we do not belong with. No one can please everyone. Those who attempt to please everyone, as the story goes, end up pleasing no one. We must stop worrying about who we are pleasing and simply live to please ourselves, and, in effect, please those who belong around us, the law of attraction working its natural order, grouping people who belong around each other together and keeping those who do not belong around each other apart. In this, only worrying about being ourselves and not about being anybody else, we develop confidence. And with this confidence, we begin to attract more and more people, as it is realized all that we have to offer them. There is room for many different people to coexist symbiotically, to gain something from each other once we are open about who we are and accepting of each other's differences. We must never question if we belong because we all belong, that's why we are here. It is not your job to find where you belong—simply be yourself, love yourself, and exude confidence, and you will end up where you belong by sheer force of nature.

It can be hard for someone who is so learned in the art of judgment to eschew beauty standards and realize that there's more to a human being than first impressions. Sometimes we have gone our whole lives thinking that way, and now we must realize that we have very little to show for it but a huge stinking pool of negativity. The universe works in strange ways, and it is nearly impossible to define specific things like who has value and who does not. So we must realize that this simply isn't up for us to define. It is something that is so ingrained in our culture; it really is a huge slap in the face once you wake up to it if you are privy. In the media, on television, in movies or magazines, so much of what is expressed to us is centered on the vanity. And, ironically, those who consume this media the most are people who are very lonely, consuming the media as some form of replacement for human connection. Thus, this negativity in the media is preaching to the choir in this way. If you wish to be negative and to judge others, know that you will have plenty of company but know that that company is not a good company, and you will have very little to show for your loyalty to it at the end of the day. It's best to turn your eye away from others and focus on yourself, and not on judging yourself, but of being forgiving towards yourself and your flaws. No one sees the flaws in us as we do. We are our own harshest critics; it comes with the territory of being the ones who spend the most time with us. We are the ones who have to deal with ourselves day in and day out, and thus it is we who have the greatest power to either be our greatest lovers or our greatest detractors. It is always better to be loving than to be hateful, as has been expressed in this book over and over again because it applies to everything. We must love ourselves and love others as we love ourselves.

Next time you are feeling insecure, really think about what it that you are feeling. How do you perceive yourself? How does what you perceive differ

from what you perceive in others that you may envy? Is there some idyllic standard of beauty that has been ingrained in you by an outside source that may not have really been the one with the power to define what is beautiful and what isn't? Are they really worth taking the suggestion from to define your own self in this way? It would help to change the method of thinking. Maybe consider what someone might possibly perceive about you in a positive light. Focus not on your perceived negative attributes but find a new attribute that can be imbued with positivity. Do this, and in this new context, maybe you can begin to reexamine those perceived flaws that you would call the initial catalyst for your insecurity. Let's say you are looking in the mirror and your eyes immediately, every time, go to a blemish on your shoulder, a birthmark. Something you have that others don't, something that sets you apart from others. Begin to look somewhere else. Look at different parts of yourself that you may not have paid as much mind to before. Or just look into your eyes and smile. In your peripheral vision, that birthmark might be freed of the negative connotations you have put on it over the years of negative overthinking. That birthmark is just another part of you that makes up the whole. Any perceived flaw is just one small part of you, and we are infinitely more than the sum of our parts. Never dwell on the negativity and always be positive.

Tell yourself that you are good and you are beautiful, and, by deduction, every small part of you is beautiful in that it makes up the whole, which is beautiful. No part of you ever exists on its own without you. And you are beautiful because you exist and because you choose to love.

And while it is never wrong to take care of yourself, to exercise, to watch what you eat, to wear the clothes that you want to wear and fashion yourself and your hair to the image that you most desire to be, know that you should do these things for love and positivity, not out of fear and negativity. Don't do these things because you don't want to be ugly anymore, do them because you want to continue to be beautiful, and to be the best you that you can be, the way that you choose, as you are always changing and growing and self- improving. Love yourself for what you do, and do what you love. Physical perfection isn't even half of the battle without also realizing yourself mentally and spiritually. The eyes are the windows to the soul, and when someone looks into your eyes, the way a person sees you can change drastically depending on how you are feeling at the moment, about yourself, about life, about others. A strong smile and open eyes with lots of love can go infinite ways towards making a person very beautiful, regardless of any physical or material attributes. Be the best that you can be, dress the way you want to, work towards bettering yourself, feel good about yourself and others, feel loved, and smile. Then you will be the total package—beauty and brains.

Let us examine some specific ways to put this into an application. Perform your induction into the trance-state, having prepped the goal already, that goal being to increase your self-esteem and your confidence. Now, visualize yourself, as you are. Comment to yourself that you are beautiful. Tell yourself that if anyone sees you and says that you are not beautiful, they are merely looking in a mirror and saying that they do not view themselves as beautiful. Visualize yourself smiling and happy. Tell yourself that you are attractive, you are happy and beautiful, and you will attract whatever it is you need to by continuing to be your best self, being happy and free and open and accepting of yourself. Visualize yourself with another person, laughing, having a good time, and enjoying each other's company. Tell yourself that you deserve to be loved, and others enjoy being around you because they enjoy who are you. You are a positive and loving person, and you have a lot of love to give to whoever wants it, and whoever wants it will be an equally loving and positive person because that is what a loving and positive person attracts. Visualize yourself as the center of attention and everyone is looking straight at you. Tell yourself that the people who are watching you are amazed at what they see when they look at you and feel in their hearts a positivity and self-love inspired by your being. These people want to know you and want to be around you, and would like to share with you what they have to offer, and receive from you what you have to offer. Visualize yourself naked, lying in the grass, a totally natural extension of the Earth itself, exactly as you were meant to be, however, you are. Tell yourself that you are a manifestation of the universe, and you are beautiful and full of love. You and it are working in each other's best interest when you hold that love and positivity upfront in your daily being. Now, lastly, visualize anyone and everyone who has ever put you down and said or done things that you have remembered and held onto and used in your own definition of yourself to tell yourself that you are not an attractive person. Tell yourself that these people do not have the power to define you, and are merely afraid to define themselves; hence they are lashing out at you, blindly, imposing on you their own constrictions that they feel when they view themselves. Tell yourself that these people are envious of you, and were only trying to bring you down in their own mind by defining you as something that is less than them, so that they can feel superior to you in their own mind, to satiate their desire not to feel undefined and empty personally. Tell yourself that these people feel they are ugly first and foremost and are unloved, and it is this pain that causes them to define others in their steed, to impose on other people a definition that suits their needs to feel better about themselves in some unnatural way, that only serves to further their loneliness and isolation and inability to feel fulfilled in their daily lives, in their quest for love and their desires to be known and understood. It is hate and fear that causes others to bring you down. This hate and fear will not stand in your light and evaporates before your being because your own definition of yourself is so strong and positive that any negativity shatters before it. Tell yourself that the only reason anyone would ever try to convince you that you are unattractive is that they are trying to convince themselves that you are unattractive in a fruitless jester to deny the envy they feel when they look upon you. If you allow this false definition to impede on you, no one benefits from it. By allowing yourself to be the beautiful person that you are, you are standing for love and light and positive understanding that will wash away all fear and doubt.

CHAPTER 19: START YOUR SELF-JYPNOSIS JOURNEY

Now, we have defined hypnosis, specifically self-hypnosis, along with its practical application and use, and 10 easy steps that lay the foundation to practice it. Let us now peruse over to the more playful territory of putting it into practice, or practicing it. Practicing it as in applying the 10 steps, and practicing the knowledge, not only by putting it into practice, but, also, practicing it in the way one would practice for an exam—we are getting better, learning, training, and understanding.

Simply put, practicing something is to do something. So to begin, you must start doing it. Start your self-hypnosis journey. You may have cold feet. All you have to do is follow through with all that we have already talked about. Prepare yourself, prepare a time, prepare your space, and begin. You never know until you try, and until you try, you don't have the experience necessary to envision the specific areas in which you will then have to grow to become a master of the subject, as an individual. We are all different, and we will all have different workflows that help us succeed at a masterful session of self-hypnosis. Transformation is different for each individual, and therefore, each individual will have a different set of totally specific steps towards a transformation that they must gradually memorize. Over time, they have come to memorize the steps like they know the palms of their own hands. You don't have to jump right into the deep end; just go out and dip your feet in. Feel the water. When you're ready, let your feet touch the ground in the shallow section, wave your arms back and forth, feel the physics of this new environment. Acclimate yourself to your new surroundings. There is no room for fear here.

Given that one of the key necessities of self-hypnosis is the absolute comfort of the subject, you, as both subject and practitioner, must allow yourself the absolute highest level of comfort possible with whatever the situation happens to be. Don't be nervous, don't be stressed out that you don't have what it takes to perform the key journey. Just allow yourself to be whatever you will be and find yourself the patience to allow yourself to blossom without interference into what you desire here and now.

Just as the child, when they are learning to swim, they might fear the water first. It is crucial that the parent doesn't become frustrated and throw the child in the water, hoping this forced total submersion will "get over" their initial fears. Despite the intentions, this is the kind of traumatic situation that makes the unfounded, curious worries of a child permanent. Ironically, the type of traumatic memory that any given person might wish to theoretically "undo" in their self-hypnosis ritual. The right thing to do as a parent is to have the patience to allow your child to come to terms with the fear on his own, his curiosity will subsist, and he will, in his own time, become the master of his worries, as that is the nature of life. Now, you, as an adult, master of your domain. You must learn this lesson two- fold, you must give yourself, as your keeper, the absolute patience required to allow yourself the time to let the natural order of things occur. Now that you have your sights set on self-hypnosis, and you are curious, it is only natural that you will come to master the act, and yourself, over time. It won't occur all in one night. It will happen naturally, as trees grow and forests rise, as stone fades into the sand. Sort of like a Chinese finger trap; you must be okay with the paradox that is the desire to become the results of your greatest wish overnight and the futility of this wish in general. It is the desire that helps you grow, and the growth itself that enables you to succeed towards the desire. In perfect harmony, you must accept your fate here. While we have talked a great deal of the ability to change anything in your path, sadly, but not regretfully, time is not one of those things. Self-hypnosis won't take you back to the Stone Age. It won't take you to a utopic future where all diseases are curable at the snap of a finger, and it won't take you to an alternate reality where all your deepest desires have been instantly realized. Everything is changeable but only over time. Time cannot be removed from the equation, and while some may find this to be a curse (as many have cursed time, a tale as old as time itself), those in the know realize it is a blessing. Without the cushion of time to allow us to acclimate to the changes in store for us gradually, we might well go insane. Imagine if you closed your eyes for one second and when you opened them, you were on the other side of the world. You would be quite ill!

Now, beyond this desire to achieve instant success and perform the most transformative self-hypnosis session the world has ever known, awakening powers in yourself is equivalent to learning you came from the planet Krypton. There is the other side, in which you have zero faith that any form of self-hypnosis will ever do you the tiniest simulacrum of good. If you don't believe that any kind of self-hypnosis will benefit you, you might not even try it. You are not going to convince yourself of anything if the part of yourself that you are trying to convince isn't having it—isn't listening. However, given that you are showing some tiny interest in the subject, even as a skeptic, I will say, continue your research. Play around with it. A part of you is just as interested as the other part is disinterested. Allow these parts to both have their say but know that until you become absolutely, unabashedly invested in the outcome, and the possibility that self-hypnosis will guide you towards a positive one. You will see very little in the way of a convincing experience. And this isn't because there is no power to self-hypnosis, no; it is because the power of self-hypnosis is derived from you. If you do not give self-hypnosis all the power that you have to give it, it will have none. You must be invested in the experience. You must give it your all. Like the child in school who is disinterested in the class, he is attending gets a report card with barely passing grades, so will you, as a practitioner of self-hypnosis, get barely passing results if you show up with minimal interest or care for the act itself. That doesn't mean that I'm telling you to leave now; there is room for plenty of skeptics and skepticism in self-hypnosis. It's our differences and our unique perspectives that allow the trees of knowledge in life to grow upwards into oblivion. But as a curious skeptic, don't expect to learn all there is to know in one day, the same message as to the enthusiastic believer. Don't expect to have such an overwhelming experience, either positive or negative, that you instantaneously come away with any real answer. Self-hypnosis is a realm unto itself, a realm that exists in a different form within every individual. As its rightful explorer, you will not be able to fully map its terrain for a near lifetime. Get comfortable with that.

Now let us get creative! Once you have set a style for your self-hypnosis and gone through that a couple of times, start playing around! And keep playing around! Like with any form of self-expression, self-hypnosis should be a playground for the mind and body that never stops drawing from and refilling the creative wells of the psyche. There are infinite possibilities for both what can be achieved through self-hypnosis and how you can achieve it. Self- hypnosis is a term that is about as broad as can be. Once you've found an essential oil or essential oil blend that pleases the palette and helps you relax, try a new one! Keep trying! What damage can be done? Life is an experiment, as we all know, and a constant struggle to find whatever works for the individual. So, there are life's creative forces. Never stop exploring every new point you reach, every new height scaled, every new planet and solar system, the universe, and dimension. Never stop exploring yourself. Do you find you like the chants of Tibetan monks? Make a habit to go around to all the CD stores in the area and find as many unique and different Tibetan monk chant CDs as you can find. Use a different one each session. You'll find the one you like the most, and maybe you'll find that even though the other ones aren't your absolute favorites, they all have their own time and place for use. Maybe one has an edge to it, an edge that will help you take down bigger demons in the battleground of self-hypnosis. Maybe one is softer, calmer, which will allow for a more serene, prolonged, lightweight self-hypnosis session to abate the stress of the day. Maybe one is two hours long, and maybe one is only an hour. There is no specific time that a self- hypnosis journey must take; so all wide varieties of times are encouraged. Could you imagine the power of performing a daylong session, maybe on the cusp of a spiritual fast? The shamans of the ages don't have to imagine it because it is something that has already been achieved. Try it for yourself. Try anything you want. Be a kid at the playground; renew yourself completely. There is no room for adulteration here. Become the child and explore this new life. Some people say during times of meditation, it is best to face toward the sunrise. Others say the sunset. I say, face wherever you want, and move five degrees the next session, or ten, or twenty. Do it on your head, do it on your butt, do it on one foot, do it on your hands, or knees, do it every single way you can imagine! Because we are here to expand our imaginations, which brings us to our next point.

Expand your imagination! Nothing will help with the act of self-hypnosis more than expanding the imagination. Imagination is the ammo that loads the gun that is self-hypnosis. Without imagination, how can we see anything more than what we presently are? How can we see the infinite possibilities of existence? How can we dream? How can we grow? How can we achieve any higher level of success than we have without first imagining it into existence? There are, as well, an infinite number of ways to expand your imagination. Self-hypnosis itself is a way to expand your imagination, just by the practice of practicing it! It's a self-fulfilling prophecy. I am a huge advocate of play. I love to pretend. I love to fool around. I love art, I love to create, and I love to do whatever I want whenever I want. Sometimes I want to sit totally still for an hour; sometimes I want to tell my body to move as fast and as wild as possible, flailing in every possible direction with no purpose, a wild, ecstatic dance, like a burning flame. I like to go to playgrounds at midnight and play on the equipment like I'm five years old. I talk to myself very often when no one is around. I create art that is only meant for me to see, just because I like the act of creation. There is no purpose, besides to grow and to be. Take a page from my book. Again, let us go back to an age of innocence before our souls became muddied and adulterated. Let us play. Find this new world to be a playground, a beautiful forest, a landscape of infinite incredible things to do for no other purpose than to feel the pure joy of doing them, incredible things, new ones every day. Feel around and find what makes you happy, what makes you satisfied, what makes you feel strong and fulfilled, and do it more. Do it in wide varieties, each and every day, and never stop. Even when you are stuck in a cubicle, find time for play. Download a proxy server and bypass the time-waste management firewalls on your computer that prevent you from watching cat videos. Work for an hour and then spend five minutes doing something that you love, that makes you happy. Imagine that your boss is a corrupt monarch, who has you imprisoned as an indentured servant, and your transgression is an act of heroic rebellion. Share it with your co- workers; allow them in on the game. Let love grow and let minds be renewed. Just like a child at the playground, going up to another one, touching them on the head and screaming, "Hi, will you play with me." There is a child inside every single one of us, and, although we may not see it or believe it, or even have the idea, once you hand the keys over to them, they'll know exactly what to do. You'll just be along for the ride. And what a joyous ride it will be. Live ecstasy.

One of the keys of this whole endeavor is just purely to live. Go out and there and start taking everything in. Take in all the information, all the stimuli, and all the experiences that you can possibly find, process them through your individuality, and make up your own mind. Never stop bettering yourself. Never stop experiencing as much as possible. Read lots of books. Read books on history, read self-help books, read fiction, read manga, read a comic book. Watch movies you've never heard of, that most people would think you are strange for watching. Try new things with your partner, get kinky, and get weird. Try new foods. Learn how to cook new foods. Grow your own garden. Take in all the art that you can find, put out all the art that you can make. Make conversation with strangers. Listen to them without talking back. Learn as much from them as possible, so you have that much more ammunition when it comes time for you to define your own self. Every experience, positive or negative, is a chance to learn and to grow. This is one of the fundamentals of ultimately positive existence, the kind that self-hypnosis as an art form strives for. The philosophers of the time, they were all so very wrong, yet so very right because they asked questions, and were curious, and defined life for themselves. Now it is your turn.

As you perform self-hypnosis, and come back to life, rejuvenated, and go back in, and come back out, and go back in, and come back out, it is like gliding through the seemingly infinite fractal surfaces of a crystal shard. These are the infinite realities that exist within us all. It is human nature for one to grab ahold of a single reality like they would a plank of wood in the ocean when they are lost at sea, but here, we must embrace the never-ending waters we see before us at all angles, we must relax, float on our backs, and go where the flow of the water takes us. We will close our eyes and tell ourselves, "The water will take us to the shore," and have faith that we will awake on the shore, over time. It does no use to struggle; struggle only consumes energy. It is best to allow the flow of nature to do what it does best and allow our guardian angels the freedom to do what they think is best for us for the time being. And this is all to say, don't be intimidated! Just practice. Practice and practice with no end in sight, when you open your eyes and see no land in sight, practice some more! There is no desperation, there is no need, there is only practice itself, and the acceptance of the many possibilities that life and love might throw your way tomorrow, possibilities you could never have imagined, however great your imagination has become, because life always knows what it will take to give you what you need, all you have to do is really ultimately focus on what that is. If we are ever going into the paradoxical territory, feel no surprise! What we are dealing with here is an elastic and flowing concept in an elastic and flowing reality. It is a dance, like that of the cosmos. Sometimes Mars is over here, and sometimes Mars is over there, and sometimes the moon of the Earth overshadows the sun. What works for one person will only hurt another if they see the positive results the other is getting and envy them. They will be perplexed, but it is the nature of our individual realities that our own precise definition and prescription need to be filled. And we can only take so much from others before we must begin to make up our own minds. Words can only do so much to convey the information necessary; a lot of it is up to you, to fill in the blanks with your own journey. So begin the journey, set forth, and practice self-hypnosis for yourself.

So while self-hypnosis is a grand and glorious and miraculous thing that can change the very boundaries of reality itself, it is also an art form, and, like any art form, practice makes perfect. Consider the martial arts. While you can go to an exhibition as a voyeur and see masters of the arts partaking in daring feats that defy your momentary comprehension and rope you right into becoming a believer and eventual true follower, becoming the thing that you see before you is not something that occurs overnight. It is something that occurs gradually and is the result of true, unbroken focus and great, ever- growing discipline. However, unlike martial arts, self-hypnosis is a realm where there is no objective rank. There are no black belts in self-hypnosis. There are practitioners, with varying degrees, there are schools, there are licensed professionals with better reviews than others and better credentials, bigger offices, more certificates, and diplomas hanging on their walls, customers, but, at the end of the day, there is just theory, practice, and proof positive. It is up to us, and all of us, to theorize, and it is up to us, and all of us, to practice. The proof will be in the pudding, so they say. Some will always be better than others. Some will be faster to relax because they are more predisposed to be relaxed. Some will be faster to discipline themselves because they are more predisposed to be self-disciplined. Some will have loftier and more ambitious goals because they are more predisposed to be ambitious and to aim higher than some others might feel comfortable. Here, in this practice, it is best to just "do you," as they say. Be who you are, and be comfortable, and let this new art form find it's fit on you, just as you find your fit in it. It will be different for everyone.

With keeping in mind all the benefits and lofty dreams of what self-hypnosis can achieve for you, try it with very clear-cut and deterministic goals in mind. For the smoker, the aim would be not to be smoke-free tomorrow but eventually. It will take its time to work in the way it is supposed to, for you and your specific situation. You will know better than anyone how it is to be for you, your limitations, your strengths, and your rightfully tiered goals. If you can do it all in one night, then good for you, but if you can't, then still, good for you, just for starting. Feel good about what you are doing. Feel good about just being there and putting in the effort to progressively better your position. This will help you in the long run. Never get tired of doing what you love, and if you get tired, try something else. Love is a multi-faceted thing. Don't get bogged down in specifics, in times, or material goals. Immerse yourself fully in practice, for the sake of practice in and of itself, and you will find yourself eventually in a greater position than you could have ever imagined. As you are reading this book, take it all to heart, and add to it and subtract from it as it suits you. You must find your own workspace and your own workflow. If you are feeling good, then it is working. If you are not feeling good, then keep trying, and try different things. The end result is for you to feel confident and secure. However, that will be for you and however, you can. Never feel insecure about your own manifestation of trying. Never compare yourself to others, or say that you should be something that you are not. Be what you are and grow that thing towards what you wish to be, gradually, over time, with practice. And, as has been expressed, have a good time with it. No part of your self-hypnosis journey should be anything but fun and pleasant. Even if what you are trying to rectify is the most horrific traumatic event known to man, it should be a pleasant and positive experience for you to vanquish this evil from your eternal kingdom, your temple, your mind, and your body. With traumatic memories, do not break the dam and open up the floodgates and let too much feedback come pouring down on you all at once. Be graceful and playful, and work towards eventual proficiency. There should be absolutely no negative feelings associated with your adventure into self-hypnosis. If you are to make the steps and the choice towards a better you, you must completely accept who you are and who you have been, what you have done and what has been done to you. When all of those things have been put up against time, they will be rightfully rectified with the psyche and the physical being, and they will become no longer things that are holding you down, but, in deduction, freeing things that allow you to reach higher and higher than ever before. Just as a trainer who wears ten-pound bands around each limb every day while performing daily tasks finds their limbs to feel weightless in comparison when, at the end of the day, they take their bands off, so too will the practitioner of the self-hypnosis, in comparison, feel stronger and lighter than they would have otherwise when freed from the things that are holding them down, whatever those things may be. The heavier the thing, the lighter they will feel, and the stronger they will have become. With this said, let us lastly cherish these things that weigh down on us, for once, something that so few people choose to do. It is all a part of you and your journey, you and your journey being two great, grand and very important things. Every single part of your life will come together to make you who you are going to be, in synchronicity with your will, and all that is involved, however ugly, however painful, must be loved. Love is the light that casts the shadows out. Love everything about yourself, even the things you hate the most, for, through loving them, they will become allies in your quest for strength. They, too, will change in your new image, the image of love. All weaknesses become strengths; all negativity becomes a positive force expanded by its own negative force tenfold. This is the power that we speak of, the power of self-hypnosis. But more than that, it is the power of knowledge of self, and the ability to control the self—yourself—the ability to be who you want to be, the ability to be yourself, your ultimate self, and create a future which is all the more brighter just for having you in it, as you are, too, for it.

CHAPTER 20: CBT IN ACTION

Facing Your Fears

For many people, a big part of their desire to deal with their mental health issues comes from the fact that their fears of objects, places, people or situations is starting to affect their life in an undeniable way. While it is normal to want to avoid things that you are afraid of, at a certain point avoidance actually starts to be counterproductive as it can make it much more difficult to realize that your fears are, generally speaking, not nearly as bad as you might think.

Practice exposure: In CBT, exposure is the process of gradually putting yourself into scenarios that trigger your fears in a controlled way to allow you to face them head on, leaving you less anxious and more in control as a result. Don't worry, when done properly, exposure doesn't ever actually put you in any danger and it is done in phases to ensure that it doesn't fully cause the trigger to activate in the moment.

What's especially useful when it comes to exposure is the fact that it allows each person who uses it to proceed at their own pace, building up confidence around trigger situations in their own way. Even better, you won't need to actively work to improve from encounter to encounter, the improvement will happen whether you focus on it or not, who knows, you may even end up enjoying whatever it is that you were previously afraid of. For example, if a person has a phobia when it comes to large bodies of water then they could start by standing in a swimming pool then slowly but surely immersing more and more of their body under water until they were eventually able to start taking swimming lessons and are some day able to swim in the ocean without issue.

If you have previously tried to shake yourself out of your fear and found that exposure did not work well for you then, it could be that you simply tried to rush the process more than your mind was willing, or able, to handle. Alternately, you may have simply not kept up the practice long enough to dull your fear to the point where it could no longer control you. Regardless, you don't necessarily need to believe that exposure therapy is going to work for you this time, you only need to start practicing it and keep it up for a long enough period of time to ensure you will start seeing results.

Seeing optimal results from exposure is possible, it is just going to take the proper planning, and plenty of patience. Remember, conquering your fears is a marathon, not a sprint, slow and steady wins the race.

Making a list: The first step to utilizing exposure properly is to know exactly what it is you are up against which means making a complete list of the objects, places, people and situations that you are afraid. This shouldn't be a general list either, it needs to be as granular as possible. For example, if you are afraid of dogs, your list may include petting a puppy, standing near a dog in someone's home, standing near a dog on a leash on the street, standing in an open space with a strange dog not on a leash, pictures of dogs, the sound of dogs barking etc. Each item on the list will then eventually become an action item that you will acclimate yourself to.

If you have multiple fears that are interacting with your life in a noticeable way, then you are going to want to make a separate list for each. While you will want to write all your lists at the same time in order to determine just what you are going to need to deal with, you are only going to want to focus on exposing yourself to one fear at a time. Don't kid yourself, kicking a fear, especially one that is deeply ingrained in your psyche, is a big task and you don't want to bite off more than you can chew, especially when you are just getting familiar with the process.

Organize your list: After you have created each of your lists, you are going to want to determine which you are going to want to tackle first. If the answer isn't clear up front, the best place to start is with a fear that is impacting you noticeably, but isn't necessarily the most intimidating on the list. This will provide you with a manageable goal to accomplish first to make sticking with the practice of exposure easier in the long-term, especially when you get to the more difficult fears on your list.

With your desired list chosen, the next thing you are going to want to do is put the items on the list in order starting with the most manageable and ending with the least manageable. Additionally, you are going to want to give each item a number on a scale between 1 (little or no fear) to 10 (crippling fear). With your list made, you will then want to start with the first, and least intimidating item. As you move through your list you will find that the things farther up it start to seem more and more manageable as you complete the tasks below it.

Once you have found a specific task to focus on, the next thing you are going to do is to make a list of all of the steps you would need to successfully take in order for you to successfully face your fear. For example, if you were dealing with a fear of social situations then eating a meal alone in a crowded restaurant may seem impossible, at first. However, it could then be broken down into steps that could be more easily accomplished such as:

- Go to a restaurant and get a coffee to go

- Have a coffee inside the restaurant but sit by exit on the patio

- Eat an appetizer at the restaurant and sit near the door

- Eat a salad at the restaurant and sit in the dining room

- Eat an entire meal at the restaurant on the patio near the exit

- Eat an entire meal at the restaurant in the dining room

You will then want to create a fear ladder for every one of your fears on your chosen list. Take note of each time a fear has an overlapping task, each of these will compress the overall amount of time required significantly and may even allow you to kill two or more fears with one fear ladder-based stone. Each ladder should include starter steps that you can do while only feeling a little bit of anxiety, before slowly scaling to scenarios that previously caused you moderate anxiety after between eight and 10 mild encounters. You will then want to up the ante to extreme anxiety situations, again, after another eight to 10 encounters. This is just an estimate, however, don't be afraid to take as small and gradual steps as you feel you need in order to find success.

Facing your fears: When you start utilizing exposure, the first thing you will need to keep in mind is that you want to push yourself past the point where you stop feeling comfortable, but not so far that your fear pushes you past the point of logical response. If the first thing you are afraid of isn't something you can do for a prolonged period of time, then ensure that you keep at it for a long enough period of time for the anxiety or fear about the activity to completely vanish. Alternately, you could try looping a shorter scenario by doing it several times in a row with only 10 or 15 minutes in between.

While the first or second time you attempt something, your physical response might be so intense that you can't react positively and have to retreat, once you are able to stand your ground you will find that your anxiety, while likely extremely high at first, will eventually subside. This isn't a question of if, it is a question of when, as remaining in an extremely anxious state consumes a lot of energy and it is simply not something the body can sustain indefinitely. Once you are able to handle a situation to the point where your physical reaction begins to subside then you can rest easy, the hard part is over, the rest is simply inoculating yourself to the specifics of the situation and moving on to the next fear on your list. It is important to do everything in your power to set up scenarios that allow you to remain in as much control of the events as possible, to ensure that things go according to plan. The more in charge of the proceedings you feel when you start, the easier it will be for you to retain that feeling of control throughout.

Diaphragmatic breathing.

Abdominal Breathing is a very effective way to heal yourself. It not only helps in improving your immune and the digestive system, but it also helps in improving your emotional health.

277

Our gut has almost the equal number of neurons as our brain. Most of the crucial functions of our body are control from here. Even the biggest decisions in your life get affected by your gut feeling. It is the gut that is generating the fight or flight response in critical situations. If you really want to improve your emotional health, this breathing technique is one of the best ways to do so. This meditation helps in stabilizing your emotional health. It makes you more decisive and balanced.

Abdominal breathing is very easy and calming. You may use this technique in any stressful situation to calm and relax quickly. It has a very soothing effect on your body.

Take your position at the place of your meditation Take your seat

Sit in a completely relaxed manner Don't do anything immediately Ground yourself first

Just sit completely relaxed for a few minutes

If something important comes to your mind write it down If there is something that is bothering you, write it down Get into a comfortable position

Keep your back straight

Ensure that your shoulders are also straight Your back and neck should be in a straight line Now, close your eyes

Lean slightly forward and then backward Lean-to your left side and then to your right

Now, bring yourself to the center and find the best and most comfortable position

Feel your head positioned on your neck Raise your chin slightly upwards

This will help you in placing your focus between your eyebrows Try to feel your whole body

Notice if there is tension anywhere

If you feel any part tense, release the tension Adjust your body to release the pressure

Put a hand on your chest and a hand on your stomach Begin with breathing normally

Let your breathing stabilize Breathe in

Count 1...2...3...4

 Breathe Out Breathe in Count 1...2...3...4 Breathe Out

We will now begin with smaller inhalations and longer exhalations Start inhaling from your nose to the count of 4

1...2...3...4

Hold your breath to the count of 4 1...2...3...4

Release the breath slowly through your mouth to the count of 7 1...2...3...4...5...6...7

Fill in the air

Let it reach your abdomen Hold it there for a while

Then, release it through your mouth With each breath you take

Observe the expansion of your chest Feel your abdomen rising

Holding the breath oxygenates your body It prepares the pressure to get released When you slowly exhale for longer

Try to push out more air than you have taken in This will helps in releasing tension along with air You will immediately start feeling relaxed

Your abdominal muscles will get the exercise Your digestion process would improve

Your immunity levels would improve

 The process is very simple Inhale from the nose

Hold the breath a little

Then release it slowly from your mouth

We will now repeat this process a few times Start inhaling from your nose to the count of 4 1...2...3...4

Hold your breath to the count of 4 1...2...3...4

Release the breath slowly through your mouth to the count of 7 1...2...3...4...5...6...7

Repeat

Start inhaling from your nose to the count of 4 1...2...3...4

Hold your breath to the count of 4 1...2...3...4

Release the breath slowly through your mouth to the count of 7
1...2...3...4...5...6...7

Observe if your mind is wandering off Don't worry it can happen very often

Don't pay attention to the thoughts coming to your mind Simply acknowledge them and then push them aside Center your attention to your abdomen

Start inhaling from your nose to the count of 4 1...2...3...4

Hold your breath to the count of 4 1...2...3...4

Release the breath slowly through your mouth to the count of 7

1...2...3...4...5...6...7

Your breathing is more important than anything else

Every breath that you are taking is helping in releasing tension There is no much emotional stress in the body

It keeps accumulating in your gut Your appetite gets affected

Your eating habits change

Too much stress can lead to emotional eating It can also lead to eating disorders

Pay attention to this breathing

Start inhaling from your nose to the count of 4 1...2...3...4

Hold your breath to the count of 4 1...2...3...4

Release the breath slowly through your mouth to the count of 7
1...2...3...4...5...6...7

If the train of thoughts is causing any distraction let it be You don't need to resist them

Simply acknowledge those thoughts and bring your awareness back Don't get involved

Pay attention to your gut

Start inhaling from your nose to the count of 4 1...2...3...4

Hold your breath to the count of 4 1...2...3...4

Release the breath slowly through your mouth to the count of 7 1...2...3...4...5...6...7

Now it is time to breathe normally

Take a small breath Hold it for a moment The release it slowly

There is no need to count now Let it be

Simply breathe in and breathe out

Let your body find a natural rhythm of breathing Fix your awareness above your head

It is time to feel the beauty of nature

It is time to get lost in the relaxation you are feeling at the moment Enjoy the euphoria

Feel the ecstasy of the moment Imagine yourself at a lakeside

It is a peaceful but cold mountain lake There is greenery all around

The environment is so tranquil You simply want to settle here

Everything about this place is mesmerizing

You had always wanted to live beside such a lake The place is so calm like the waters of this lake There are small ripples in the water but no big waves There is certainty

You can know just about anything you want to know The length of the lake

The depth of the lake The extent of the lake

There is nothing that can scare you

You always wanted to be at a place where you were always in complete

control

This is the place you have been looking for

This lake will take away everything you want to discard Sit by the lakeside

Feel free to dip your feet inside the water Be careful, it is cold

Now start throwing your worries in the late We will inhale to the count of 3

Gather the things we want to throw one by one to the count of 4 And disperse them in the late on the count of 5 as you exhale Think of the first thing you want to get rid of

Any habit, memory, or a feeling for someone It can be anything

Contempt, grief, hatred, jealousy, the feeling of loss, Don't worry

This lake will take anything

It won't tell about it to anyone Your secret will be safe

There is no point bearing such things on your person They are weighing you down

They are taking a toll on your physical and emotional health They are affecting your life

Inhale 1...2...3

Gather the thoughts 1...2...3...4 Exhale and disperse 1...2...3...4...5

Doesn't it feel relaxing? Let us do it again Inhale

1...2...3

Gather the thoughts 1...2...3...4 Exhale and disperse 1...2...3...4...5

Now that you have done the practice Let us gather your deep fears

The ones that are deep in your heart Take one of them out

Inhale 1...2...3

Gather the thoughts 1...2...3...4 Exhale and disperse 1...2...3...4...5

Let us now try regrets

Your most profound regrets They might have hurt you

But they are a thing of the past now

There is no purpose of holding them to your heart Let them out

Inhale 1...2...3

Gather the thoughts 1...2...3...4

Exhale and disperse 1...2...3...4...5 You are doing great

The feeling is ultimate You can do this every day

It takes away the stress from the heart It feels so light

It is time to go now It is getting dark Let's get back

Bring your awareness back to your stomach Resume breathing normally

Hold on to the state for a bit long Let your breathing normalize Don't open your eyes immediately Give yourself some time

Slowly start feeling your surrounding Feel the cushion on which you are sitting Now open your eyes slowly.

You are feeling completely relaxed now.

Progressive Muscle Relaxation

Progressive Muscle Relaxation technique is a great way to release the tension in particular muscles in the body. In this technique, you will progressively tense each muscle group in your body and then release the tension from the muscle. At the end of the meditation session, you will feel completely relaxed and the tension in the muscles will be gone.

If there is some pain or discomfort in any specific muscle group, you can choose to skip exerting tension in that muscle group. The purpose of this technique is to provide complete relaxation.

Take your position at the place of your meditation Take your seat

Sit in a completely relaxed manner

You can also choose to do this meditation lying down Don't do anything immediately

Ground yourself first

Just sit or lie down completely relaxed for a few minutes Get into a comfortable position

Keep your back straight

Ensure that your shoulders are also straight Your back and neck should be in a straight line Now, close your eyes

If you are sitting

Lean slightly forward and then backward Lean-to your left side and then to your right

Now, bring yourself to the center and find the best and most comfortable position

Feel your head positioned on your neck Raise your chin slightly upwards

This will help you in placing your focus between your eyebrows If you are lying down

Ensure that your spine and neck are straight Keep your palms open facing upwards

Try to feel your whole body Notice if there is tension anywhere

If you feel any part tense, release the tension

Adjust your body to release the pressure

Your attention should focus completely on your body If your mind is distracted by the thoughts

Observe them but do not pay attention to them Start by breathing normally

Breathe in

Fill the air through your nostrils Let the air fill your abdomen Hold it there for a few seconds

Then, slowly release the air through your mouth Repeat this process a few more times

Breathe in

Hold your breath in the abdomen Exhale longer through your mouth As you breathe in

The oxygen will fill your body It will energize you

When you exhale

You will feel more relaxed Breathe in

Hold your breath in the abdomen Exhale longer through your mouth Breathe in

Hold your breath in the abdomen Exhale longer through your mouth Breathe in

Hold your breath in the abdomen Exhale longer through your mouth

Breathe in

Hold your breath in the abdomen Exhale longer through your mouth Now, focus on your forehead

Begin by raising your eyebrows as high as possible This would create tension on your forehead

Hold your eyebrows in this position till the count of 5 1...2...3...4...5

Now release the tension

This needs to be done in sync of your breathing As you start inhaling through your nose

Start raising your eyebrows

Hold the eyebrows in the position for 5 seconds 1...2...3...4...5

Now release the tension Exhale longer

Enjoy the sensation of tension getting released Focus your attention on your eyes

As you inhale, start squinting your eyes tightly Hold your eyes in this position for five seconds Release on the count of 5

1...2...3...4...5

Release the tension

Feel the relaxation in your eyes Now, bring your focus to your face As you inhale

Start forming a wide smile

Stretch your lips in a smile as wide as possible

 Hold your smile in this position for 5 seconds Release it on the count of 5

1...2...3...4...5

Release the tension as you exhale Relax for a few seconds now

Pull your neck backward as you start inhaling Keep it in the stretched position for 5 seconds Release the tension on the count of 5 1...2...3...4...5

Release the tension as you exhale

As you inhale, tense your shoulder muscles

You can raise your shoulders making them touch your ears Keep them stretched for 5 seconds

Release the tension on the count of 5 1...2...3...4...5

Release the tension as you exhale

Start clinching your bicep muscles as you inhale Feel the muscles clinching

Keep them in the tensed state for 5 seconds Release the tension on the count of 5 1...2...3...4...5

Release the tension as you exhale Repeat the same exercise with your arms

Tense the muscles in your arms as you inhale Keep them in the tensed state for 5 seconds Release the tension on the count of 5 1...2...3...4...5

Release the tension as you exhale

Create tension in your hands as you inhale Stretch your palms as far as possible

Hold them in the position for 5 seconds Release the tension on the count of 5 1...2...3...4...5

Release the tension as you exhale

Now, create tension in the muscles in your upper back as you inhale You can stretch them towards the center of your spine

Keep them in the tensed state for 5 seconds Release the tension on the count of 5 1...2...3...4...5

Release the tension as you exhale

Start creating the same tension in the muscles of your lower back as you inhale

Hold the tension for 5 seconds Release the tension on the count of 5 1...2...3...4...5

Release the tension as you exhale Bring your focus on the chest

Create tension in the chest muscles as you inhale Hold the tension for 5 seconds

Release the tension on the count of 5 1...2...3...4...5

Release the tension as you exhale Shift your focus on your abdomen

Stiffen your abdomen muscles as you inhale Hold the muscles for 5 seconds

Release the tension on the count of 5

1...2...3...4...5

Release the tension as you exhale Shift your attention to your buttocks Clinch your buttocks as you inhale Hold the tension for 5 seconds Release the tension on the count of 5 1...2...3...4...5

Release the tension as you exhale Bring your focus to your thighs

Tighten your thigh muscles as you inhale Hold the muscles for 5 seconds

Release the tension on the count of 5 1...2...3...4...5

Release the tension as you exhale

Now tighten your calves as you inhale again

Hold the calve muscles in the same position for 5 seconds Release the tension on the count of 5

1...2...3...4...5

Release the tension as you exhale

Now flex your feet towards your body as far as possible Do this for the whole duration of your inhalation

Hold the feet in the same position for 5 seconds Release the tension on the count of 5 1...2...3...4...5

Release the tension as you exhale

Now start creating tension in all your toes

Stretch them outwards or bend them as far as possible as you inhale Hold them in this position for 5 seconds

Release the tension on the count of 5 1...2...3...4...5

Release the tension as you exhale

Now leave your body loose for a few seconds Enjoy the sensation of a stress-free body

This position helps you in releasing all the stress in the muscles It will help you a lot in sleeping peacefully

Now once again bring your focus to your abdomen Breathe deeply

Inhale

Fill your abdomen with air Let it expand

Hold your breath for a few seconds Now exhale slowly

Let all the air escape through your mouth

This will help you in relaxing your body completely Repeat the process once again

Breathe deeply Inhale

Fill your abdomen with air Let it expand

Hold your breath for a few seconds Now exhale slowly

Let all the air escape through your mouth Breathe deeply

Inhale

Fill your abdomen with air Let it expand

Hold your breath for a few seconds Now exhale slowly

Let all the air escape through your mouth It is time to stabilize your breathing

Start breathing at a natural pace

Do not try to alter the breathing pattern Simply inhale and exhale

You will find yourself completely relaxed

Enjoy the sensation of a completely stress-free body Now you can open your eyes gently.

Mind-Body Relaxation to Decrease Stress and Anxiety

The purpose of this mind-body relaxation meditation is to get rid of fear and anxiety. This guided meditation session will take you deep inside your mind. You will be able to get rid of your fears and anxieties. You will get a chance to face them and defeat them.

This guided meditation is very helpful in relieving stress and anxiety. It helps you in sleeping better and provide complete physical, mental, and emotional relief. You can practice it anytime you like.

Take your position at the place of your meditation Take your seat

Sit in a completely relaxed manner Don't do anything immediately Ground yourself first

Just sit completely relaxed for a few minutes

If something important comes to your mind write it down If there is something that is bothering you, write it down Get into a comfortable position

Keep your back straight

Ensure that your shoulders are also straight Your back and neck should be in a straight line Now, close your eyes

Lean slightly forward and then backward Lean-to your left side and then to your right

Now, bring yourself to the center and find the best and most comfortable position

Feel your head positioned on your neck Raise your chin slightly upwards

This will help you in placing your focus between your eyebrows Try to feel your whole body

Notice if there is tension anywhere

If you feel any part tense, release the tension Adjust your body to release the pressure

This meditation will help you in relaxing your body and mind You will let go of all your stress and anxiety

Throughout the meditation session

You will breathe in through your nose slowly Hold your breath for a few seconds

Breathe out through your mouth making a "Haaaaa" sound It might look like you are testing your breath

This process helps in taking out all the spent air from your body It takes away the stress and anxiety

Breathe in slowly through your nostrils Let it fill your abdomen

Let it light your body

Hold the breath for a few seconds

 Now exhale with the 'Haaaa' Repeat the process 5 times

Breathe in slowly through your nostrils Let it fill your abdomen

Let it light your body

Hold the breath for a few seconds Exhale with the 'Haaaa'

Breathe in slowly through your nostrils Let it fill your abdomen

Let it light your body

Hold the breath for a few seconds Exhale with the 'Haaaa'

Breathe in slowly through your nostrils Let it fill your abdomen

Let it light your body

Hold the breath for a few seconds Exhale with the 'Haaaa'

Breathe in slowly through your nostrils Let it fill your abdomen

Let it light your body

Hold the breath for a few seconds Exhale with the 'Haaaa'

Breathe in slowly through your nostrils Let it fill your abdomen

Let it light your body

Hold the breath for a few seconds Exhale with the 'Haaaa'

You are feeling much relaxed and composed now

There is no stress and anxiety in the body You are feeling comfortable

You are feeling calm

If there were thoughts bothering you? They have disappeared now

It is time to relax your breathing There is no rush now

There is no fear now

You can bring your breathing to normal Breathe in slowly

Hold the breath

Exhale through your mouth Don't count

Don't bother

Let your body find its breathing rhythm Let's not bother about it

Shift your focus between your eyes Keep your eyes comfortably closed Do not squint your eyes

Simply try to see the light between your eyebrows Somewhere in the center of your forehead

You might see the white fog a bit above the center of your nose bridge Enter this fog

There is something beyond this fog It looks very peaceful

You should explore it

There is no need to be anxious Enter the fog

The fog is not very dense

On the other side of the fog, there is a green pasture It's a lush green grassland

It's so green that even a single yellow blade of grass can be spotted You haven't seen such lush green pasture in years

It is mesmerizing

It is so soothing to the eyes You are loving the scenery

You wanted to visit such a place for so long It is like a dream come true

Look all around yourself

There are some sheep grazing the green grass They are so white as if wearing snowflakes Not even a single sheep has patches of color Looks like they have been painted

But they are real

They are not inanimate They are moving Making noise

At the other side, there are some kids They are playing

The kids are trying to throw stones as far as possible It is such an amusing game

They are small kids Not very powerful

They can't throw the stones very far Their stones fall very near

You like this game

But you don't want to disturb the kids You look at the other side

There is a valley Very deep

Very steep

It looks like you are at the edge of a cliff You find some stones lying there

You want to play the same game You want to test your throwing arm You used to be really good at it There is no harm in trying again There is no one looking at it

There is nothing to be ashamed of You pick up a pebble

It looks small But it is heavy

Just like your fears and anxieties

They are also small and insignificant in size But they keep you anxious

They keep you worried

You just can't seem to stop thinking about them It is a good time to get rid of them

No one is here to notice you

Pick up each stone and fling it hard Throw it from here

It cannot return

You can get rid of all your fears and anxieties here No one will notice you

You will come out of here fearless You will not have these anxieties You will be able to get rid of them Pick up a stone

Think of it as some generalized fear Begin with small things that worry you Pick anyone

Now throw it hard It feels good

You are feeling relieved This is an amazing feeling

You can get rid of all your fears and anxieties here You have all the time and opportunity here

Let's try another one

Pick any of your bigger worries Look at it fearlessly

Face it

It can't scare you anymore

You can throw it away at any moment Now get rid of it

Isn't it an exhilarating feeling?

You have started enjoying the process now Let's try a bigger one

Pick the things that make you anxious

Pick the things that have been making you insecure The things that scare you the most

Weigh it in your hands

It didn't weigh that much after all

Yet, you remain scared of it Face it now

Look at it for the last time

It should know that you are victorious now You have conquered it

Now, let's try something that makes you really restless Don't be afraid

There's nothing that they can do You are in complete control

You are not afraid of anything now

You have taken the matters in your own hands now Pick it up

Face it

Call out its name loudly Louder

Even louder so that you can hear it Louder so that even the kids can hear you There is no shame in facing your fears You are challenging them now

You are one step away from conquering them all Fling it forward into the deep abyss

It's gone now Gone forever You have won

You have become victorious over your fears You are feeling great

It is an amazing feeling You are radiating brilliance

You are radiating courage

You want to admire the scenery a bit more You can't get enough of it in your eyes But it's getting dark

It's time for you to go home

The kids have also started returning to their homes with their sheep You must also return

But you will be returning victorious You have conquered your fears Beyond that fog is your home Come back

Become aware of your surrounding Become aware of your breathing You are doing great

You are feeling completely relaxed There is no fear now

There is no anxiety There is no stress

You can open your eyes now

Or choose to sit in this position for a bit longer Relish the feeling for as long as you want.

CHAPTER 21: IMPROVED SELF-HYPNOSIS

Exercise 1: Perform Physical Relaxation Techniques

The physical relaxation techniques that we have gone over and explored during the 10 steps don't need to be explicitly relegated and only to your core journeys into self-hypnosis. They are concepts and ideas and actions that can be taken and applied anywhere you happen to find yourself in life, without the specific intention of any self-hypnosis whatsoever. There will never be a time when practicing these things in any way, shape, or form doesn't pose some benefits.

For example, when I wake up in the morning, I start taking control of my breathing. I become aware of my body, and I will be still for a good couple of minutes, charging my being with my breaths, before I get out of bed. And it will continue over the day. There is generally not a time over a day where I am not exercising my awareness of my breathing. I perform conscious breathing on the way to work while at work, on my way home, and when I get home. This is just going on in the background while I perform my daily tasks. I am aware of my breaths, and I am keeping them slow and steady. Then, when I have legitimate downtime, for instance on my lunch break, or when I am home either before or after work, I will have an amount of time where my awareness of my breathing shifts to the forefront and I will evaporate all other thought from my being while I focus only on the slow and steady breathing, to relax and recharge my physiology. This type of exercise will make it not only, so you are better at the act of controlling and being aware of your breathing when it comes time specifically for a session of self-hypnosis but it will pose all sorts of benefits to you besides and apart from the ones posed specifically by self-hypnosis, such as increased focus, easier handling of daily stress, less anxiousness, increased performance, better health, a stronger body, less lethargy, feeling more awake, and just all-around feeling much more relaxed and comfortable in your body. What an idea that relaxing your body would help you feel more relaxed in your body! And what problems in daily life would such a concept not go a million miles towards bettering, purely and simply, just by performing a few simple and moldable actions in the background of your daily life? It can be as intensive or as subtle as you wish, you can put your life on hold for five seconds and take a couple of deep breaths, either by counting them out ("1, 2, 3, inhale, 1, 2, 3, exhale") or by measuring the internal rhythm by some other means, or you can constantly be honing your awareness of breaths, such as I have described doing in my personal life, measuring your breaths at every second, always practicing making them slower, stronger, and steadier. You can also perform daily yoga, added to any kind of exercise regimen that you are beginning or already in the process of maintaining in your daily life. Yoga is a very positive means of getting better at the awareness of the body while also making the body stronger and steadier through this very awareness. There are all sorts of schools and methods of different forms of yoga that you can practice, and, just like with self-hypnosis techniques, you can personalize them and pick and choose which ones help you be the most comfortable and proficient in your skin. Just be relaxed and try to feel good about yourself. Eat a healthy diet and take care of your body, and always be aware of what your body is telling you.

Exercise 2: Relax Your Mind Every Night

Just as with the physical relaxation techniques, mental relaxation techniques don't end and begin specifically and only when you are to make a concrete journey into self-hypnosis. They can be practiced in varying forms and to varying degrees and all different periods and place, and one great time and place is in bed before going to sleep. And similar to the use of physical relaxation techniques outside specific and designated sessions of self-hypnosis, the exercising of mental relaxation techniques poses many more benefits than simply becoming more proficient at the mental relaxation techniques themselves, for purposes of more successful self-hypnosis. Many people alive today have great trouble sleeping, either getting to sleep, staying asleep, feeling that the type of sleep they are getting is as rejuvenating to the body as necessary or all three. As soon as you lie down for sleep, relaxing will pose extreme benefits with all three of these problems. As soon as you lay down, make a concentrated effort to leave all the troubles of the day behind you. They are neither here or now. They can be dealt with at another time. Now and now, it is time for you to relax and rest so that you may be stronger in the morning and tomorrow when it comes time for you to deal with whatever has to be dealt with. Set aside your troubles, clear your mind, and begin a pattern of deep and conscious breathing, inhaling peace and serenity, and exhaling all your worries and stress and troubles of the day. Let them leave you. Maybe they will return, maybe they will not. That is not for you to worry about right now. Relax your mind both with a concentrated effort of breath and concentrated effort of visualization. Go to your relaxing place internally, mentally. Find a visualization that works for you. For some, they might see themselves sleeping on a peaceful cloud in the night sky. Some might see themselves on a hammock in a secluded paradise, listening to the birds' songs. Some might see themselves floating downstream in the bluest of waters, carried away by the hands of some divine deity into an ocean of pure and relaxed ecstasy. Be still, and be quiet, in your body as well as in your mind. If your mind begins to wander back towards oppressive thoughts, thoughts that awaken you, simply and gracefully guide your mind back to the stream. Do this as many times as it takes until you are solidly and comfortably at peace. It is a very similar concept as to the old practice of counting sheep. If your mind is focused on the very simple task of counting, it cannot begin to race towards the thoughts that agitate and awaken it and will become successfully lulled. Maybe if your worries persist in breaking through the veil of peace, you can incorporate them into the fantasy that diminishes them, then proceed to throw them out more peacefully and effectively then simply shutting them up. For instance, if you see your boss yelling at you while you are trying to lie in your hammock, visualize a glass box being put down around him, so his yelling becomes silent. Visualize his mouth moving angrily but no words coming out. This might seem comical. Laugh at him while you are relaxing on your hammock, then, naturally, your attention will shift elsewhere, to a pleasant breeze, to a bird landing on a branch nearby. Next, time you look in the direction previously occupied by the yelling man, he will be gone. Your mind will have excised him as a total and unnecessary use of its faculties to fantasize.

Exercise 3: Visualize Positive Energy Flowing Towards People You Interact Within Day-to-day Life

The previous thought carries right into this one, involving reframing troubling aspects of daily life into a more positive and manageable position. The same kind of visualization you perform for yourself either when attempting to enter the trance or mid-trance, as a form of a post-hypnotic suggestion or spiritual cleaning, can be performed at any time for yourself and for anyone you know. If you are having trouble with a person at work or cuts you off during your morning commute and flips you off, visualize those people being swarmed with the most positive energy the universe has to offer. This can be therapeutic in two ways. For one, it transforms all hate and resentment, you might feel into a positive force. For another, it might actually do them some good! While it is very typical to wish pain on the people around you who you view as oppressive forces, sometimes this is totally the wrong way to go about things. Generally, the people in your life who are negative forces are already in extreme amounts of pain, be it physical, mental, or spiritual, and adding to the pain will only make matters that much worse. The answer, as per usual, is love. Agape love is the name for the kind of love that God has, another term for what we would call unconditional love; love for all living things. It is something we should all work towards exercising, however, complicated the limitations of our physical bodies and our current physical realities and situations may make it. Just as love has the power to turn a negative thought into a positive one, love has the power to turn a negative force into a positive one, and a negative person into a positive one. Maybe loving your enemy will turn that enemy into a friend, or, at least, a much more neutral party. It is rare that anyone in your life is "out to get you", however much you may feel that they are. Generally, we are projecting something onto them when we feel this way. It

306

is much more common for a person to be, like you maybe, out to get themselves, and just lashing out blindly all around them, unable to control the pain and venomous negativity coursing through their veins. It will always prove a very tough thing to love someone who has hurt you, but, here, in our journey towards betterment, specifically in the astral fields and the field of self-hypnosis, it is a totally necessary step. In the small way of just visualizing a little bit of positive energy flowing towards the people you interact with on a daily basis who pose you any mild grievance, we can make great strides internally in regards to our ability to constantly be emanating love and positivity, for ourselves and for others, for life. This will come back in many ways over the course of your journey. For many, they will have to confront a past or current abuser, someone who has done much worse than just cutting you off in morning traffic. There are many great myriad of terrible things that have been done over the course of history, but, as is the definition of agape love, God still loves all his creations, however much darkness shrouds them in the current moment. It may seem totally counter-

 intuitive to love your abuser, but know, this is no submissive love; this love is an absolutely powerful and dominating force. You must never allow yourself to forgive in any way that will compromise your own future, but you can turn your back and walk away and still turn all the hate and resentment in your heart into the positive force that is love.

Exercise 4: Continually Ask Yourself What You Would Most Like to Be Doing Right Now Instead of What You Are Doing

This will not only give you a very personal idea about what you should be working towards but will help you get to know yourself better, as well as your current circumstance. Think of it as a good conversation starter to help you bond with yourself. It doesn't have to be entirely negative. Hard at work, you might ask the question, and get an answer such as "Be on the beach, drinking a hard drink," or "Be at home in bed." These kinds of answers will tell you, simply, what you already know; that sometimes you can be stressed. This is not news to most people, as most people are stressed and it is very apparent to them, yet they aren't sure quite what to do with the stress or where to put it. But the answers can also be more interesting. Say, you are out for smoke break on the job, you might ask yourself the question, and the answer could be, "I'd like to be inside, drinking a cup of tea." Or on the subway, staring off into space, you might ask the question, and the answer could be, "I'd like to be reading a really great novel." Maybe you haven't been reading enough lately, and your mind is craving a thrilling read yet hasn't had the opportunity to express it in terms your body can put to work. So start making that small talk with yourself. Don't be afraid to find out more and more about yourself, however much that may change your perspective for the immediate better or worse in regards to your current situation. There is no knowledge that hurts. Ignorance is only bliss in the immediate short term, and that bliss gives way in the long-term to wounds that are not taken care of and begin to fester under the façade of complacency. We must always be vigilant about our own mental and physical wellbeing. If our body or soul or mind is in need, it is our duty to know, and to understand, and find a way to give ourselves whatever it is that we require to be happy, to be comfortable so that we can be that much more powerful in working towards our self- betterment. Never be surprised to find out something about yourself that you don't already know. It is very common. We are very complicated beings, in that we can desire a great many things that we may not even know the words for, but we are also very simple, in that all it will take for us to be feel satisfied is generally, in some way, shape, or form, very much attainable. You might feel a desire for something that isn't totally attainable right now in this very moment, such as to be on vacation at a time when there is much work that needs to be done or to be a millionaire in the morning when there is only a thousand dollars in your bank account, but these desires can be satiated all the same in a fulfilling way for the psyche in creative ways that lay the groundwork for more and infinite betterment in the future. If you feel you need a vacation, make plans for one! This will serve two benefits, as you will be excited about the future and have something to look forward to and work towards and you will also be able to tell that part of yourself that is very tired and needs a break that a break is coming soon. So don't fret! Similarly, while you may not see a direct deposit into your bank account of a million dollars first thing tomorrow morning, you can deal with the desire for a greater income by simply beginning to explore your options, the many that there are for all people the world over, and see what it might take for you to increase your monetary value in some way that you can begin working on immediately. There are many ways to supplement income. Part-time jobs, freelance work, turning your hobbies into a profit, such as selling artwork that you may make for your own enjoyment in your spare time, or investing. Investing is something that all people can do, but many are afraid to. Just putting a little bit of money aside each paycheck and investing it in some way can satiate that part of you that yearns to be working towards something more. These internal desires, they should never be ignored, regardless of how large of a task satiating them seems to be at the moment. There is always room for working with them for some sort of healthy compromise, that takes fully into account the desire and where it is coming from and uses the desire to slowly work toward betterment.

Exercise 5: Empathy

Being that a goal of self-hypnosis is self-betterment, here we can take a look at the people around us, either immediately or even in the media and find things about them that inspire us, things that we may aspire towards. These things are like looking in a fun-house mirror, providing alternate reflections of potential selves. Given that a large part of self-hypnosis is really having a much more positive outlook on who you already are, and who you have been, it may seem counter-intuitive to indulge blatantly in comparing yourself to others in such a fashion. Finding attributes that you are lacking and what others seem to have in spades but we must accept that although we are great, and we have great power to do the things that we want to do, there is always something we can admire in others that we would like to see more in ourselves. It is only natural. That's why there is such a culture of idol- worship as we see in the world. While there is a negative tendency to praise the greatness of others while knocking down ourselves, saying that what others have that is great is something to only be worshipped externally through them and not something personally attainable. Let us turn that around on its head and say that the things we admire in other people are admirable through empathy, through seeing them achieve something that we ourselves could also, and maybe should also be working to achieve for ourselves. Go back to the analogy of martial arts. If you are a new practitioner of the arts sitting back and watching a black belt performing their training regimen, you might feel slightly intimidated, albeit incredibly impressed. Let us worship in them not their accomplishments for themselves but their accomplishments for humanity in general and their display of the infinite potential of the human body and the human spirit to achieve such great things. The things that you see in others that you find impressive do not feel satisfied in experiencing second-hand, realize that the power in seeing them is to become aware of their existence, to expand the limits of what you previously thought attainable. We can easily revel in admiration in this way, and it will be a very healthy thing. It is easy to feel negative when you see someone accomplishing much more than you, but if you reframe it, so you are not shamed, but inspired, realizing the potential in yourself if you yourself were to put in the same amount of work as the person you find so impressive, then the act of idolizing someone can become a very powerful tool towards your own personal journey towards self-betterment! So while you are out in the world, look around you, and look at what everyone else is doing. Find something to celebrate in your fellow man. And instead of comparing yourself to them, feeling any kind of shame, or even feeling pride in the fact that you may be better in some ways than this person, just sit and think about what these things tell you about human existence, about your own human existence, and the potential in you for both positive growth and to possibly in some circumstance be less than you are now. Appreciate yourself through these lenses, appreciate what it shows you about the power of the human will, and use these feelings as a catalyst for your own dreams and aspirations and goals, and your own working towards self-empowerment and self-betterment. There is always something we can admire in our fellow man, and there is always something that someone else is doing better than us. You may not be as great at everything as someone else is at something, but you can always be better at something than you were yesterday, through the sheer act of will. In celebrating the accomplishments of others, we can become inspired to better ourselves in the same ways.

And so, in these five simple exercises that you can do in your spare time, or even in the back of your mind while you are busy with more seemingly pressing tasks, we can be always working towards self-betterment, both in the realm of our practice with self-hypnosis, and in the very act itself of bettering ourselves through exercise and growth! What helps us become better at self- hypnosis will also help us in every aspect of our lives to become more positive and productive people, less held back by our own negativity and more empowered by our constant strides towards becoming the best person that we can be. You will begin to notice that as you practice self-hypnosis and work on exercising your power to hone your mind and your will and your body towards the specific goals, you become more powerful and productive in ways you didn't even intend.

Exercise 6: Meditation to be more present

This meditation session's objective is to physically release the tension from the body through self-massage and mentally release the tension through meditation. It is going to be a completely relaxing session. You can sit in any comfortable position you want. If you wish you can sit on a chair or even in the cross-legged posture.

Simply follow the guided meditation session and you will feel completely relaxed at the end of it.

Take your position at the place of your meditation Be seated

Sit in a completely relaxed manner Don't do anything immediately Ground yourself first

Just sit completely relaxed for a few minutes

If something important comes to your mind write it down If there is something that is bothering you, write it down Get into a comfortable position

Keep your back straight

Ensure that your shoulders are also straight Your back and neck should be in a straight line Now, close your eyes

Lean slightly forward and then backward Lean-to your left side and then to your right

Now, bring yourself to the center and find the best and most comfortable position

Feel your head positioned on your neck Raise your chin slightly upwards

This will help you in placing your focus between your eyebrows Try to feel your whole body

Notice if there is tension anywhere

If you feel any part tense, release the tension Adjust your body to release the pressure Start by inhaling through your nose

Breathe in deeply

Let the air travel through your body Feel the areas of tension

Hold the air for a while

Then, release it through your mouth Your inhalations should be shorter Your exhalations should be longer Breathe in

Breathe out

Breathe in the positive energy Feel the love and compassion Let your worries dissipate Don't bother about things much Simply enjoy the moment Breathe in

Breathe out Breathe in Breathe out

Breathe out Breathe in Breathe out

Think of the areas in which you are feeling the stress Direct your breathing to those areas

Try to release the tension mentally Breathe in

Breathe out Breathe in Breathe out

Now rub your palms together vigorously This should comfortably heat your palms Devote some time to it

Don't rush the process

The longer you rub your palms together The more energy they will accumulate

They will also get smoother and provide more warmth and good sensation Now take your index finger and the middle finger of both hands

Use them to touch at the sides of your neck

Start massaging the sides of the neck in a circular motion Start massaging gently

Move both your fingers in a circular motion Massage this area for a minute or so

Adjust the pressure you want to apply to the area You shouldn't press very hard

Gently hold both sides of your neck and massage Stop after a minute or when you start feeling relaxed

Give yourself some time

Now start pressing under your chin with your thumb circularly move your thumb gently

This action will provide a soothing sensation

Messaging this area will provide a soothing sensation to your whole head Now, take your index finger and middle finger together again

Press them right below your ear lobes Move them gently in a circular motion

This will provide a soothing sensation to the back of your neck Your face would also start getting relaxed

Bring your fingers at the joint of your jaws Start massaging your jaws in circles

This will help in relaxing your facial muscles You will feel a great rush of energy here Repeat the motion for a minute

Relax for a moment

Bring your fingers to the back of your ears Massage in this area for a bit

This is very relaxing for the back of your head You will feel utterly relaxed all of a sudden All the pain and tension goes away

Relax for a moment

Now hold your ears from the top Gently rub the top of your ears

This is also very soothing and relaxing You can repeat this motion a few times Relax for a moment

Now cup your ears completely

Rub your ears in a soft circular motion with your palms This also feels very soothing

Keep rubbing the ears as long as you feel comfortable Relax for a moment

Now bring your fingers to your temple

If you are feeling headache, running your temples in a circular motion will help a lot

Simply rub with the tip of your fingers in a gentle circular motion

It releases all the tension that might have built up while messaging the jaws It will relax your head completely

Relax for a moment

Now put your thumbs at the side of your base bridge

Your thumb should be placed beside the nose bridge and the side of your eyes

Place your index fingers at the top of your forehead together Now your fingers will be forming a bridge of their own Start massaging both the points together

This is a very relaxing exercise

You will feel your eyes getting completely relaxed

If you wear glasses, this will be really soothing for you

The glasses put a lot of pressure on the nose bridge that we don't usually realize

Doing this exercise releases that pressure

Now, you can put the index finger and middle finger of one of your hands at the center of your forehead

Place your other hand at the top of your hand

Now move your fingers in a circular motion at your third eye chakra which is at the center of your forehead

This is a very relaxing exercise

The hand placed on the top of your head is supporting your crown chakra Take deep breaths as you rub the point of your third eye chakra

Be gentle

Press this area for a minute or so

This will relax your mind completely as this point is the seat of your third eye Your power to sense things improves with this exercise

In the end, you can also massage the back of your head with both your hand Place your thumbs at the back of your ears

Take your fingers at the back of your head Now gently rub the back of your head

It will release any kind of tension retained by your head You will now feel your head completely relaxed

If there is any stress on your shoulders and upper trapezius you can rub these areas too

Cup the shoulders of the opposite sides by your hands Now move them in a circular motion

This releases the tension in the shoulders

If there is any tension in the upper trapezius Hold it by your hands and massage it very gently This will relax your shoulders completely

Now, again focus on your breathing Breathe in

Breathe out Breathe in Breathe out Breathe in Breathe out

Relax your body completely and become aware of your surroundings You will feel completely relaxed and calm.

CHAPTER 22: WE DESIRE TO BE HAPPY AND FULFILLED

Now we will discuss the secret of everything—the holistic manifestation of the self. We desire to be fulfilled, to be happy, to be satisfied, and to be always creating. Let us put to work our entire selves for the betterment of our entire selves, and find how we can achieve happiness through creation.

Given everything that we have already gone over in our initial journey into and introduction to self-hypnosis, we have obtained the tools necessary to begin our trek and work towards bettering ourselves in any way we see fit. We will begin by assessing damage that has been done internally and diagnosing it so as to create a new path in which we can rectify the damage and turn it on its head to actually become in and of itself an accessory to our betterment, by redefining it, and, in effect, it's effect on our wellbeing, to be something more useful and productive in our psyche. For a while, you will be repairing damage and healing wounds. But then, after an even longer while, you will find that you have greatly come to terms with your past and your present, and you are wondering where the knowledge and experience you have gained in the realms of self-hypnosis can take you now. Imagine you were a cave dweller, being pushed underground by the negative thoughts that made you afraid to see the light of day. Now you have made it to ground level, and you have acclimated to the sunshine, and you are no longer afraid, you are joyous, and you are grateful, and you are wondering what the next step is. Well, then, the next step would be to keep going up, by building towers into the sky. Once we are at a comfortable place internally, we will turn the power of self-hypnosis away from healing and damage control and into further betterment for its own sake, up and out, just as one who has healed an atrophied limb through physical therapy will continue their exercise regimen once the limb has been healed back to the status-quo, strengthening their limb with the new habits developed through the traumatic experience to become something more than the status quo. We have achieved health, and it will be simple and easy for us to maintain health, so now we focus our intention on the accumulation of wealth and general abundance in our daily lives.

Wealth, of course, as has already been discussed briefly before, is not just material. Wealth simply refers to an abundance of something. Vaguely, let us consider our future endeavors to be our drives to become rich and abundant in spirit. If we focus purely on spirit and positivity, then the wealth of spirit and positivity will naturally transfer over to become a wealth and abundance of anything we could possibly desire in our lives, as spirit and positivity are invaluable currencies that never decrease in value, and can always be traded for whatever it is we need or desire in our daily lives. When we are at our fullest faculties and then some, mentally and spiritually and physically, life will have a habit of taking care of itself, through synchronicity with the universe. What we desire and strive for when totally honed in on and made the purest focus of our being, becomes magnified into existence by our sheer force of will.

Let us consider life. There are key things in life that everyone needs. These

things can be put simply, money, health, and a reason for being. Money, as it is, is merely the physical manifestation of our value. If we have value, the value that we create through being ourselves and working towards our own betterment, that value that is increased will be mirrored, naturally, by an increase in, and abundance of, money. Health, likewise, is born from positivity and proper function, if we are true to ourselves and living life for positivity, health will have a way of working itself out. When the body is listened to and understood, and all our needs are digested and met, health will follow. The reason for being is the most complicated of all these things. There are many very rich people monetarily who become depressed and complacent, continuing to accumulate wealth through their daily rituals or invested interest while their body and spirit atrophy through a feeling of not having anywhere to go now that they have "made it." There are sick people who are more fulfilled in their reason for being than people who have never been sick a day in their lives, this struggle through sickness creating positivity and appreciation for life through its own juxtaposition with it. If we never know pain, how can we appreciate pleasure? And if we never have to struggle to achieve what we have achieved, how can we appreciate it? The reason for being, then, is simply, as you may have already guessed, to keep working towards being better than you are now. You are always growing. There is no finish line, there are goals and marks along the way, and there is always room for the celebration of accomplishments that you have met, but there is never a time to sit down and stop working towards bettering yourself. As far as life goes, there are many, many tasks to complete, and when those tasks are completed, there is always more to be completed down the way. If you feel you've run out of things to do to improve your own self, for the time being, go out and work on improving the lives of others! This very reason is why you see so many healthy and very rich people out there investing a great majority of their energy into charity and kind acts towards others who do not have it so well as they do. Their needs in life have been so thoroughly met and machinated that they no longer feel any kind of great reward in providing for themselves or their families the basic human necessities, or even extremities beyond that. So do the same! Follow their example. Go out and meet someone new, and share yourself with them, and, in that new chemical process, you will find a new tangent opened up in your life for you to work on and develop. Or, as said, volunteer! Accumulate wealth not for yourself but for others by working for a charity. Wealth creates wealth; the same as positivity, and it is always a good idea to spread wealth, positivity, and love as far as you can. You reap what you sow, so the saying goes. An abundance of spirit, when planted in the right soils, will bring back an even greater abundance of sprit tenfold, and then twentyfold, and then a hundredfold until the positivity you have generated through your work, starting at the bottom and then gradually and slowly building towards a better you, than a better world, will have touched the entire planet. Once having done so, the positivity will come back around the globe to you, filling you with such a purpose and drive in life that you will become a veritable superhero, turning everything before you into gold, living health, wealth and abundance for yourself and for all the world to bask in the glory of.

So, back to the atrophied limb, work it back up to its initial functioning level, or, if it was never at a functioning level, to begin with, find a functioning level and define that functioning level for yourself. And once you have done so, and thus feel comfortable, continue to imagine greater and greater levels of strength that you could achieve, practically and realistically, by continuing to exercise and focus on the betterment of the limb. Over time, and with great effort and positivity of the spirit, the limb will grow to be strong, and, in its

strength, its desire to be stronger will be self-fulfilling; it will continue and continue to grow. Once the limb has fulfilled all your needs, go out in the world, and use it to help others, and you will spread the seeds for infinite and greater love to grow out of the Earth and come back to you, giving you a sense of never-ending fulfillment.

It's not all about money, and it's not all about being the strongest person on the block. You can have all the money in the world and still be miserable, having no idea what to do with all the material wealth you've accumulated, that seemingly positive force remaining stagnant around your being and turning against you as it strives to escape into more knowledgeable and positive hands. Wealth means nothing if it is not flowing, and abundance is useless if it is not put to great use and shared. And you can be the strongest person on Earth, a marvel to behold, lifting buses with one hand and wrestling grizzly bears on your days off, and you may still feel weak and insecure on the inside—a small child who never came to terms with their own sense and definition of the self. What really makes a person wealthy is an abundance of fulfillment, to have the feeling that all your hunger in life are satiated and then some, so that you are an overwhelming beacon of positivity, with love and light pouring out of you at such a rate so as to affect and better, by extension, every single person that you come into contact with in your daily life. In this sense, the richest person in the world can be very materialistically poor in the moment and still have an overwhelming abundance of wealth, and the strongest person in the world can be so weak at the moment that they cannot even lift a glass of water into their mouths to stay hydrated. The difference is that, over time, these truly rich people, of body, spirit, and will, will come to surpass those who do not appreciate what they have, regardless of however much they have of it. Let this inspire you, then, wherever you are in your life, to become rich and wealthy and find an abundance of spirit in yourself tonight, at this very moment. Through the act of self-hypnosis, you may not accumulate one hundred pounds of muscle overnight, or a million dollars, but you can flip the switch immediately that makes you spiritually and mentally rich, and wealthy, with an abundance of positivity, love and light, that will go on to fuel you to have all these things that you desire, that you crave, that a human being needs to not only to survive but to be happy, fulfilled, and always progressing.

So we will work towards our betterment. Once having achieved a level of comfort, we will immediately rise past complacency and up into the stratosphere, to keep bettering ourselves to new heights and greater sights that will never cease to be filled by the giving gods of the universe. If we ask for it, and we have the purest of spirits, our desires for fulfillment will always be granted, and in our fulfillment, we will begin to develop health, wealth, and abundance. You can always be healthier. Your body can always be stronger; your mind can always be faster to come up with those great answers, you will always be able to jump just a little bit higher than you can now, even and especially if you are the world's greatest athlete, or sharpest scientist, or both. You can always be wealthier, in all aspects of your life; there is no cap to the abundance of wealth you can achieve in any aspect of your life. And, importantly, wealth will not just be about the accumulation of resources for resource's sake, but the wealthier expenditure of such resources. It is not about the size of your house or the size of your body, but how you put it to use. If your house is the largest mansion in the world, but it is dead and empty than that is not true wealth. If you have a normal-sized house with loving and loved residents in each and every room, with bustling positivity beckoning forth from it every single day of the year, that is truly wealth. And it is wealth generated through a pure abundance of love and positivity. All your needs will be met, and then some. You will never struggle, and you will always grow.

So let us perform one last exercise, in which we give ourselves the ultimate script to achieve further health, wealth and abundance at any time and place in our lives, however much we already have, however much we many need. First, enter into the trance, relax your body and mind, and find your hypnotized state. Then, visualize yourself, in an abyss, no ground, or celling, and no possessions or clothing. Slowly and surely, with yourself as your paper doll, build the scenery around yourself that you desire. Wherever you would like to be, make that the background, whatever you would like to be wearing, make those your clothes, whatever you would like to have in your possession, pepper these things all around you. Whoever you would like to be in your company, place them adjacent to you. Put a smile on your face. Stand yourself up tall and fix your posture. Go as far as you would like; there are no limitations here as to what you can have, in this dream, in this internal manifestation of your true desire. Get it all out. Now, once you have totally set the scene, tell yourself these words:

"This is what I have because this is what I desire. Because I desire these things, these things are mine, and I can attain them because that is my goal. The very act of realizing what I want is the first step to getting it. I am healthy, I have an unlimited reservoir of energy that my body draws from, coming from a source that will never run dry, this energy powers my body and heals my wounds, it cures any ailments that might ever overcome me, and it fuels me towards anything I might ever need to do to keep myself and my loved ones safe and secure and to get anything that I might need or desire in my life. Because of this infinite reservoir of spirit, I am incredibly wealthy, very rich in all manners that a person could require to do what they need to do to flourish in life beyond the necessities of survival. Because of my unlimited reservoir of spirit, of positive love and light, I will always have in life the access to whatever it is that I desire. If I desire for things, I have the health and strength and positive will to attain these things. If I desire for money, I have the health and strength and positive will to earn money through any means that are functioning in synchronicity with my desires. If I desire for company, I have the health, strength, and positive will. Self-esteem and confidence will attract anyone into my life that belongs in my life, and the people that I will attract will likewise attract me, by the law of attraction, and we will achieve a positive symbiotic relationship in which neither takes more than they give. We will flourish together and fulfill each other's desires for love beyond any possible amount that they will need to be satiated. If I desire a new location, there will always be a new location waiting for me. The world is a vast and loving place, and I am a vast and loving spirit. It is up to me to find the things that I require so that the universe may show me the way to attain them. I will keep an open mind, and I will be self-loving and ever vigilant in my quest to be my best self. I will, therefore, always be deserving of the grand gifts that life has to offer me as I follow this path towards the light. I am loved."

Affirmation for your lifestyle

I want to provide you with positive affirmations in this audio guide. You have come a long way and I want you to confirm these affirmations with yourself frequently. Remember to choose a comfortable space to sit. Perhaps a space that allows you to speak out loud now. Keep your breathing exercises in mind, always maintaining an even rhythm in your breathing. This is a fun exercise, an exercise that will reassure you of your worth. Now, allow me to guide you.

I want you to participate in this section by repeating my words. Please do repeat these words out loud because it's essential to hear your own voice. I will pause briefly after each affirmation and you will have the time to repeat the sentence. Shall we begin?

I acknowledge my own value and my confidence continues to grow each day. I strongly believe in my own abilities and skills to attract a positive outcome. I am fully capable of reaching any target I set for myself with my newfound confidence.

I will aim to make memories I treasure because I refuse to live a robotic life.

I will walk into the spotlight with my head held high because I no longer fear the crowd.

I'm not afraid of meeting new people because I'm interesting and have so much to offer.

I don't need to compare myself to another person because I'm unique.

I have the confidence to speak to anyone because my voice is a powerful tool. I'm confident in my knowledge and refuse to doubt my own words.

I will take some brief time off now and then because life can become hectic for anyone.

I will finish my tasks one by one and not become overwhelmed. I will own my mistakes instead of punishing myself.

I'm a powerful force and nothing in the world can shove me off track. I will not allow myself to take on more than I can handle.

I acknowledge the fact that I cannot control everything. I acknowledge that I'm not perfect because no person is.

I won't allow my fears to control my thinking and prevent me from living life to the fullest.

I have complete control over negative emotions that plague me at night. I will create what is best for me because I control my imagination.

I am strong enough to defeat any addiction or pain.

I'm a strong, confident, kind, and loving person who is capable of anything I set my mind to.

Thank you for repeating these affirmations.

CONCLUSION

You know now that the first step is the most difficult, but it is also crucial. Once you take it, you set the wheels in motion, and all the rest falls into place like dominos. In this first step, you have to prepare the groundwork and create a clean, receptive environment to build your self-esteem. During this first step, it is necessary to connect yourself to the world of which you are a part and which has been either a silent or active partner in all that has happened to you. While you take this first step, remind yourself of the little things that give you pleasure and can make your journey enjoyable--something that can erase, even momentarily, all your concerns and will give you a few moments of pleasant respite.

Once you take your first step towards building your self-esteem, you need to be applauded for your courage. It takes nerve to accept that you need to change and take a step forward. And if you have accepted the necessity of this endeavor, then you certainly are a person who will one day achieve your goal. Start now to believe in yourself and your self-worth. Try to understand what lies at the root of low self-esteem, and then identify ways to assess its level. If you are dissatisfied with the degree of self-worth you possess, it is undoubtedly time to rectify it.

Once you evaluate the origin of your low self-esteem, you will realize that most of it spring from a lot of negative thinking to which you are submitting yourself. You blame yourself for what goes wrong, and if someone fails to respond to you in a way that you want, you think you are responsible. First, do not have

331

unrealistic expectations from others. Then understand that you are not responsible for other peoples' actions and choices. If a friend does not invite you to her party, it does not necessarily mean that you are a terrible person or are to be blamed for it. It is her liability. Your happiness should not depend upon other people's choices. You should know your worth and stick to it. You are the right person. Do not let anybody else tell you otherwise. To challenge this pessimism and bring to your notice the importance of your self-worth, you have to reflect. Just telling yourself that you are good can become redundant after a while, and you may question its validity. So don't just say that you are good. Prove to yourself how good you are. You may doubt a baseless statement, or an enforced chant of I am good. But you cannot deny it if it's proven to you. Start making a list of your positive attributes for you to see. Jot down all your strengths, then set goals for yourself. This will give you a purpose. A person with purpose thinks highly of herself. She sets goals because she feels inside that she is capable of achieving them. You will see a glimpse of that self-esteem rising on the horizon, just like the sun at dawn.

Understand that you are not perfect. No one is. We all make mistakes, and we all have the right to be forgiven... first and foremost by ourselves. Try to see yourself in a new light. Eat a healthy and balanced diet, exercise regularly, maintain good personal hygiene and a good appearance, and meditate for peace with your inner self. Also, be sensitive towards the hardships of others now that you have overcome yours. Engage with the community and local charities.It will give you a sense of wellbeing but will also help you to give back to the world that which you have taken from it. Try to be around positive people and not shrink from positive feedback: it can only help you grow. Getting a bit of professional help wouldn't be unwise.

If You Believe, You Will Achieve

Please understand that belief is the cornerstone of your life. If you believe you will achieve. If you don't believe it, it's going to be a much harder road for you.

This may not necessarily mean you would fail, but you're going to have a harder time. You have to have your mind in the right place before you go on this journey of overcoming your anxiety. Otherwise, your mindset will sabotage you, undermine you, and constantly get in the way. Before you know it, because of your mindset, you just run out of steam.

What's So Important About Your Mindset Anyway?

Your mindset dictates your life. Mindset equals selective perception, selective analysis, selective response, selective action, which triggers selective reality.

How does mindset impact your reality?

Believe it or not, your mindset helps you edit your reality. I know that's a strong word because when you edit something, you change its form. You change its direction. Eventually, you change its quality.

We all are editors of our realities. Just because most of us don't step up to this responsibility and take full ownership of it, it doesn't make this fact go away. All of us have this capability.

This is how it works. You have a mindset. Believe it or not, you have chosen it at some point in time. It may not seem like it, but that's the way it is. It's chosen. You're not going to hang on to your mindset if you didn't choose it.

This mindset is not neutral. When you take in all these objective stimuli from the rest of the world, you process them through your mindset, and you give them meaning. This is called analysis.

It may seem natural, it may seem like this is the objective reality, but don't kid yourself. This is subjective because two people with two different mindsets can look at the same set of facts and walk away with two different conclusions. That's the power of mindset.

Your childhood, upbringing, how people treated you, any kind of abuse you suffered, and what kind of beliefs you have all impact your mindset. And it's yours.

We learned about what hypnosis is, its origins, and its applications, specifically in regards to the self, upon the self. We learned the power hypnosis can have and the benefits that can be gained specifically through the practice of self-hypnosis. We learned how to perform self-hypnosis in 10 simple steps, from beginning to end, what we should do to prepare for self-hypnosis, how we should enact self-hypnosis, why we should enact self-hypnosis, and what we should do when we are done. We learned how to continue the practice of self-hypnosis and develop a workflow over time that works towards mastering self-hypnosis and always working towards and honing your craft. We learned five simple exercises that we can do outside of self-hypnosis that will both further our work in self-hypnosis and also peripherally benefit us in our daily lives. We learned how to use self-hypnosis to overcome negative aspects of our subconscious mind that might be inhibiting us from positive growth in our everyday lives. We learned how to use self-hypnosis to increase or self-esteem and our confidence, the way we are perceived in our being, and how we present ourselves to other people. Lastly, we put all our knowledge together and learned how to use self-hypnosis to achieve all-around health, wealth, and abundance in our daily lives and constantly be bettering ourselves. I hope you enjoyed reading this book as much as I enjoyed writing it, and I hope you can use the information learned to better your life as much as possible;

And congratulations, you have now risen from the ashes of your low self-esteem to build a new confident image. You can think of yourself as worthy and valuable. Your self-esteem has been reborn and restored from its crushed vestiges, just like the phoenix's comeback.

CPSIA information can be obtained
at www.ICGtesting.com
Printed in the USA
BVHW091920171220
595878BV00010B/483